# Women and the Public Sphere

in the Age of the French Revolution

# Women and the Public Sphere
## in the Age of the French Revolution

JOAN B. LANDES

*Cornell University Press*

*Ithaca and London*

First published 1988 by Cornell University Press.
Second printing 1990.
First published, Cornell Paperbacks, 1988.
Fifth printing 1994.

International Standard Book Number (cloth) 0-8014-2141-1
International Standard Book Number (paper) 0-8014-9481-8
Library of Congress Catalog Card Number 88-3723
Printed in the United States of America
*Librarians: Library of Congress cataloging information appears on the last page of the book.*

⊗ The paper in this book meets the minimum requirements of the American National Standard for Information Sciences— Permanence of Paper for Printed Library Materials, ANSI Z39.48-1984.

To my father and to the memory of my mother

# Contents

# Acknowledgments

This book has been very long in the making. I could not, at the outset, have foreseen its final contours. Like a latter-day Scheherazade, I have found myself continuously producing narratives, each one leading to a new point of departure, each involving an element of self-definition and survival. *Women and the Public Sphere in the Age of the French Revolution* is the outcome of nearly two decades of work on modern feminism, during which time I have become increasingly emboldened to revise both the subject matter and writing of political theory from a feminist standpoint. To be sure, it has been a humbling experience. All along the way I have needed to acquaint myself with ever larger bodies of knowledge, both substantive and critical. This has not been a solitary endeavor. I belong to a generation of women whose journey into academia was propelled and assisted by the rebirth of the women's movement. I have never been forced to choose between a political and an intellectual path, nor have I been constrained by the boundaries too often imposed by the disciplinary organization of knowledge. This project was nurtured at a critical stage by the opportunity afforded me to spend a year sheltered among a community of women scholars at the Mary Ingraham Bunting Institute. For this, and for its generous financial support, I thank the Bunting Institute, as well as the National Endowment for the Humanities, which twice awarded funding to this project.

My greatest debt is to Theodore Norton for his loving support, intellectual companionship, and practical help at every step along the way. I have profited enormously from his expansive knowledge of critical theory, modern European history, and political thought, and I have learned from him how necessary it is to take risks if one is to pose and try to answer urgent and complex questions. His work on Jürgen Habermas' theory of language, communication, and society first oriented me to the concept of the public sphere. Even now it is difficult for me to determine where his thoughts end and mine begin. Without our constant dialogue, I doubt that this book could have been completed.

Nancy Fitch has been throughout a loyal friend and colleague. Whatever modest knowledge of French history I have attained I owe in good measure to her patient guidance, incisive remarks, and enormous generosity. She has given unselfishly of her time in reading various versions of the manuscript. Her own interdisciplinary outlook has been a constant source of inspiration. I am especially fortunate to have had the encouragement and advice of Lynn Hunt. She offered valuable insights and concrete suggestions on the manuscript which helped immeasurably in the revision process. In addition, perspicacious readings and stylistic suggestions for all or part of the book have been contributed by Erica Harth, Sarah Maza, and Dena Goodman. At an earlier stage, I was aided by the responses of Carol Kay, Robert Rakoff, Mary Ryan, and Anna Yeatman. The comments of all my readers have pushed me to make connections that I otherwise would not have attempted. I only hope that I have been able to satisfy at least some of their concerns.

I have benefited from my participation in the Five College Women's Studies seminar and project and by collaborative teaching with scholars from other fields in the humanities and social sciences. I am grateful to my colleagues at Hampshire and the Five Colleges with whom I have shared some of these ideas and from whom I have learned a great deal about both cultural and feminist studies: Myrna Breitbart, Susan Douglas, Sura Levine, Jill Lewis, Andrew Parker, Mary Russo, Miriam Slater, Doris Sommer, and Susan Tracy. Over the years, my students have offered a congenial audience for the provisional formulation of this project. Jean Bethke Elshtain, Penina Glazer, Bertell Ollman, and Peter G. Stillman gave their endorsement at the beginning of my endeavors. Hampshire College provided faculty development funds. I could not have been favored with a finer editor than John G. Ackerman. I appreciate his unflagging confidence in this work. The editorial staff of Cornell University Press expertly guided the final production of this book. I owe special thanks to Margaret McKenna, former director of the Bunting Institute, for her keen interest and support, and to Ellen Bassuk, Hemalata Dandekar, Barbara Johnson, Sumie Jones, Diane Middlebrook, Susan Shell, and Linda Williams for shared study and discussion. My daughter, Eleanor, who has literally been raised along with "mommy's book," has provided me with endless hours of joy, a fair number of interruptions, and even a few phrases that have found their way into these pages.

JOAN B. LANDES

*Pelham, Massachusetts*

# Introduction

How difficult it is to uncouple women from domestic life. How much more difficult, once uncoupled, to imagine a world in which women's proper place is in the public sphere. Why this paradox endures, and how it may have come to pass, are among the questions I confronted in writing this book. By refusing to accept as inevitable the given pattern of political life, I assume a consciously feminist stance to my subject. Advocates of women's equality have clearly made vigorous claims on "the political," and feminism itself is a quintessentially political avenue to female emancipation. Although recent research reveals how widespread and long-standing are feminist impulses, "modern feminism" as a distinct political genre seems to be a product of bourgeois society. While a comprehensive survey of feminism is beyond the scope of this study, I remain impressed by the fact that in the century between 1750 and 1850 women were confronted with a new, and hitherto relatively inconsequential, source of discrimination, the constitutional denial of women's rights under bourgeois law. During the last half of the nineteenth century, women's movements emerged throughout Western Europe and North America as a response to this situation. Here, I discuss the incipient stages of these developments. I relate the genesis of feminism to the fall of the politically influential women of the absolutist court and salon of Old Regime France.[1]

1

What follows is an interpretive essay in which I rethink, from a feminist perspective, the decisive historical passage from French absolutism to bourgeois society. I argue that the shift in the organization of public life is linked to a radical transformation of the system of cultural representation. I do not offer a causal explanation, but rather an account of the way experience is organized differently in modern times. I propose that the collapse of the older patriarchy gave way to a more pervasive *gendering* of the public sphere. Despite the excessively personal and patriarchal character of Old Regime monarchical power, women of the period participated in and influenced political events and public language. They were largely unconcerned with the bourgeois norms of domestic propriety. Furthermore, because rights were not universal, women's exclusion from formal channels of power was not deemed to be particularly exceptional. This was a situation women shared with most men in early modern France. I explore the mechanisms of violence and seduction, indeed the entire ideological configuration, by means of which women in the past came to be politically silenced. I investigate the enormous obstacles, discursive and institutional, which feminists confronted in their efforts to advance women's position in public life. I discuss the paradoxical relationship between feminism and republicanism, and thereby consider the fact that feminism emerged in tandem with a specific, highly gendered bourgeois male discourse that depended on women's domesticity and the silencing of "public" women, of the aristocratic and popular classes. My goal, then, is to reconceptualize the problematic relationship of women to the modern public sphere from the standpoint of politics itself, rather than from the family or economic relations, and to illustrate how politics is mediated by the vocabulary and patterns of cultural existence.

If we think about the public sphere at all, it is difficult to ignore its gendered meanings. One can point to an etymological connection between gender and politics. According to the *O.E.D.*, the early Latin *poplicus* — from the feminine *poplus*, later the masculine *populus*, 'people'—appears to have given way to *publicus*, "under the influence of *pubes*, in the sense of 'adult men,' 'male population.'" On the one hand, our inherited term "public" suggests the opposite of "private," that which pertains to the people as a whole, to community or nationwide concerns, to the common good, to public opinion, to things open to sight, and to those things that may be used or shared by all members of the community. Public is that which is open, manifest, common, and good. A public man is one who acts in and for the universal good; a public thing is that which is open to, may be used by, or shared by all members of the community (that which is not restricted to private use by any person). On the other hand, a public woman is a prostitute, a commoner, a common woman.[2]

A public action is then one authored from or authorized by the masculine position. Only the latter is truly general, community-spirited, and universal in its consequences. Surreptitiously, language works to effect a closure, one that dictates women's absence from political life. As male and female speakers, we take up our positions on either side of the sexual divide. By second nature, we occupy territories segregated into public and private zones. Only rarely are the historical determinations of this semiotic code of language and place opened to investigation. Yet we are speaking here of Latin words that resonate with modern meanings. Why that should be so is itself a vast topic. It is of some consequence, however, that modern republicanism—born of the Renaissance city-state, carried forward by aristocratic opponents of absolutism, and achieving its greatest heights in the bourgeois revolutions of the late eighteenth century—reinvents the classical world's commitment to civic virtue and inherits its affiliated prejudices for a gendered patterning of public and private life.[3]

Stated baldly, the early modern classical revival—with its political, linguistic, and stylistic overtones—invested public action with a decidedly masculinist ethos. Curiously, this was compounded, not undermined, by the eighteenth-century bourgeois repudiation of aristocratic splendor and artifice in favor of the values of nature, transparency, and law. Certainly the bourgeoisie were not alone in favoring classical values. The monarch and the aristocracy were equally enamored of a classical vocabulary. Their claims to nobility accorded well with the classics. In the allegorical system of truth favored by the aristocracy, it was possible to image the king as Hercules, as if there were no difference between the two. In contrast, the bourgeoisie sought to represent the world not as it seemed but as it was. They upheld the equality of all human beings by nature and looked to a nature governed by objective law. In their efforts to represent human nature, they found an agreeable template in the ancient world, which seemed to possess the values of virtuous simplicity and natural nobility. Thus the bourgeoisie's esteem for objective truth and transparent, immediate signification did not go unadorned. Indeed, they appropriated what they needed from the dominant representational system of the Old Regime, harnessing certain elements of classicism to their own purposes.

In their preferred version of the classical universe, bourgeois men discovered a flattering reflection of themselves — one that imaged men as properly political and women as naturally domestic. In the traces of both political tradition and language, however, the possibility of an alternative structure of politics is occulted. Even today, long after the discovery of "society" in the writings of such nineteenth-century theorists as Hegel, Marx, Comte, Durkheim, and Weber, the dominant schools of American political thought persist in celebrating a utopianized version of ancient Greek and Roman politics.[4] Only recently has the Western canon been scrutinized by feminist critics, but this literature is so preoccupied with an appraisal of liberalism that the profound impact of republicanism on the construction of modern political discourse has been greatly underestimated.[5] In short, a full discussion of the implications of classical subject matter and norms for a feminist reconstruction is still required.[6]

In this context, Jürgen Habermas' novel contribution to political theory and political history deserves special consideration. Some twenty years ago, the young philosopher and sociologist published *Strukturwandel der Öffentlichkeit* (the structural transformation of the public sphere).[7] By way of an immanent critique, Habermas held up liberal society to its original ideals *and* institutional practices. He argued that the rise of a liberal democratic public sphere was central to the modernization of late-eighteenth-century societies, but that commercialization, bureaucratization, and the "culture industry" progressively limited the scope for action of the autonomous public.[8] The book had an immediate and far-reaching impact on both scholarship and politics in Germany. It served as a direct inspiration for the German New Left, and it provoked a debate that is still in progress, opening up new lines of research in history, political theory, and culture studies.[9] In Germany and Western Europe, its impact was comparable to Max Weber's famous thesis on the Protestant ethic and the spirit of capitalism. What Weber had done for the social and economic historiography of the seventeenth century, Habermas provided for the historical sociology and cultural history of the late eighteenth and early nineteenth centuries.[10]

The subtitle of the German book points to the "public sphere" as a "category" of bourgeois experience. Habermas is here using the term "category" in an emphatic sense, that is, as a socially shared organization of experience constitutive of modern societies. In a German setting, Hegel's tripartite distinction between family, civil society, and state had long served to organize reflection on modern politics. Transmitted through both Marxism and the sociological tradition, it continued to define the parameters of this reflection. But thanks not least to American theorists, Habermas was able to reconstruct a *fourth* fundamental category of social organization, one by which both politics and culture had been organized in the modern age. And he showed how early modern societies had also incorporated a public dimension. The "public," as an informal association of private persons oriented to general interests, served to mediate between the economy and network of intergroup relations and the state (including its own public representations). Thus Habermas enriched our understanding of modern society by highlighting autonomous regions of political association not centered on the state or the family and not reducible to the principles of labor. His concept of the "public sphere" also alerted us to the possibility of a political life beyond the state, and one that does not take its standards from the ancient polis. He opened up new lines of research into the continuing transformation of the category of the public sphere in the West and revealed why the category itself now must be reconstituted: because the quasi-autonomous public of the bourgeois era has been progressively colonized and coopted by agencies of civil society and the state.

Habermas' thought on the public sphere took an increasingly less historical, and more formal, turn, eventuating in his *Theories of Communicative Action.*[11] Subsequent contributions to theory and history have, however, served both to enrich and to displace his original thesis. If the public is a fundamental category, it cannot be so easily effaced. Other German writers soon began to examine the rise and transformation of "counterpublics," both revolutionary and reactionary. Their studies prompted yet other debates, on the "proletarian" and "fascist" public spheres.[12]

In the meantime, in France historians and critics investigated phenomena related to those examined by Habermas.[13] Following Marx's references to the "political and literary representatives of the bourgeoisie," Habermas (and Peter Hohendahl) had viewed the public as a cultural as well as a political formation.[14] The French investigations further explored the cultural aspects, with reference to a wider range of symbolic representations (theatrical, graphic, scientific, literary-journalistic, and political). They postulated a link between the rationalism of early modern thought and the increasingly efficient forms of surveillance and power over the lives of individuals developed by the modern state. In effect, the French discussions challenge the utopian bent of Habermas' argument on the classical bourgeois public sphere. Although they do not employ the Habermasian category, they are clearly relevant to the enlargement of his initiative — and they have had an impact on the present study nearly as great as Habermas' work.

Yet, for all its diversity, the post-history of *The Structural Transformation of the Public Sphere* failed to give rise to any extended reflection on what appear to be two crucial aspects of the formation of the modern public — the relation of the public sphere to women and to feminism. In the present study I focus on both aspects. In so doing, I aim to redirect the entire discussion. I argue that the exclusion of women from the bourgeois public was not incidental but central to its incarnation, and that, however marginal, feminist theory and practice supply important historical and theoretical vantage points from which to re-view the modern public's emergence. By reconsidering the public sphere from the perspectives of women (both real and as represented, both feminist and otherwise) and of feminists (not all of whom were women), I am led to propose significant revisions — of Habermas' initial thesis and of later contributions. I claim that the bourgeois public is essentially, not just contingently, masculinist, and that this characteristic serves to determine both its self-representation and its subsequent "structural transformation."

The significance of this intervention goes beyond a revision of Habermas and his successors, for it touches on our existing ideas about feminism and women in politics. The reconstitution of the category of the public sphere can help us to make better sense of the history of modern feminism. Feminism is now, and always has been, as much a creature of the public sphere as of the other "categories" of modern society. Additionally, the entire situation of women in modernity needs to be reconsidered from this perspective. The relation of women to the family and the economy cannot be well understood apart from the problematics of women and the public sphere. Finally, the entire system of political representations and practices, including "theoretical" representations, is incomprehensible in isolation from the public fate of women and feminists. It is no news that political theories, institutions, and practices have remained enduringly sexist. *How* this sexism plays itself out, and *what* motivates the specifically modern varieties of masculinism, are questions that cannot be adequately posed apart from an investigation of the "public and its problems." The burden of this study is to reorient research and reflection along these lines.

The status and scope of this book are necessarily restricted by its main concerns. Although it contains many references to the historical literature and offers readings of political texts, it is intended neither as a historical monograph nor as a feminist rereading of the political theory tradition. My goal throughout is to provide an interpretation of the genesis of the modern public sphere from a feminist perspective. To lend weight to this revision, I have narrowed my focus to the period 1750–1850, the era of the classical bourgeois public sphere. And, in light of the significant French contribution to the discussion after Habermas, I have concentrated on French historical examples. But I keep in mind the wider scope of historical and theoretical issues, and I discuss writers who were not French but who figured in contemporary European debates, in the later history of feminism and the public sphere, or in both. Also, although I do not believe that what happens elsewhere necessarily follows the French model, I appreciate the status that Old Regime and revolutionary France held in the eyes of contemporaries both inside and outside the nation. Indeed, down to the present, French developments are everywhere discussed as paradigmatic of the specifically political determination of modern society.

I offer no survey of women's, political, or cultural history, no survey of the history of political thought or of Habermas and new French theory. Instead I attempt a *reconstruction* of public-sphere theory from the vantage points of women and feminism. This reconstruction necessarily involves rethinking the relations between history and theory, theory and symbolic representation, and symbolic representation and action. Theoretical texts may enter history as forces in one of three ways: immediately, through later effects, or in terms of recasting earlier conceptions. Theoretical texts, too, may serve as counters in symbolic representation. In my view, theories are representations. To use a dramatic metaphor, they provide scripts according to which human action may be staged. They can play a (variable) role in recodifying or reworking prevailing systems of symbolic representation, as exemplified perhaps by the way Rousseau and Rousseauist images served the revolutionary movement in France. By reading theory as a form of symbolic representation, then, I hope to displace at least some of the dilemmas encountered in current discourses concerning text and context. I do not make rigid separations between history and theory; rather, I observe that every text is always part of the context, while appreciating that the context is—before, now, and after—internalized in the text. Theory belongs to history, and history is internal to theory.

In turn, symbolic representations are counters in symbolic actions.[15] As Marshall Sahlins proposes, they are "risked" in action.[16] And action cannot be conceptualized apart from the deployment of representations. The issue then, is not symbolization (including theory) versus action but the conjoint quality of both. I have attempted, with a level of success that only the reader can assay, to observe the fluid interaction of theory, representation, and action.[17]

One aspect of this characterization deserves special comment. The precise temporal locus of a representation does not limit or exhaust its significance. I take David's 1785 painting *The Oath of the Horatii*, discussed in Chapter 5, as a prefiguration of the problematic of the nineteenth-century bourgeois public and its representation of women. Similarly, I introduce the 1983 film *La nuit de Varennes* in Chapter 4 as a recent instance of that which works to transform our understanding of the Old Regime. What comes first changes our notion of what comes after, and vice versa. What is important is that we are not obliged to privilege either of these relations. Above all, although we can criticize representations, we can never escape the web of representations. Criticism takes the form of reading representations. Additionally, there are *parallel* as well as *sequential* processes. What Mary Wollstonecraft or Edmund Burke write on the contemporaneous French Revolution may not influence its course directly, but these parallel processes, of revolution and the British reaction to it, may converge, as in the later history of feminism and bourgeois society. I seek to exemplify these possibilities, without exhausting them.

This book belongs preeminently to the overlapping areas of current research in women's studies, feminist theory, and cultural studies. The "Weber thesis" directly influenced the work of early modern historians, but also of people in many other fields; so, too, the "Habermas thesis," together with its German and French supplements. And just as whole books have been written on, and thereby established the tradition of, the first thesis, so the present study continues that of the second. Yet, as I have suggested, what counts here is less the unfolding of a scholarly argument than the political and cultural destinies of societies that have claimed to command universal membership while preserving their partiality. To confound such claims is not necessarily to construct a better universal but to envision a public "whole" that no longer needs shamefacedly to conceal its private "parts."

In Part I, I address the dynamics of political and cultural representation in Old Regime society. In Chapter 1, elite women's public influence, especially their role in shaping public speech and behavior, is juxtaposed to the iconic world of the absolutist court. I discuss the urban salon as an alternative sphere of cultural production within late absolutism and locate the *salonnières'* extreme mannerism as one aspect of the dominant representational system of early modern France which valued manner and artifice over means and object of representation. I observe how male complaints against women's social power and evasion of domesticity are linked in turn to worries about excessively stylized discourses and to the emasculating effects of monarchical power. The chapter concludes with a consideration of Montesquieu's views on the relationship between domestic and political order.

The entire complex associating language, gender, and politics sets the stage for an examination in Chapter 2 of the emergence inside absolutism of what Habermas terms the classical or oppositional bourgeois public sphere. I expand on Habermas' discussion by looking at the shift in systems of representation away from the iconic imagery of the father-king to symbolic politics: for example, a more abstract, ex-centric system of representation based on writing, the law, speech and its proclamation. I consider the impact of the print revolution on the ethos of individualism and on the construction of the bourgeois interior. I ask about the gender preferences of those who inhabit the bourgeois public sphere and propose that the central categories of bourgeois thought — universal reason, law, and nature — are embedded in an ideologically sanctioned order of gender differences and public-private spheres which grounds the institutional and cultural geography of the new public sphere. Finally, I address the role of women in the eighteenth-century ("enlightenment") salon, women's impact on epistolary fiction, and their place within the oppositional press of Old Regime France. A brief exploration of Rousseau's contribution to the active textualization of life — the production, distribution, and circulation of texts — within the eighteenth-century oppositional public sphere segues into Chapter 3, where I discuss in greater detail Rousseau's aversion to public women. I orient my reading of Rousseau to the shift from an iconic, spectacular public life to a textualized symbolic order. I am especially interested in the mechanisms by which Rousseau elicits women's support for a project of domestic virtue; that is, I take seriously the fact that Rousseau writes to and for women, not only about them. Finally, I propose that the figurations of women to be found within Rousseau's texts are constitutive of the organization of public and domestic life in the post-revolutionary world of bourgeois propriety.

In Part II, I consider the fate of women and feminism in the bourgeois public sphere. In Chapter 4 I pose the struggle for authorship which ensued once the king was dead; I ask who gets to be included as "the people" (as authors of the revolution), especially once those on the margins begin to make claims that the principles of the revolution ought to be extended to their logical conclusion. The chapter opens with a reading of the film *La nuit de Varennes* in which I address the ambivalent implications for women of the dramatic shift in political and cultural life that accompanied the fall of the old patriarchy. Against the shift from liberalism to republicanism within the Revolution, I read the discourse on women's rights produced by the Marquis de Condorcet, Olympe de Gouges, Etta Palm d'Aelders, Theodor Gottlieb von Hippel, and Mary Wollstonecraft. I also look at women's role in the Revolution, from the dramatic march on Versailles to their participation in revolutionary clubs, societies, the press, and, finally, the Society of Revolutionary Republican Women—a novel, cross-class radical organization of women, committed to the program of the Terror, which existed briefly during the height of the popular revolution in Paris and whose suppression occasioned the banning of all political activity by women. I reject the claim that this outcome was inevitable; rather, I ask how it is that women revolutionaries (as political women) *became* unnatural during the course of the Revolution. I feature the representations of women as frivolous, disorderly, emasculating, and sexually dangerous or endangered which surfaced during the Revolution, and I am careful to distinguish the class divisions that separated women at this time. In summary, however, I try to establish that the Republic was constructed against women, not just without them.

In Chapter 5 I counterpose the Revolution's outcomes to a more systematic discussion of the symbolic representations of women produced during the Revolution, for example, Liberty but also the figuration of domestic and public life in David's masterpiece *The Oath of the Horatii*. David's visual rhetoric symbolizes the oppositions between family and state, private and public life, characteristic of the new republic. Liberty functions as a representation of the extent to which gender relations were submitted to republican order. Yet "unrestrained" public women and their sexuality threatened the harmonious community of the gendered republic. I ask, therefore, how virtue operates within the language and practice of republican motherhood—and consider the possibility that political women and feminists shared a common discourse with their republican brothers.

In Chapter 6 I contrast Auguste Comte's positivist philosophy to Flora Tristan's socialist feminism in light of the revival of feminist activity during the 1830s and 1840s and the legal barriers to women's freedom which resulted from the passage of the Napoleonic Civil Code in France. I acknowledge the shift in representations of women that emerged in post-revolutionary culture—specifically, a new regard for women's nature, which was credited as a source of difference *and* a cause of women's presumed superiority over men. Although women failed to achieve political emancipation, the Revolution bequeathed them a moral identity and a political constitution. Gender became a socially relevant category in post-revolutionary life. Indeed, both domesticity—including republican motherhood—and feminism might be viewed as two variant but interrelated outcomes of the transformation of the absolutist public sphere. Whereas liberalism was for the most part eclipsed, republican ideology in nineteenth-century France continued to display an enormous force and protean character, a capacity indeed to encompass both feminist and antifeminist alternatives. My readings of Comte and Tristan, therefore, are intended to reveal the positivist and socialist imprint on nineteenth-century republican and feminist discourse. I conclude this book with some reflections on the relationship between women and the public sphere.

# PART I

# WOMEN AND THE
# ABSOLUTIST PUBLIC SPHERE

In France the nation is not a separate body, it dwells entirely within the person of the King.

Louis XIV

The rights and interests of the Nation, which you dare to make into a body apart from the Monarch, are of necessity one with my own, and lie in my hands only.

Louis XV

## CHAPTER 1

# Woman's Voice in the Old Regime

A central metaphor of early modern political discourse was that of the body politic. Since it was thought to be self-evident that no body could be divided into competing interests or factions without risking the life of the whole, it followed that only a unitary and hierarchical organization of society could achieve peace and prosperity. The life of the organism depended on the integration of the parts; so, too, the good of the whole required the rule of one. The Great Chain of Being that stretched from heaven to earth was an order of families, each ruled by a benevolent father. Moreover, the divinity of the greatest earthly father was granted by the Father of us all. And, as the absolutist Christian rulers of France were quick to insist, the power, rights, and interests of the nation were coterminous with the person of the king. The body politic was inscribed on the king's own body.

The theater of absolutism raised the father-king from lord to central icon of the regime. Yet this excessively personal and patriarchal political universe tolerated arenas of public speech and performance by women. Indeed, many contemporaries exaggerated their importance. Still, elite women achieved a public position that had little if anything to do with their domestic roles. (Of course, a woman's public position was conditioned by her "family interest" in a wider sense, that is, by her location within a lineage system or a series of kinship relations.) Women's involvement was in society, in a public life outside of the household and increasingly distinguished from the court as well. It is this paradox within absolutist society which frames my discussion in this chapter.

## Body Politics and Spectacle in the Absolutist Public Sphere

According to medieval juridical theology, the king's body was a double one: kings might come and go, but the king's body persisted across time, providing the physical and intangible supports of the kingdom.[1] The doctrine of the king's two bodies bridged the gaps between the natural and political world and between the impersonal, immortal dynamics of rulership and the intensely personal, even intimate features of the exercise of absolutist power. The legal mechanisms of kingship which distinguished between but also linked the person of the king and the demands of the court were further buttressed by an immense iconography of power—a whole ritual culminating in the coronation, the funeral, and the ceremonies of submission. The absolutist court functioned as a vast visual and theatrical spectacle, a machinery whose royal retinue functioned to authorize the king's superior and indivisible power. Like a god, the monarch was memorialized and imaged in ceremonial court practices and in artistic representations ranging from the most lowly on coins to the loftiest royal portraiture.[2] The king's touch was even said to cure scrofula. His was a magical body.[3] In a world in which all political authority was mapped onto the body of the king, the center acquired a deeply sacred status.

The official public sphere of the absolutist court achieved and maintained its sacred status by virtue of its performative character. It is precisely this feature of the absolutist public sphere which interests Habermas; for example, the need for repeated reenactment of the sources and conditions of public power, hence its "re-presentative" character.[4] The grand spectacle of absolutism required a repeated reenactment of the sources and conditions of public power. The court, with its festivals, balls, banquets, royal chambers, coronations, and entry ceremonies, operated to place the visual aspects of theater in command. Ancient symbols were invoked to magnify the king's past and future power; for example, the figures of Apollo and Hercules were employed in France to make tangible the mystique of kingship at the heart of absolutism, to lift the monarch from mere humanity to supernatural myth.[5]

The metaphors of the stage and stagecraft describe best the genius of Louis XIV: "As a virtuoso performer in the elaborate piece of baroque stagecraft that was his reign," writes Joseph Klaits, "he wanted Europe to believe that he also had composed the script, built the set, designed the costumes, and directed the action. By identifying himself totally with his role of monarch, Louis gave dynamic life to absolutist ideology."[6] A theatrical performance, however, would be nothing without its audience. And in the "artwork of the absolutist state" French society was not merely passive. The king's subjects participated in the ceremony of monarchy. Corporate groups were molded into vehicles of royal grandeur. Academies, for example, were founded under royal auspices so that the creations of their members would serve the reproduction of absolutist power. Under the Bourbon monarchs, and especially during the reign of Louis XIV, even the great nobility became one more resplendent appurtenance of monarchical power. Life was lived at court, far away from provincial responsibilities and powers.

All state occasions were invested with religious and courtly pomp. And no matter how privileged and restricted the audience, the events were public happenings. The royal family and the nobility enjoyed a kind of publicity, a publicness, which defined their status and position within the state. Indeed, the nobility was by definition a social class whose private actions had public consequences for the whole nation. Their living quarters were less a private retreat than a semipublic household whose codes of behavior, dress, personal comportment, forms of pleasure, and social attitudes were mimed by other social groups in the nation jealous for recognition and status. Everywhere in old Europe elites adopted the behavior, language, and architecture of the court of Versailles.

Whereas the court was the home of the monarch and his immediate family, it also represented the state to its subjects. It was not strictly divided according to public and private spaces. Although the king's chambers were not accessible to all, neither could they be considered private in a modern sense. Moreover, the mechanisms of influence were such that intimacy with the king, his ministers, confidantes, family members, or personal favorites usually favorably swayed political outcomes.[7] The monarch's family and the court nobility served as a royal audience, to be sure, but they also functioned as part of the elaborate machinery of absolutism. Their own actions represented the king's power before the broader audience of the entire nation.

In the grand spectacle of royal absolutism, the figuration of power was tied ineluctably to the masculine subject of the monarch. All circuits of desire pointed in the direction of the king's body. Accordingly, visual representations of power dominated all other forms of communication.[8] The object of this iconic structure of representation was at once a divine king and an intimate father. Power was enacted and tied to the king's person in a theatrical system of communication. Patriarchal norms were strongly embedded within the routine practices of absolutist society. Nevertheless, women were very much in evidence in the impressive spectacle of royalty. For one thing, they were absolutely essential to the generational reproduction of class power. Moreover, through sexual intrigue or marriage, women achieved a jealously guarded intimacy with the monarch or his personal representatives. They often served as conduits or mediators for aspiring courtiers and socially ambitious gentlemen. Over and over again, one hears men decrying the influence of female powerbrokers—not only in the court, but in the salon, a novel institution of Old Regime society soon to be discussed.

In a society in which one man was so far elevated above all the rest, it would seem that all subjects, male and female, shared a subordinate posture. The effect of the king's supremacy in the grand household of the kingdom, therefore, was to "domesticate," even un-man, those who ought to have been his peers. This, as we shall see, was the angry protest of those who celebrated the virile constitutions of republics and despised the "effeminized" status of men under absolutism. The metaphoric language of the complaint suggests a link between gender and power, and indeed many proposed to cure this intolerable state of affairs through a kind of "domestic reform" in which the king would be restored to a more modest position as one among equals and women would be returned to the aristocratic and bourgeois households to which they properly belonged. No longer would men find the corridors of power blocked by influential women.

## Gender Relations and State Structure

The enormous centralization and concentration of power which accompanied the growth of the absolutist state in the West, along with the creation of the privatized nuclear family, have been identified as key factors in accounting for a shift in gender conceptualizations in early modern Europe.[9] The historian Natalie Zemon Davis argues that avenues for women's freedom were foreclosed rather than expanded with the rise of the modern nation state, secular culture, private property, and even Protestantism.[10] Her research highlights the manner in which culture mediated structures of economic and political life for women. Within early modern society, women of urban artisanal classes participated in a range of public activities and also shared work settings with men (even though they were generally disadvantaged in terms of tasks, wages, and access to property). On the other hand, noble-born women were experiencing a real loss in status and position which has been attributed to such factors as the consolidation of modern nation states, republican ideology, and changing family structure.[11] Recalling that medieval women had borne arms and governed jurisdictions, Joan Kelly denotes two respects in which the process of state formation affected women—the loss of power women of rank suffered as states eroded the military, juridical, and political powers of aristocratic families, and the formation of the preindustrial, patriarchal household as the basic social unit, as well as the economic unit, of postfeudal society.[12]

I have no quarrel with the general outline of this argument. Indeed, I insist that the eighteenth century marked a turning point for women in the construction of modern gender identity: public–private oppositions were being reinforced in ways that foreclosed women's earlier independence in the street, in the marketplace, and, for elite women, in the public spaces of the court and aristocratic household. But we also need to account for the emergence of a very impressive social institution in which women exercised a considerable degree of power—unmatched in subsequent or prior eras. Women appeared to organize according to certain fixed rules of comportment and speech, a terrain upon which manners and talk were decisively altered. In the salons, men of the aristocracy mingled with writers, artists, scholars, merchants, lawyers, and officeholders. A novel pattern of interchange existed between educated men and literate, informed women who functioned not just as consumers but as purveyors of culture. This culture remained an elite affair, but it represented a potent alternative to court society, a gathering so all-important that the French called it *le monde*, literally, "the world."[13] The salon was associated in the public mind with a new shape of life which integrated alternative sources of status into the culture of the traditional social elite. These new cultural arrangements were not greeted with equanimity by all. Even those who basked in their atmosphere complained about unwarranted female influence. Many identified women with an egregious trend toward overconsumption and luxury. In other words, precisely at the moment when the monarchy was amassing national power—with the effect of restricting the independence of the old nobility—and displaying national wealth on an unprecedented scale, a group of women rose to social prominence. They themselves were drawn overwhelmingly from the aristocracy and the haute bourgeoisie. They attended court, but also belonged to the city. In fact, they were part of a movement to define a new center, that of the capital.[14]

Although the salon shared many features with the emerging oppositional, bourgeois public sphere of the cities, on some points—not least of which is the position of women in society—the two were in conflict. I prefer, therefore, to regard the salon as a rather unique institution of the early modern period. The salon has often been compared to the press and cited as a "vast engine of power, an organ of public opinion."[15] In this role, it was displaced in part with the creation of a modern publishing apparatus; as a mode of cultural production which survived in shadow form into the later modern age, it failed to make the same successful adaptation as the press. Neither strictly bourgeois nor aristocratic, this much is certain: like other institutions that flourished during the classical liberal phase of the late absolutist public sphere, the salon declined in importance with the rise of the mass media and modern industry—what Habermas terms the "structural transformation of the bourgeois public sphere." In what follows, I focus on a prominent feature of absolutist public life, the existence of performative and vocalizing roles for women in salon society, and attempt to locate this feature within the larger political and cultural geography of the age.

## Salon and Salonnière

The women against whom men revolted were distinguished by their participation in and leadership of urban salons. Established in France during the seventeenth century, salons flourished in France and elsewhere in Western Europe for two centuries. To some extent, the salon was merely an extension of the institutionalized court, which already accorded royal women positions of leadership in matters of taste and pleasure.[16] But it also allowed for the extension of the culture of polite society to an ever-widening groups of persons, persons often outside the traditional nobility, brought to prominence by the growth of the absolutist monarchy and especially by its venal officeholding system.[17] As non-nobles acquired land and office, gradually usurping noble titles, they consciously imitated the noble way of life. And since the central feature of upward social mobility depended on one's ability to live like a noble, salon women were particularly important in teaching the appropriate style, dress, manners, language, art, and literature to these newcomers. Indeed, the salon was central to making this usurpation possible.[18] The salon, then, contributed to the consolidation of the elite by introducing new members into its folds. Even so, it remained a highly restricted affair. One participated by invitation, and to attend a salon was to know and be known by those who counted in society.

Salonnières, then, were a social force that abetted the integration of new individuals into the elite. They encouraged social assimilation by marriage of previously unaffiliated groups—whether new and old nobility, bourgeois and aristocrat, or Jew and gentile.[19] Romantic love was used as the justification for these new arrangements, which challenged the old ways of custom and rank. In the process, however, women began to redefine nobility and virtue. Not birth but commerce, venality of office, and intrigue at court became the new coins of power. Women functioned as adjuncts, then, of a system of advancement for merit. Circles at court and salons in the city became centers of female power brokers.[20] In effect, what was occurring was the cultural integration of new groups within a *mondain*, or worldly culture of the nobility. But, in the process, noble values came to be dissociated from birth and attached to behavior.

Thus the salon belonged to a wider urban culture — beyond the sphere of the court proper. It was distinguished by its "worldliness," its cosmopolitan character. And it was a factor in the important evolution of the status system toward money and away from the land.[21] Connections, rather than formal invitations, provided one access to a good salon. Conversation, new works of art, bureaucratic patronage, status, wealth, and even daughters were exchanged at these gatherings. Wit, urbanity, conversation, politesse, and pleasure were the earmarks of salon society. Here, literature passed into life, and life into literature. Verbal portraits originating as salon games made their way into novels, while novels and other printed materials were read aloud inside the salon. In this aristocratic world of spectacular relations, where seeing and being seen was an overriding concern, a favorite sport was to play dress up. Disguised as characters from their favorite novels, members of the salon circle produced amateur theatrical productions for their own entertainment. The salons became schools for assimilation into aristocratic manners. From women, bourgeois gentilhommes learned how to comport themselves. And what they learned was the polish and affability required to exist and to succeed in a world of exteriority — a world dominated by appearances in much the manner of Versailles. So the *précieuse*, the purportedly affected woman of the Parisian salons, was deemed the female counterpart of the *honnête homme*, "the man of whatever social origin who appropriated to himself noble *civilité*."[22]

Carolyn Lougee observes that those who welcomed a wider definition of the social elite were typically advocates of women's education and rank, whereas those who rejected it (whom she terms antifeminists) were opponents of women and especially of their public role, favoring instead a project of domestic reform for the nation as a whole. We must, however, distinguish two distinct, though often overlapping, complaints. First, noble resentment toward the rise of the bourgeois gentilhomme surfaced in arguments against the salon, the institution deemed most responsible for the disruption of traditional social stratification. Nobles denounced salon society for contributing to a general social upheaval, for unregulated luxury that left undifferentiated properly unequal ranks and undermined the traditional system whereby different social groups had distinct dress, manners, and customs. Even aristocratic women of the court complained of the cost of dressing themselves in the face of their urban bourgeois competitors, and men feared their ruin by well-to-do and ambitious wives.[23] Second, then, criticisms of the institution easily gave way to complaints against those with whom it was most associated. Attacks were leveled against women for their frivolity, luxury, and impropriety. The style of the précieuse was perceived as "a mask worn on occasion but not defining the lady's whole self," something to be shrugged off when inconvenient.[24] The women were accused of masquerade and imposture; their fault, that of changing themselves, leaving their proper station. Félix de Juvenal aptly protested, "There is not one who does not believe her condition to be far higher than it actually is." And François de Grenaille objected, "We see coquettes who are sometimes not even noble and who wish to be better treated than Queens."[25]

Disgruntled members of the traditional aristocracy accused the salons of being merely elegant brothels. They linked illicit love, the reign of women, and the breakdown of traditional social stratification. They denounced theaters, assemblies, operas, and novels. Antoine Arnauld, for example, feared the potential of all these manifestations of his culture to "inflame the passions," to deify love.[26] The public role of women, and the ideal of leisure it represented, was thought to corrupt society. Even the promenade, an institution of le monde where people of different ranks might be seen walking together in public, was accused of violating the norms of order in society. Antifeminists denounced the effeminates (of their own class) who adopted the refinement and leisure ethic of women, abandoning their military professions and thus weakening the state. In Jacques-Joseph Duguet's assessment, "gradually, the court where they have power . . . degenerates into a court full of amusements, pleasures, frivolous occupations. Luxury, revelry, gambling, love, and all the consequences of these passions reign there. The city soon imitates the court; and the province soon follows these pernicious examples. Thus, the entire nation, formerly full of courage, grows soft and becomes effeminate, and the love of pleasure and money succeeds that of virtue."[27]

What we are witnessing here is the articulation of a cultural complaint (against bourgeois ennoblement, and the institutions—especially salons—which made it possible) in political and gendered terms. The metaphor of "the reign of women" signified the corruption of society at its heights. (By implication, only a corrupt and inadequately virile ruler would allow himself and his kingdom to be disarmed by the exercise of female power.) In response, therefore, antifeminists argued for social regeneration from below. Their vision was one of population growth, moral reform, and sound management of family income. Marriage was proposed as an antidote to préciosité and polite society. The isolation of woman in the home was offered as a way to preserve the world from feminization and a way of saving individual women from the corruptions of le monde. Woman's love would then become a private bond between the domesticated woman and her dependents, children and servants, rather than a social force uniting large groups of people. This decentralized vision of the moral regeneration of France was one in which the state would emerge stronger as the sum of its private (familial parts), and social status by birth would be restored.

It is not enough to say, then, that we owe the origin of a new family ideology in the West to the rise of the bourgeoisie, and to the corresponding decline of an older code of aristocratic sociability.[28] Since the seventeenth century, noble reformers had embraced the cult of the family: François de Salignac de la Mothe-Fénelon incorporated a vision of domestic woman into a wider understanding of aristocratic reform.[29] Moreover, aristocratic reformers were enamored of Rome. Repudiating Christian ascetic morality and the neo-Platonist form of mondain moral philosophy, they discovered in the "ancient republic" an attractive model of reformed sexual morality, female chastity, simplicity, and frugality with which to counteract the excesses of feminine luxury. Actually, both the monarchy and the traditional nobility employed classical motifs, but the monarchy tended to prefer the symbols of imperial Rome over those of the republic.

Fénelon despised both the court and the city. He deemed both to be parasitic institutions, especially on the luxury trade. He proposed a regeneration of society from below through agriculture. Likewise, he objected to the professionalization of courtiers and of polite society. For him, "courtly culture based upon leisure was a type of feminization which created men incapable of diligent application to their professions."[30] By reviving the Aristotelian notion of family as the fundamental unit of civic life, Fénelon and other antifeminists would return women to the family, balance their role by broad domestic duties (including for elite women, the management of estates), and impose rigid spheres without which only social disorder would reign.

By the seventeenth century, then, a vision of the "domestic republic" was being articulated by disgruntled nobles who tied their resentments against the breakdown of traditional social stratification to complaints about women's cultural power.[31] Many of the terms of this attack on women would come to be shared by the bourgeoisie, so it is noteworthy that the metaphor of "women out of place" to signify a corrupted society and an emasculated state power was first used by members of the traditionalist aristocracy. I propose, therefore, to explore more systematically some of the cultural implications of the political figurations of women during the Old Regime.

## Language, Gender, and Politics

Women, especially salonnières, were accused repeatedly of artifice and authorship of stylized discursive practices in conflict with nature. Yet the artistry of these cultivated women was in the employment of mannerisms in language, history, painting, mythology, and drama which were widely celebrated during the classical age in France. The salonnières displayed their pictorial wit by drawing verbal portraits of one another and of their friends. History and mythology were regular features of their parlor games. Their extreme mannerism was an aspect of the dominant *ut pictura poesis* representational system of early modern France, which assigned a disproportionate influence to manner over means and object of representation. As Erica Harth observes, "The value of representation came to consist in the 'artifice,' or skillful manner, of its imitation. From the ancient concept of art as imitation the moderns evolved an art *of* imitation."[32]

It is appropriate to locate these complaints against women alongside the all-determining opposition between preciosity and classicism in Old Regime France, in which the former signified female influence and the arbitrary, overly refined and excessive uses of language. Although precious speech did not wholly depart from the rules of grammar, its pleasurable play with language stood out. Preciosity shared with the wider system of aristocratic artistic representation an aesthetic sensibility uniting the verbal and visual arts by analogy. Not absolute truth but verisimilitude, the simultaneous imitation and enhancement of life, was the adopted goal of all artistic practice. But, the précieuse subscribed to moral philosophy, not Christian morality or the secular ethics of the ancients, as a way of knowing how to live in polite society. Also, by focusing on the particular—as in her parlor games, costumed excursions, or even historical novels that were thinly disguised portraits of contemporaries—the précieuse undercut the central principle of absolutist representation, that is, the glorification and celebration of the royal subject. As Harth points out, "The 'precious' aesthetic centers on the particular; the classical aesthetic soon to take over prescribed the depiction of things according to 'nature,' for it centered on the general or the universal. . . . The portrait's value as a parlor game derived from the particularity of its reference, for only the initiates could either appreciate the artifice in the imitation of a known model or guess the model from the artfulness of the imitation."[33] Finally, in the place of pedantry, the précieuse stood for spirited and pleasurable conversation. For all these reasons, it is not inappropriate to think of the précieuse as a modernist. Unlike many of her male contemporaries, she had little patience for classical models of virtue and behavior.

As rhetorical figure, then, the name "précieuse" constructs an illusion charged with ambivalent associations and fears about woman's capacity to displace power within a phallic order — an order composed by male social dominance and by masculine authority over the Word. Molière's satire of woman's "unnatural" attacks on language in *La critique de l'école des femmes*, like his memorable title *Les précieuses ridicules*, comically captures masculine anxiety that "the woman who tampers with language does violence to the natural order."[34] The impulse to recuperate this disorder by evoking the sin of female pride is evidenced in the following remark by Abbé Michel de Pure, the seventeenth-century author of *La prétieuse; ou, Le mystère des ruelles*: "They have invented a haughty and glorious name for themselves to imitate truly learned women," he protests. "They call themselves précieuses, form salons, hold meetings, debate issues, judge books, give their opinions about other people's works, and by an unparalleled tyranny, cannot tolerate a book that is not to their taste, nor a mind that does not resemble their own."[35]

Indeed, the same women who willfully and unnaturally oppose marriage are accused of extending their empire by a willful and unnatural control over language. This brings us back to a very basic fact. The salonnières existed as public women outside the institution of marriage. They were hardly enamored of the maternal function. Above all, they advocated love matches, within or outside marriage. Marriage for them was primarily a situation of convenience, even a game of strategy. In the place of privatized bonds among family members, the salonnières authorized purely social activities—happiness, friendship, social polish, and pleasure. They subscribed to an ethos of sociability, not domesticity. In this light, Pure's charges against these women are even more arresting—that they "invent a name" for themselves, form salons, hold meetings, debate issues, judge books, give their opinions about other's works. The women are accused of acting as critics and arbiters of cultural production—worse, they are guilty of altering the masculine monopoly on linguistic meaning and usage.

Because of their presumptuous manipulation of language, the précieuses traversed the male monopoly of pure mind. They are unnatural, therefore, in the further sense of yearning to be men. And where women are men, there is nothing left for men to be but women. We seem to have come full circle to the dilemmas of everyman in the absolutist public sphere in which one man claims a complete monopoly on all power and prestige. And man's effeminization is even more troubling if the source of emasculation is identified as a woman. In some deep sense, then, women's violation of the codes of language is associated with a fantasy that such women are also capable of breaking the contract that structures family life, that ties women to (their) men, and that undermines women's capacity to act in concert with other women.

## Revolting Women

In the *Persian Letters*, Montesquieu cleverly narrates the tale of a revolt against domestic despotism by the wives in an oriental harem who have been abandoned to the untempered rule of eunuchs during their husband/master's travels in France.[36] The *Letters* feature a strong moral lesson regarding what can happen if women are either too free or too suppressed. The challenge is to discover their proper place.[37] Usbek, a Persian nobleman, leaves Persia in 1711 in the company of his friend Rica. Their travels take them to

France during the reign of Louis XIV and the first years of the regency, where they remain until 1720. During the nine years of Usbek's absence, his wives become increasingly unruly. Usbek first seems an especially enlightened and loving husband. Yet after his wives' revolt he authorizes the use of force in the seraglio. The head eunuch undertakes a violent course of action, destroying whatever fragile chances for peace remain. Usbek upholds the eunuch's rule, despite his favorite wife Roxanne's appeal that "horror, darkness, and dread rule the seraglio; it is filled with terrible lamentation; it is subject at every moment to the unchecked rage of a tiger" (Letter 156). Tragically, Usbek learns that Roxanne has taken a lover. She denounces Usbek's tyranny and kills herself.

The novel's harsh parable of the effects of despotism on public and private life is punctuated by witty and arresting portraits of French Old Regime life. It consists of a series of letters written and received by the Persian travelers. In this parody of the conventional European travel narrative, outsiders view the inside and readers are made aware of what, to a foreign sensibililty, are their own excessive social practices—not least of which is the unusually liberal role of French women. As Usbek tells Roxanne, "The women here have lost all restraint. . . . Instead of the dignified simplicity and pleasing delicacy of manner that is the rule among you, a crude immodesty prevails" (Letter 26). Rica mocks women's witty conversation and the extremes they go to in publicizing their ideas: "Making a witty remark is not enough: it has to be publicized and distributed. Otherwise it's as good as lost. I can tell you that there is nothing more dispiriting than to see a well-turned remark that one has made going to its death in the ear of some fool of a listener" (Letter 54). In addition, the Persians identify women with some of the most distasteful French customs, openly public forms of pleasure such as gambling and fashion. "But the hardest thing of all to believe," writes Rica, "is how much it costs for a husband to keep his wife in fashion." After further ridiculing French women's obsession with fashion, Rica goes on to

link this abuse with courtly life: "It is the same with manners and modes of behaviour as with fashion: the French
change their ways according to the age of their king. The
monarch might even manage to make the nation serious if
he were to attempt it. The sovereign imposes his attitudes
on the court, the court on the town, and the town on the
provinces; his mind is the pattern which determines the
shape of all the others" (Letter 99).

Fashionable women, through the promotion of luxury and
excess, have an equally malevolent effect on the economy.
"Paris, which is perhaps the most sensuous town in the
world, is where pleasures are most subtly cultivated, but it
is perhaps also the place where one leads the hardest life. For
one man to live in luxury, a hundred others must work without respite. A woman gets it into her head that she must
wear a particular outfit on some occasion, and at once it
becomes impossible for fifty craftsmen to get any sleep or
have leisure to eat and drink; she gives her commands and
is obeyed more promptly than our monarch, since self-
interest is the greatest monarch on earth" (Letter 106).
Speaking through the Persians, but reflecting the prejudices
of the parliamentary nobility to which he belongs by birth,
Montesquieu alerts us to the want of order and propriety in
the public and private life of France. France, too, calls out for
a reconstructed domestic regime. In its absence, there exists
nothing but weakened marriages, uncontrolled social
mobility, declining population and prosperity, prostitution,
excessive celibacy, and both abortion and excessive anti-
abortion laws.

Virtually everything is perverted, but worst of all are the
political consequences of this overly feminized atmosphere:
a king and a kingdom ruled by women. As Rica complains,
"For every man who has any post at court, in Paris, or in the
country, there is a woman through whose hands pass all the
favours and sometimes the injustices that he does. These
women are all in touch with one another, and compose a
sort of commonwealth [*république*] whose members are always busy giving each other mutual help and support." So,

he concludes, invoking the most fearsome political meta-phor of his day, "it is like *another state within the state,* and a man who watches the actions of ministers, officials, or prelates at court, in Paris or in the country, without knowing the women who rule them, is like a man who can see a machine in action but does not know what makes it work" (Letter 107; emphasis added). France has been re-duced to a situation in which women operate *in consort* to exercise authority and to allocate power.

Yet none of this can excuse the Persians and their life-style. Oriental polygamous marriage practices appear espe-cially backward and uncivilized from the vantage of French society. Attempting to straddle both worlds, Usbek deludes himself into thinking he has a modern, romantic relation-ship with Roxanne, even while he has reduced her to a con-dition of absolute bondage. Breaking the ban of silence imposed on the seraglio, Roxanne achieves authentic speech only at the novel's tragic conclusion. Her words burst forth in fury, exposing the hypocritical sentimentality and sham liberty of all women (and men) subjected to the rule of abso-lute dominion: "Yes, I deceived you. I suborned your eu-nuchs, outwitted your jealousy, and managed to turn your terrible seraglio into a place of delightful pleasures. . . . How could you have thought me credulous enough to imagine that I was in the world only in order to worship your caprices? that while you allowed yourself everything, you had the right to thwart all my desires? No: I may have lived in servitude, but I have always been free. I have amended your laws according to the laws of nature, and my mind has always remained independent" (Letter 161).

Usbek learns the meaning of love tragically. He has mis-taken submission for virtue, resistance for desire, and mod-esty for faithfulness. He has overlooked the fact that to be a partner in love, one must be free to return another's affec-tions. Men are not exempt from the consequences of domes-tic despotism. As Rica confesses, after observing the French, "Our wives are too exclusively ours; . . . being so firmly in possession leaves us nothing to desire, or to fear; . . . a certain amount of fickleness is like salt, which adds flavour and prevents decay" (Letter 38).

## Virtuous Wives

The seraglio represents a society untempered by the civilizing influence of civil society, an essential feature of which is marriage. Marriage can establish the necessary boundary between the natural and the social; and although marriage in civil society may well be based on property, its distinguishing feature is that of a contractual union between two consenting partners, man and wife. Women are offered the opportunity to transcend the fate of compelled subordination through the dynamics of domesticity within a monogamous match. Montesquieu explores the possibility of yoking femininity to masculine desire through the device of sexual love. But love alone is not sufficient. Left alone, it might result in a romantic, adulterous passion. Montesquieu upholds unequivocally the law of the fathers. As Usbek states in the *Letters*, "It is noticeable that in countries where fathers are given wide powers to punish and reward, families are better run. Fathers resemble the creator of the universe, who, although he could lead men by love, also binds them to him by the motives of hope and fear" (Letter 129).

Montesquieu addresses the temperizing qualities of marriage within civil society more directly in his major political treatise, *The Spirit of Laws*. In the *Letters*, we are led to condemn the effects of despotism. But the outcome is not meant to be perfect liberty either. It is worth recalling that it is the women's expression of egoistic individualism, their particular interest inside marriage, or what Roxanne calls her freedom, that unleashes this awful cycle of anarchy and violence. Montesquieu strives to find the appropriate public and private institutions (including marriage) that will moderate the passions and strike a middle course between absolute liberty and despotism.[38] In *The Spirit of Laws*, he painstakingly correlates political forms such as monarchy, despotism, and republicanism with the effects of climate and marital customs, guiding attention to the effect on public and private virtue of "the condition or state of women in different governments."[39] His conclusion is simple: the vices of aristocratic luxury lead to female corruption. Women's unrestrained liberty and vanity spill over into the public domain of the court whenever ambitious courtiers are compelled to seek advancement through the offices of powerful women. In contrast, he praises the virtue and freedom of women under republican constitutions wherein liberty is constrained by manners, luxury banished, and with it corruption and vice. But, he warns, where women are out of their proper place, men are reduced to an effeminate posture and disorder necessarily ensues.

The danger is ever present. Women's weakness, according to Montesquieu, is not pride but vanity. "Luxury," he insists, "constantly attends them."[40] There is a further link between women's natural vice and the corruption that flows from excessive luxury. According to Montesquieu, luxury derives either from inequality or from the desire to distinguish oneself in the eyes of others. The reader is warned against ills associated with a specularly oriented society and encouraged to see woman's narcissistic display as both symptom and cause of aristocratic corruption. Like other members of the parliamentary nobility, Montesquieu objects to that sector of his class who have been absorbed into the machinery of absolutism, fated to live a life of complete appearance, existing for a glimpse of the royal presence.

Montesquieu applies the metaphor linking women and civilization in this way: in despotic government women are enslaved; in monarchies women are free. In his words, "The despotic power of the prince is naturally connected with the servitude of women, the liberty of women with the spirit of monarchy."[41] Carefully distancing himself from these two poles, and therefore from the sexual conventions of Old Regime France as well, Montesquieu notes that, where liberty abounds, women are less apt to act virtuously. He presents a third possibility: there is, he argues, a qualitative difference between the liberty of women within monarchies and within republics. He favors a chastened, less sumptuous, more continent ideal of womanhood, one that places women within the domestic realm. He scorns the deceitful display and staged appearances of a theatrically structured public realm. His contempt for luxury and for that peculiarly urban desire to distinguish oneself in the eyes of others, along with his belief that in republics a loss of virtue signals decline, explains some of the praise he lavishes on a custom of the ancient Samnites to reward their virtuous young men for services to their country with a wife: "Love, beauty, chastity, virtue, birth, and even wealth itself," Montesquieu writes, "were all, in some measure, the dowry of virtue."[42] Thus he treats women as the coin of stately service, as nothing more than a gift-commodity to be exchanged among men. Recalling Aristotle's praise for a moderate constitution, Montesquieu concludes that democracy is compromised and corrupted as a result of either too much equality, which breeds despotism, or too much inequality, the mark of aristocracy. And like Aristotle, he insists on the patriarchal presuppositions of republican rule.[43] This is the real meaning of private virtue, at least for women. The corrupt desire for complete equality in a republic turned despotic has its analogue in the private sphere. He protests: "If respect ceases for old age, it will cease also for parents; deference to husbands will be likewise thrown off, and submission to masters. This licentiousness will soon captivate the mind; and the restraint of command be as fatiguing as that of obedience. Wives, children, slaves, will shake off all subjection. No longer will there be any such thing as manners, order or virtue."[44]

Respect is the law, the very glue holding together all forms of duty, obligation, and submission. Wives, who are otherwise promised the contractual freedom to will their own marital destiny, are reduced here in a most revealing manner to the level of children and slaves from which they ought to have escaped forever. Montesquieu fears that, without respect, society will be reduced to chaos. But is the binding power of duty yet another form of servitude? As Georges Bataille warns, "Respect is really nothing but a devious route taken by violence. On the one hand, respect keeps order in the sphere where violence is forbidden; on the other, it makes it possible for violence to erupt incongruously in fields where it has ceased to be permissible. The taboo does not alter the violence of sexual activity, but for disciplined mankind it opens a door closed to animal nature, namely, the transgression of the law."[45] It is, however, just such constant transgression for which Montesquieu believes he has found a permanent solution. The forward march of civilization, he cautions, requires the domestication of women; in a more advanced society, women will be sure to occupy their proper place. The domestic woman is accommodated to her new surroundings, her narcissistic vanity and licentious use of freedom are curbed, and her nature, like that of a domesticated animal, is made to fit a depoliticized domestic environment. In compensation, Montesquieu proposes that republican women will be neither slaves nor libertines. They will be emancipated from the abhorrent domestic slavery typified by the oriental seraglio, just as they will be harbored from the temptations of the absolutist public sphere in which women weave their influence in the courtyards and boudoirs of the monarchy. Private virtue within the male-defined, restricted family, Montesquieu hopes, will provide the foundation for a patriotic and virile political constitution. "Society," along with its female actors, will be superfluous in the new republican polity.

As we shall discover, many of the arguments against women's speech and power originally articulated by Montesquieu and other members of the ancient nobility were redeployed in the symbolic politics and theories of the emerging bourgeois public sphere, and Montesquieu's dream of the domestication of women was enacted by the male leadership of the French Revolution and their post-revolutionary successors. Indeed, the new symbolic order of nineteenth-century bourgeois society was predicated on the silencing of public women.

CHAPTER 2

# The New Symbolic Politics

The changes associated with the long transition from feudalism to capitalism have been frequently rehearsed, but
rarely from the perspective of the introduction of new patterns of cultural and political communication. As Habermas argues, new communication systems fostered by the
cosmopolitan culture and economic infrastructure of the
cities worked to liberate political discourse and contributed
substantively to the revolutionary atmosphere of the last
decades of the century. Stated otherwise, "the town was a
form of acculturation in itself." The main theme organizing
the cultural geography of eighteenth-century society was
"this very ancient definition of the town as the home of
Enlightenment and civilization."[1]

The great capital cities functioned as major nodes within
a national and international system of exchange in which
cash purchases of unfamiliar goods were possible for growing numbers of people. For the eighteenth-century urban
dweller, the "public" came to mean an arena of strangers and
acquaintances, a life passed outside of the sphere of family
and close friends.[2] And the new cultural institutions arising
in urban centers — coffeehouses, clubs, reading and language
societies, lending libraries, concert halls, opera houses,
theaters, publishing companies, lecture halls, museums,
journals and newspapers — were all distinctive products of a
swelling verbal and written culture. Suspended between

39

civil society and the state, they brought into existence a new public world, what Habermas calls the classical or oppositional bourgeois public sphere.

Although salon society was also a feature of this new public universe, the salon was among the most traditional of these new institutions. It represented, as I argued in Chapter 1, an alternative sphere of cultural production inside absolutism. In addition, the salon was set apart from all the others by its pronounced feminine character. It is precisely this feature of salon society on which contemporaries remarked. This suggests an implicit gender dynamic within the institutional and cultural geography of the oppositional bourgeois public sphere. Moreover, the secret power of bourgeois formalist and universalist rhetoric may be seen to derive from the way it promised to empty out the feminine connotations (and ultimately, the women as well) of absolutist public life. Thus questions arise as to how the bourgeois public sphere was constituted. To whom and for whom was the rhetoric of public opinion addressed? Any discussion of these issues must begin by identifying how the symbolic politics of the emerging bourgeois public sphere was framed from the very outset by masculinist interests and assumptions.

## Symbolic Politics

Habermas' category of the classical bourgeois public sphere denotes an oppositional formation inside Old Regime society which contained the seeds of a radically new social order—that of modern bourgeois society itself. Thomas Crow emphasizes the dynamic character of this public sphere, suggesting that the eighteenth-century bourgeoisie was itself a product of, just as it helped to create, the *new* public spaces of the cities.[3] Moreover, the bourgeois public sphere of the cities, unlike the visually absorbed absolutist public sphere, was oriented around language—its textual production, discussion, and proclamation. There occurred a vastly expanded production of printed texts, or what Robert Darnton calls a heightened demand for the printed word.[4] Other writers identify a shift away from the stable iconic imagery of Old Regime authority to an entirely new discursive economy, one characterized by a regime of words, printed and spoken.[5] Marie-Hélène Huet refers to the opposition between an iconic and a symbolic universe. Adapting François Furet's conceptualization, Huet writes of a progressive shift during the century, culminating in the Revolution, away from the motivated, iconic imagery of the father-king and toward an abstract system of representation in which the impersonal order of law, writing, speech, and its proclamation prevailed. And Keith Michael Baker adds to Habermas' formulation of the public as a political tribunal, arguing that the concept of the public took on meaning in France in the context of a crisis of absolute authority. Both the crown and its opponents appealed to a principle of legitimacy beyond that of the traditional political system to press their competing claims.[6]

Together, then, these critics have outlined the contours of the new symbolic politics of the bourgeois public sphere. We will have recourse to the full range of issues raised here, especially if we are to confront the fact that none of the changes in political and social life associated with the emergence of the bourgeois public sphere seem to have resulted in a situation of gender equality. To the contrary, during the celebrated "Age of Woman," the period of her purported "empire," forces that would eventually limit women's access to public speech and power were already under way. To begin, it is useful to set forth Habermas' formulation of the classical bourgeois public sphere. Most important, he associates it with the rise of public opinion. He argues that informed public opinion began to function as a weapon in the battle against the arbitrary dictates, privileged corporations, and secret practices of the absolutist state. Critics of the Old Regime demanded publicity, not secrecy, in the judicial and legislative sphere. They appealed to the sovereignty of the public against the public claims of the sovereign ruler.

Habermas also proposes that a seeming equality arose among discoursing subjects who claimed the right to speak and judge in "the translucent space of the public sphere" on the basis of universal reason, not social power, privilege, or tradition.[7] Thus, owing to the exercise of rational judgment and enlightened critique by private citizens, a universal public body with great political force was forged.

Of course, this category of the public sphere is itself an ideal representation of a form of discourse Habermas credits with the historical triumph of the bourgeois constitutional and legal order over absolutism. Through such social institutions as the coffeehouse, the literary club, and the free press, private individuals assembled for the free and equal interchange of reasonable discourse. In the process, they produced a social product, public opinion. For Habermas, eighteenth-century public opinion is an entirely new phenomenon—neither Plato's private doxa, nor Locke's private conscience. First of all, opinion was now the outcome of many conversations, many words on the printed page. It was a social product of the first order—all the more so because it was the result of an open form of communication. In principle, no one was barred from joining in its making; access was open to all citizens. Moreover, opinion was not mere opinion (prejudice or habit). It was the result of deliberation on matters of the "general interest." As Habermas states, "Citizens behave as a public body when they confer in an unrestricted fashion—that is, with the guarantee of freedom of assembly and association and the freedom to express and publish their opinions—about matters of general interest."[8]

Habermas attempts to describe the institutional conditions by virtue of which "the liberal fiction of the discursive formation of the public will" was created.[9] In the social geography of the bourgeois public sphere—Crow's new public spaces—he locates the linguistic habits of deliberation, criticism, and opinion. In the communication circuit established by the circulation of words, he sees no hierarchy of speakers, no privileged statuses. In fact, the rational content of writing and speech works to emulsify whatever residue of class-bound content still exists. The differential rights among private individuals who compose this public body are suspended within the region of social discourse itself. In that way, the bourgeois liberal principle of abstract equality is reconfirmed within the new public sphere. Terry Eagleton clarifies Habermas' argument. He writes, "The truly free market is that of cultural discourse itself, within, of course, certain normative regulations; . . . What is said derives its legitimacy neither from itself as message nor from the social title of the utterer, but from its conformity as a statement with a certain paradigm of reason inscribed in the very event of saying."[10]

In practice, however, even participation in the oppositional public sphere was predicated on one's having a certain position in the property order. Habermas admits this, and he poses it as the failure of the bourgeois public sphere to realize its utopian content. Still, he insists that "the public sphere comes into being in every conversation in which private individuals assemble to form a public body. They then behave neither like business or professional people transacting private affairs, nor like members of a constitutional order subject to the legal constraints of a state bureaucracy."[11] In actuality, however, the bourgeois public sphere encouraged a rather messy interaction between the concerns of literary men, financiers, industrialists, and merchants. In that sense, the political, economic, and cultural worlds were wholly intermeshed, belying bourgeois self-definitions of a public sphere oriented around reason not power, rationality not domination, and truth not authority. Even if there was no direct discussion of property interests, such interests became the public sphere's "very concealed problematic, the very enabling structure of its disinterested enquiry."[12] To be disinterested, in effect, was to have an interest. What is remarkable, therefore, is the way the bourgeoisie discovered in impartial discourse and universal reason an idealized image of its own social relations:

Shadowing all particular utterances within this space, delivered inseparably along with them as the very guarantee of their authority, is the form and event of universal reason itself, ceaselessly reproduced in a style of enunciation and exchange which rises above and sits in judgement upon the partial, local messages it communicates. All utterances thus move within a regime which raises them at the very point of production to universal status, inscribes within them a legitimacy which neither wholly pre-exists the particular statement nor is exactly reducible to it, but which, like the elusive concept of 'capacity', is at once identical with and in excess of whatever is spoken.[13]

This predication of the category of the public sphere on a disinterested, universalizing principle of rational discussion can hardly be regarded as unproblematic. Habermas is quick to point to the shortcomings of the bourgeois public sphere. He admits that in a class society oriented to the accumulation of private property, the public sphere can only approximate imperfectly its goal of universality. Indeed, his overriding objective is to account for the loss of an informed and functioning critical public (assuming that it once did or could have existed). Like C. Wright Mills, he worries about the shift from a critical public to a pacified "mass." He argues that the incursion of private interests into public opinion, produced by the unequal distribution of property under capitalism, is illuminated best by the structural transformation of the classical bourgeois public sphere into the late bourgeois public sphere. This transformation occurs under advanced capitalist conditions of mass media and state-guided market systems. In short, he perceives how class structures have suppressed the utopian contents of liberal public opinion. But he never scrutinizes those contents themselves for their own ideological implications. Moreover, his argument is based on a retroactive point of view. It assumes that any future movement for liberation would strive to retrieve and reestablish the lost liberal political contents of early bourgeois society.[14]

Habermas' formulation fails to acknowledge the way the symbolic contents of the bourgeois public sphere worked to rule out all interests that could not or would not lay claim to their own universality. If only what is universal may wear the mantle of truth and reason, then it is precisely everything else that is reduced to the sphere of what Habermas calls "mere opinions (cultural assumptions, normative attitudes, collective prejudices and values)."[15] He ignores the strong association of women's discourse and their interests with "particularity," and he refuses to reckon with the widespread agreement during the century over the reality and force of sexual difference. To the extent that this issue was at all disputed, it was a question of determining how modifiable natural differences might be. Furthermore, even advocates of women questioned the artificial style and language of le monde and argued that education was necessary to return a corrupted society to its natural foundations.

It is striking that in this much celebrated Age of Woman so many of the men who associated with women and benefited tangibly from their society exercised a license to criticize "the sex."[16] Two brief examples help to illuminate this general observation.[17] In his (posthumously published) essay "On Women," the encyclopedist Denis Diderot offers an explanation of women's inferiority on the basis of their legal subordination and poor education. But, he objects, "women accustom us to discuss with charm and clearness the dryest and thorniest subjects. We talk to them unceasingly: We listen to them: We are afraid of tiring or boring them. Hence we develop a particular method of explaining ourselves easily that passes from conversation into *style*."[18] Similarly, Diderot's former friend and antagonist of enlightened circles Jean-Jacques Rousseau upholds the fiction of a "natural language" against the artificial, stylized discourse of eighteenth-century "society." The overly cultivated discourse of the salon is a dominant trope in Rousseau's writings for the moral corruption and social decadence of Parisian society of his day.[19] Thus Diderot accuses women of suppressing the reign of reasoned argument, while Rousseau worries over speech's lost ability to refer to a world of deep human significance.

These remarks are indicative of the manner in which reason was counterposed to femininity, if by the latter we mean (as contemporaries did) pleasure, play, eroticism, artifice, style, politesse, refined facades, and particularity. What reason offered, and from which the feminized culture of le monde detracted, was an ideal version of wholly transparent social relations—relations that conformed to nature itself, free from the soil of human conventionality and "mere opinion." Beyond the present world, another world was said to exist "of the already-seen and already-known, of physical laws and some fixed, immutable order of nature."[20] The effect of such a claim was to oppose nature to art. The imitation of ideal nature as found particularly in classical art and literature promised to combat the sensualized and artificial universe of absolutist art and society by teaching moral virtues.[21] Moreover, this symbolic order of nature was one in which all differences were fixed, where the sexes were positioned in their proper places within the contrasting but mutually interdependent spheres of public and domestic life.

Consequently, universality and reason were relied on to sustain, not to eradicate, the (sexual) differences erected by the order of nature. Bourgeois publicists shared with earlier aristocratic reformers a strong attraction to masculinist classicism and an aversion to a feminine preciosity.[22] The seeming universality of their discourse appears to descend in a straight line from pretensions to universality in classicism. They, too, celebrated the ancient version of public and private life and longed for a world that could once again be inhabited by noble, public men and domestic, virtuous women. They called on nature, therefore, to accomplish its austere purposes as it had in the ancient republic. Consequently, they perceived virtually no contradiction between a transcendant appeal to nature and a respect for the privileged books of ancient learning. If anything, the two were taken as mutual confirmation of a universally derivable set of truths. This outlook was reinforced by the Reformation discovery of the Bible as the "book of nature" or "text of creation," and by early modern scientific materialism, in which nature was approached as a text to be deciphered. In this regard, barriers to women's learning appear to be all the more important. Because women were denied entrance to male institutions of learning, they were excluded from a Latin-based classical curriculum. No matter how learned they became — and many women struggled valiantly to compensate for their inferior educations — they always remained tainted by the powerful stigma of women's preciosity.

Decisively, too, the hegemonic system of aristocratic representation was associated in the public mind with a distinctly feminized sensibility. Mme de Pompadour, for example, was singled out by anti-rococo mid-eighteenth-century Parisian art critics because of her taste for frivolous, mannered, and erotic works. Indeed, oppositional critics objected strenuously to the way style infected politics within the privileged absolutist public sphere. Highly visible public women of the court and the city were targeted as the most egregious examples of aristocratic stylistic excess and imposture. After all, they were long thought to be the violators of the order of nature in language, dress, and society. Bon ton and rococo refinement were seen by pre-revolutionary radical pamphleteers as masks for greed, depravity, and tyranny. In contrast, bourgeois rhetoric was one of unmasking; critics urged the public to attend to outward signs of virtue or vice in individuals. As Thomas Crow observes, "This unmasking, this laying bare of true character, is most often reduced to questions of style — style in manner, in appearance, in written and spoken expression."[23] The virtuous man of the oppositional public sphere aimed to awaken the public to the falsity of bon ton. By society's standards, his speech was an "awkward, overly direct, embarrassingly impassioned discourse." But, as Crow points out, this merely served as a symbol of virtue and nobility, as a sign that he spoke the language of truth as found "dans la Nature toute seule."[24]

To ask, then, how the eighteenth-century bourgeois saw *himself* in the world, or what went into the production of bourgeois ideology, we need to attend to the way audience, rhetorical style, and ideology were all converging. In effect, the bourgeois model of public opinion predicated on universal reason, nature, and truth was a product of the bourgeoisie's idealization of the immediate, instantaneous forms of communication which seemed to exist between writer and public, and especially between artist and audience (in the Salons, the biennial exhibitions begun in 1737, mounted by members of the Royal Academy of Painting and Sculpture) in the new public spaces of Old Regime society. In other words, the transformation of the public sphere passed through a cultural grid. The symbolic and political changes I have been discussing would have been inconceivable except for the actual institutionalization of new forms of public existence which joined audience and critic and fostered the growth of liberal reason.[25] Both language and style were ingredients in the making of bourgeois ideology. Thus Crow proposes, first, that the pre-revolutionary radicals had to invent a language powerful enough to oppose the formidable symbolic structure of the Old Regime, since every form of expression was deemed tainted by privilege. Strikingly, the opposition reduced all conflicts to distinctions between good and evil based on external signs. Second, then, style was the terrain upon which these battles were fought out, and the language of nature was deployed as a substitute for all that was spoiled: "Style itself, those socially given patterns, modes, and nuances of presenting the self and receiving presentations of other selves, is equated with a hated structure of privilege, the appeal is always beyond society to nature; where an unmediated and unproblematic unity between word, action, and meaning is imagined to reign; nobility becomes a province not of society but of the natural world, the domain . . . of the awkward, the untrained, and the improvised."[26]

But style also signified the charged dimension of gender relations—the privileged symbolization of a natural world which would reverse the spoiled civilization of le monde in which stylish women held sway.[27] In this symbolization, public women were a convenient metonym for the worst sides of absolutist life. Appeals to opinion, truth, and reason and virulent attacks on style were constituents of a backlash against the privilege of public women in the absolutist public spheres of court and salon. Indeed, the antifeminist implications of the new symbolic politics did not rest merely on the actual existence or nonexistence of women in public life. This is not to say that the rhetoric of universalism appealed to men but not women, to bourgeois but not peasant and urban artisan. On the contrary, universalism had widespread influence. Its potency and ultimate hegemony derived from its ability to speak across all differences, to solicit the participation of all persons in the name of the general interest. Indeed, the very structure of implicit oppositions (universal–particular, natural–artificial, transparent–masked, male–female) within bourgeois discourse may have helped to ensure its appeal. For all these reasons, discourse was an important factor affecting the fate of public women.

Yet another aspect of this discursive shift was rooted in the material and cultural effects of writing. As Jack Goody observes in his broad-ranging discussion of communication and social evolution, "The written word does not replace speech, any more than speech replaces gesture. But it adds an important dimension to much social action."[28] Following Goody's suggestion, I am attempting to account for the consequences of changes that were taking place in systems of communicative acts, especially as they related to social institutions. Not only the book, but all printed literature, had acquired a heightened symbolic significance. Only a few women could be counted as producers of printed works, sometimes through the posthumous reception of their work as in the case of the seventeenth-century author Mme de Sévigné, whose fame spread in the next century. The majority of those who were acclaimed as literary women (novelists, moralists, memorialists, and writers of published literary correspondence: Mme de Graffigny, Mme d'Epinay, Mme de Lambert, Mme de Tencin, Mme du Deffand, and

Mlle de Lespinasse also received guests in their salons. And with some exceptions, these women were probably first associated with that role rather than with their literary efforts. Also, Mme de Graffigny, one of the most celebrated writers among them, author of *Lettres d'une péruvienne, Cénie,* and *La fille d'Aristide,* even "resisted calling herself an author, because she found the role inappropriate for a woman."[29] Women acted in public theaters, and there was an increase of women playwrights during the Enlightenment. In addition, salonnières organized private stages for the performance of theater pieces, for which Mme de Genlis and others wrote plays. Still, many of women's performances, their theater pieces, even their literature aspired to the Old Regime value of worldliness. Some of their greatest works were regarded as a refinement of the conversational arts practiced in the space of the salon.[30] Taken altogether, the dominant associations of public women were with the spectacular and theatrical functions of the absolutist public spheres. Publicly ambitious women were placed under enormous suspicion by a public increasingly integrated into the new regime or institution of textuality—that is, the production, consumption, and dissemination of printed objects.[31]

*Print Culture, Public Life, and Women*

Those who participated in the eighteenth-century oppositional public sphere inhabited a world of print culture, the product of what has been characterized as the print revolution of the early modern period.[32] The development of a market in printed materials aided in the emancipation of the author and contributed to the rise of an independent press, no longer working in the service of power—the Fourth Estate.[33] The press flourished once printed products could be bought and sold like any other commodity. As Jack R. Censer and Jeremy D. Popkin observe, "It took the Revolution to give the periodical press in France legal freedom, but uncensored periodicals were a de facto part of the French political system long before 1789."[34] Similarly, a lively market in cultural goods provided enjoyment to a public outside of the official circuits of court and high nobility. In principle, a work of art, literature, or information was beginning to be available for the price of a ticket or a subscription. Perhaps most significant, alternatives to the older patronage system — including those functions performed by salonnières — became available with the rising importance of such new figures as editors and critics.

Although the reading public in eighteenth-century France was expanding, literacy rates were extremely low, especially when judged by the standards of today's mass reading public. Only a minority of the population could read. It is even suggested that the gap between male and female literacy widened rather than narrowed during the eighteenth century. Nevertheless, literacy rates were not static. It has been estimated that illiteracy declined from 79 percent a century earlier to 63 percent on the eve of the French Revolution.[35] Even with a largely illiterate population, published materials found their way to a fairly wide audience. According to a long-standing practice, written materials were often read aloud. Furthermore, the range of readers and reading material was broad. Whereas the technically literate read almanacks, chapbooks, and cheaply produced traditional stories and tales of wonder, the more accomplished had access to philosophy, science, political debate, poetry, fiction, classical languages, and literature.[36]

Readers themselves were establishing altered patterns of communication. The prohibitive cost of books and periodicals encouraged the growth of subscription services, public libraries, reading rooms, and reading societies. In the academies, Masonic lodges, and cafes, interested individuals met to exchange impressions, to discuss and comment on newssheets, political journals, and books. Together, these institutions generated new public (literary and political) spaces, which appear to have been divided along gender lines. Robert Mandrou compares the salon to other more masculine alternatives of the day: "The academies and reading rooms are more serious gathering places than the salons, and almost exclusively masculine; their success is perhaps even greater, and certainly more characteristic." Yet, according to Maité Albistur and Daniel Armogathe, although their numbers were few, the academies were open to women.[37] And, as I discuss shortly, the eighteenth-century salons were not altogether "unserious," as contemporaries and some recent historians would have us believe.

As a consequence of these many changes, "the public life of eighteenth-century France was acted out before an expanding, nation-wide audience of informed public opinion."[38] This audience was increasingly well informed about more distant events, and its orientation to public affairs was undergoing a dramatic alteration. Chrétien Malesherbes' observation on the shift from an aural public to a reading public seems pertinent to the argument being advanced here: "What the orators of Rome and Athens were in the midst of a people assembled," he remarked, "men of letters are in the midst of a dispersed people."[39] In other words, writers could now address themselves to an invisible public; face-to-face relationships were giving way to public cultural forms of a more anonymous sort. And precisely for that reason, individuals were being called to a more privatized relationship both to an author and, as solitary readers, to a text. Still, it would be wrong to exaggerate these phenomena in eighteenth-century France. As I have already stated, texts were often read to people who assembled in churches, inns, cafes, and on street corners. Even if reading remained in part a public activity, it is also true that orality was an aspect of the new print culture. It, too, was textualized. In any event, readers were taking their place alongside audiences of the old style.

Above all, the mediation of public life by the institution of writing contrasted sharply with still firmly implanted Old Regime practices. Whereas the king and the aristocracy, along with salonnières, convened politics from above and in their presence, now dispersed and invisible publics of opinion were being created. The fact that many eighteenth-

century women writers were *epistolières* reinforces this distinction. Unlike the journalistic or philosophical criticism
directed toward the anonymous audiences in "the republic of
letters," an authored correspondence always preserves its
distinctly personal character. It is occasional writing,
addressed to a specific Other.[40] After all, a correspondence
exists only when a group of letters is collected and a decision made to publish them, or some selection of them. Usually someone other than the author *constructed* the
published work for a larger audience. Supplementing the
author function, editors began to assume a much more
assertive and self-conscious role.[41] However, this vital function was rarely, if ever, performed by women.

The oppositional public sphere was not one (universal
sphere of discourse, as Habermas implies) but many. Critical distinctions are to be drawn—not just between society
and its critics—but among the oppositional publics themselves, and between the spoken word, the written word or
letter, and the printed word.[42] I have already observed the
extent to which women excelled in the categories of speech
and letter writing; as a result of this excellence, they helped
to shape an aesthetic of preciosity or worldliness. The
seventeenth-century salons discussed in Chapter 1 flourished before the refinement of the court under Louis XIV.
Because of the ascendance of Versailles, which absorbed the
attention of good society in the last decades of the century,
worldliness emanated from a dominant model of courtliness and urban salons provided an alternative venue alongside the official absolutist public sphere. But following the
austere last years of the reign of Louis XIV, during the
regency ("when the Duc d'Orléans led the unrefined pleasures of his roués at the Palais-Royal"), there occurred a
decline of courtliness and an associated revival of Parisian
society.[43] In their influential salons, such eighteenth-century women as Mme de Lambert and Mme de Tencin skillfully practiced the conversational arts (like their précieuse
predecessors). They contributed to the tone and manner of a

renewed literature of worldliness, and they fostered a strong relationship between speech and writing.

At the same time, a gender division was exacerbated as men outpaced women in the category of print, and particularly in the highly esteemed fields of science, mathematics, and philosophy.[44] Furthermore, salonnières began to serve as promoters and managers of the careers of literary men; it is said of Mme de Tencin, for example, that "it was her influence that gave its first impulse to the success of Montesquieu's *Esprit des lois*, of which she personally bought and distributed many copies."[45] In the later drawing rooms of the philosophes—those of Mme d'Epinay, Mme du Deffand, Mlle de Lespinasse, and Mme Geoffrin—this pattern was even more pronounced. Mme du Deffand, Mlle de Lespinasse, and Mme Geoffrin were noted for their influence over publication and over the academic careers of talented men. It was women who were reputed to be the real powers behind an election to the Academy. Also, women functioned as muses, aides, and co-collaborators. Mme d'Epinay assisted Grimm in his *Correspondance littéraire*, and Mlle de Lespinasse probably did more than any other woman to encourage the encyclopedists. Still, this situation was not greeted with equanimity by all. In his *Memoirs*, the president of the Parisian Parlement, Hénault, remarked stridently of Mme de Lambert and her salon: "One had to pass through her in order to get into the Académie Française."[46]

Thus even a privileged parliamentarian could hackle at the culturally influential position of women. As I demonstrated earlier, whatever profit he may have enjoyed, Montesquieu harbored strong ambivalences toward salon society. When we look beyond the circumscribed world of privilege, male hostility toward women and their institutions appears even fiercer. Here, Robert Darnton's contrast between the high and low Enlightenments is pertinent. He observes that "the republic of letters" was beset by enormous pressures, registering the desperate situation of so many who tried and failed to earn their living as writers in the new public sphere.

In fact, to live by one's profession as a writer—that is, to sell one's wares on the market—was still a rather difficult affair.

Certainly, Voltaire and the encyclopedists had achieved positions of reknown. But a wide gulf separated them from large numbers of aspiring authors who crowded into Paris, and their success cannot be taken as simple confirmation of the salon's "democratic" function (as some would have us believe). To the contrary, one might say that it merely reaffirmed the increasing possibility of individual social mobility in the Old Regime, earlier heralded by the venal sale of titles. But in no sense was the mechanism of individual achievement a challenge to the established class order of Old Regime France. Nor did those who arrived in society open the door to all who followed them. Rather, to the extent that individuals succeeded, they became part of the very structure of privilege in response to which the bourgeois public sphere had first emerged.

According to Darnton, by the end of the century the "official Enlightenment" had been absorbed into the corporate structures of Old Regime cultural power: To be successful was to become part of le monde. Most writers of the late Old Regime remained tied to the privileged patronage system. But huge numbers of aspiring philosophes sank into desperate situations, existing on the margins of literary existence. Failing to secure sinecures, these hack writers mixed high and low literary expression. Burning with resentment against le monde, which had failed to recognize their talents, they produced biting social criticism, flavored by scandal and pornography. Moreover, Grub Street developed its own counter-institutions: alongside the formal, elitist, and privileged atmospheres of salons and royal academies, there were cafes, musées, and lycées. The latter two operated as clubhouses, formalizing the functions of the cafes, serving as counter-academies and anti-salons for the literary proletariat. If Darnton is correct, "the café functioned as the antithesis of the salon. It was open to everyone, just one step from the street, although there were degrees in its closeness to street life. While the great names gathered in the Procope or La Régence, lesser figures congregated in the notorious Caveau of the Palais Royal, and the humblest hacks frequented the cafés of the boulevards, blending into an underworld of 'swindlers, recruiting agents, spies, and pickpockets; here one finds only pimps, buggers, and *bardaches.'*[47]

In the libelous literature of Grub Street, sexual sensationalism and political opposition were indistinguishable. Sexual and moral disease signaled to a receptive audience the horrible maladies of political despotism. Even writers of the most pornographic texts deployed a powerful moral vocabulary. And where morality was at stake, a protest against public women was often implied.[48] Consider, for example, this scathing attack on Mme du Barry, a woman of the court, the climax to an obscene pamphlet by Charles Théveneau de Morande, a libelist of the first order:

> Passing directly from the brothel to the throne, toppling the most powerful and redoubtable minister, overthrowing the constitution of the monarchy, insulting the royal family, the presumptive heir to the throne, and his august consort by her incredible luxury, by her insolent talk, . . . [she insults] the entire nation, which is dying of hunger, by her vainglorious extravagance and by the well-known depredations of all the *roués* surrounding her, as she sees groveling at her feet not only the *grands* of the kingdom and the ministers, but the princes of the royal blood, foreign ambassadors, and the church itself, which canonizes her scandals and her debauchery.[49]

Morande's paroxysms notwithstanding, he speaks the language of the underground, opposition press. Indeed, in the moral vocabulary of the new publics associated with the letterization of culture under late absolutism, reproaches against feminized courtiers, diseased aristocrats, and extravagantly powerful women were virtually commonplace. Because of official censorship, this was a clandestine literature. Though members of the high Enlightenment also met the hand of the censor, they existed at some remove from the clandestine public to which Morande belonged. A distinction is required, therefore, between the public sphere and publicity. For the emergent public sphere, publicity was a problem posed by the censorship, an aspect of what Habermas refers to as the liberal moment of the public sphere. Although the official Enlightenment existed in an oppositional relationship to the state, it possessed a de facto viability by virtue of its institutional position. If part of the dynamic of the public sphere was to expand the boundaries of permissible public discourse, then the official Enlightenment succeeded only to the extent that it achieved a limited form of public space, the salon. The salon offered one way of getting around the problem of censorship, by holding public discussion in private. But it was not a solution available to all members of society. Ultimately, salons preserved a sphere of privileged discourse that could never satisfy the problem of class discrimination suffered by members of the clandestine public. The underground faced two limits, that of censorship and that imposed by the class structure of Old Regime society. Its very existence can be viewed as a response to the limits placed on the boundaries of permissible public discourse as a result of class discrimination. Nevertheless, probably the most virulent examples of an antifeminine, antiaristocratic discourse circulated in this "unofficial," clandestine counterpublic sphere. The writers and artists of the clandestine public regarded salons and their women as among the worst symptoms of the despised system of privilege whose destruction they hoped to ensure.

In spite of this situation, some women participated as journalists in the eighteenth-century counterpublic sphere. In addition, as I have indicated, the counterpublics of the late Old Regime were distributed across a wide and surprisingly nuanced spectrum, encompassing even a female public. Beginning from this premise, Nina Rattner Gelbart has reconstructed the remarkable history of the monthly paper *Journal des dames*, which appeared intermittently during the twenty years between 1759 and 1778. Immediately after acquiring a royal privilege for the journal, its last female editor, Mme de Montanclos, secretly turned the paper over in 1775 to her friend and editorial contributor Louis-Sébastien Mercier. Under Mercier, the paper became even more blatantly oppositional, supporting the parlements against the crown. The paper was not of the underground, but among the regime's permitted, tolerated journals. As Gelbart reports, however, "Unlike the Grub Street pamphleteers who could say anything, the frondeur journalists dealt daily with censors and therefore had to navigate prudently, giving particular thought to the timing of their copy."[50]

Between October 1761 and April 1775, the paper was owned and edited by three women who transformed "a trivial bagatelle into a serious oppositional publication addressing social issues, preaching reform, and attempting to make its audience think." On three occasions the paper was relaunched after being suspended by the censors. Sharing the prejudices of much opposition opinion, the *Journal des dames* was designed "to nourish the mind and discourage vanity." It is of particular consequence, then, that the journal's attack on vanity and frivolity was addressed explicitly to women, who were asked to reform their behavior in a practical direction, and to join the cause of an enlightened citizenry. In addition, the *Journal des dames* stands out from the underground and the officially authorized conservative press in its commitment to "a female public's right—and obligation—to be informed about controversial matters." It was also exceptional for its support of women's right to pursue careers in the public sphere. The social composition of the *Journal des dames*'s growing readership grew broader over the course of its twenty years, reaching beyond the ladies of a pampered elite to a more practical-minded readership. And the public's support and interest was actively elicited. Readers were encouraged to contribute their opinion in letters to the editor.[51] The *Journal des dames* also advanced the cause of the new genre of bourgeois drama, which, it believed, could inspire and lead the illiterate people out of ignorance and slavery.

The women journalists who edited the *Journal des dames* existed in a another world from the literary hostesses of salon society. In Gelbart's estimation

> women . . . played a significant role in the fight for freedom of the press. The female editors of the *Journal des dames* recognized the potential of journalism to reach and sway an audience, and they willingly embarked on a career other *femmes de lettres* scorned. The disapproval was mutual, for the editors had no use for the salon set that played hostess to great men, arbitrated matters of literary taste, and made or broke reputations of aspiring male writers. The female journalists were genuinely concerned with bettering the lot of women. They wanted immediate, frequent, frontal, and reciprocal contact with a broad social spectrum of readers with whom they could discuss their cause.[52]

The journal's first female editor, Mme de Beaumer, was perhaps the most idiosyncratic and most radical in her feminist beliefs. She eulogized great women of all levels of society, but she was especially fond of the contributions of women of the popular classes—female artists, merchants, artisans, and musicians. Mme de Beaumer subscribed to the Masonic vision of universality. She believed that through useful, constructive activity, women could begin to make a revolution in society. She applauded vigorous study and improvement and sang the praises of marriage. She adopted the feminized form of author and editor, referring to herself as *autrice* or *éditrice,* and dressed in masculine garb, dedicating herself to supporting her sex's "honor and its rights."[53] Mme de Beaumer's unorthodox demeanor, language, and actions attracted the attention of the regime's censors. Rather than put her own advancement ahead of the journal's future, she graciously stepped aside, passing the enterprise on to a more acceptable female editor, Mme de Maisonneuve.

The journal's last female editor was wiser and certainly more cautious than Mme de Beaumer. Unlike Mme de Beaumer or Mme de Maisonneuve, her two predecessors,

Mme de Montanclos was a mother, who pleaded for loving and responsible motherhood. Gelbart reports that she may have belonged to one of the female Masonic lodges that proliferated in the 1770s and often had parlementary leanings. Her letters reveal that she gave frequent reading to groups composed exclusively of female Masons. Her *Journal des dames* preached the same virtues — fidelity, discretion, modesty, purity, trustworthiness, charity, to which female Masonry was committed. Likewise, the *Journal de musique*, to which she contributed in 1777, was heavily Masonic. She was a playwright and fought for fair treatment at the Comédie Française in the 1780s. By the time of her accession to the editorship, however, Jean-Jacques Rousseau's writings had begun to work "a revolution in feminine psychology." Women — especially mothers who were made to feel socially useful — were among his most ardent fans and enthusiastic readers. Mme de Montanclos' *Journal des dames* was profoundly influenced by Rousseau — she even referred to herself as the "Jean-Jacques Rousseau of the female sex" — who she believed had done a great deal for feminine self-esteem.[54] By insisting on woman's right to a career, however, she extended Rousseau's ideas, indeed making them compatible with a version of feminism not unlike that of the 1790s (to be discussed in Chapter 4).

Under Mme de Montanclos and Mercier, the journal linked motherhood and patriotism, calling on vibrant images of Roman motherhood from the classical repertoire. Female subordination was situated as one of many social injustices requiring political reform. Mercier's *Journal des dames* published poems and articles by such future revolutionaries as Condorcet on the economy, freedom of the press, and the abolition of slavery.[55] Thus the journal combined a commitment to female rights with a celebration of republican motherhood, distancing itself all the while from the world of le monde and its women. It played a role in the development of political consciousness and in the formation of political opinion in the last decades of the Old Regime. Its language was republican and feminist. The *Jour-*

*nal des dames* styled a version of feminism that was parliamentarian, patriotic, and deeply committed to fostering a
new civic consciousness among men and women. In doing
so, it opposed the institutions of the absolutist public
sphere. It resisted fashion, luxury, and women's reduction to
objects of beauty and pleasure.

The *Journal des dames* articulated a vision of respectable
womanhood linked to the familial values of the bourgeois
interior. This early example of feminist journalism participated, then, in the restructuring of morality as a category of
private or individual rather than of communal life. To that
extent, its emergence is symptomatic of what Elizabeth
Eisenstein has identified as the long process of change associated with the print revolution in early modern Europe. In
Eisenstein's judgment,

> the new medium encouraged a sharper division between these
> two zones. An unending stream of moralizing literature pen-
> etrated the privacy of the home and helped to precipitate a
> variety of domestic dramas. The "family" was not only
> endowed with new educational and religious functions, espe-
> cially in regions where the laity was trusted with printed
> Bibles and catechisms; but the family circle also became the
> target of a complicated literary cross-fire. As book markets
> expanded and divisions of labor increased, feminine readers
> were increasingly differentiated from masculine ones, and
> children were supplied with reading matter different from
> their parents.[56]

## The Bourgeois Interior

The new print culture was a major factor contributing to
the constitution of a way of life that featured the restricted
family domain and focused attention on the interior land-
scape of the privatized individual subject. In this setting,
divisions between public and private life were strengthened.
The bourgeoisie developed a preference for comfortable

town dwellings on a reduced scale. Its invention, the parlor or foyer, a new, more privatized space for proper domestic entertainment, would eventually supplant the aristocratic salon. In contrast, aristocratic existence was organized around permeable or fluid definitions of these two spheres. Not only did the aristocracy's dwellings display an architectural grandeur, but there was little definition of private spaces inside the aristocratic household. Indeed, hostesses first entertained the social elite from their daybeds, or *ruelles*, and the word *ruelle* was the earliest term for a salon. Robert Mandrou describes the contrast in this manner: "This bourgeois existence certainly seems to be one of domestic economy, in which the great concern is with furnishings and appointments. Thus, it is quite different in its setting and particularly in its way of life from that of Versailles and the court, where, in a setting whose scale is entirely different, everyone spends without reckoning. The opposition between the town and the court is not merely a theatrical one."[57]

The architecture of privacy was replicated in a vast pedagogical literature that instructed men and women on the proper rules for family life and then tutored them on their parental duties in the business of childrearing.[58] The habit of letter writing was another important manifestation of this new symbolic culture. In letters, men and women explored their unique subjectivity and shared it intimately with a sympathetic Other.[59] Janet Gurkin Altman has traced the change from the Renaissance, when women authors published their own letter books and broached the same range of topics as men, to the seventeenth century, when authorship became a "male-dominated institution, deeply imbricated . . . in political hierarchies."[60] She examines the relationship of the collected letters of such sixteenth-century humanists as Etienne Pasquier (whose book of letters, like Sévigné's, was first published beginning in 1725) to Mme de Sévigné's singular letters (to her daughter), which forced "the rediscovery of the value of the idiolect and respect for the particular experiences that it conveys."[61] After the posthumous publication of her letters in the early eighteenth century, Mme de Sévigné rapidly became, along with Voltaire, the only epistolarian worth reading and emulating.

For Mme de Sévigné, "the letter was an essentially intimate communication, opening up on an interior space where a highly personal self evolves over time in interaction with close relations. For [her] the letter is not a political maneuver or a public exercise, an extension of salon- and court-approved conversation." Thus, according to Altman, Mme de Sévigné's letters ushered in a new kind of writing, one tied to personal and private history. Indeed, the enthusiastic reception of these letters by eighteenth-century readers was connected to changes in the topography and politics of literary space between 1670 and 1770. The new readers of the (education-conscious) eighteenth century were subtle, capable of filling in narrative blanks where they existed, and youthful. As with Erasmus' Renaissance program of epistolary apprenticeship, the child again became a possible reader and beneficiary of published correspondence. Sévigné, furthermore, can be seen as "functioning within the nonhierarchical space established by friendship, which permits infinite development of the idiolect." Altman extends the theory of Roland Mortier that the cult of idiolect, of personal style, whose eruption is usually attributed to Romanticism, can be dated to between 1740 and 1770. Her focus on Sévigné calls attention to one woman's imprint on the freeing of epistolary space from the political and cultural domination of a court-centered aesthetic. Indeed, Sévigné's letters made an enormous impact on militant writers such as Voltaire, Diderot, and Rousseau, all of whom practiced epistolary activity as a privileged form of literary expression.[62]

Surely there is no greater model of an intense quest for self-discovery than Jean-Jacques Rousseau's *Confessions*. A literary heir of Mme de Sévigné, Rousseau directs his self-observations to a new anonymous but extremely personalized audience whom he hopes to refashion in the image of his ideal text. Rousseau does not require a daughter or personal confidante for inspiration. Along with Richardson, he even extends the epistolary form to the novel. Moreover, he claims to aspire to distinction through his individuality, spurning the privileges of inherited status or property, and "worldliness." He eschews the values of exteriority and social appearances, hoping "to render the interior transparent."[63] What is most unusual is that Rousseau displays his distinctiveness through the practice of writing rather than by a series of exploits in the world or by acceptance in society. "I have resolved on an enterprise," he proclaims, "which has no precedent, and which, once complete, will have no imitator. My purpose is to display to my kind a portrait in every way true to nature, and the man I shall portray will be myself. Simply myself. I know my own heart and understand my fellow man. But I am unlike any one I have ever met; I will even venture to say that I am like no one in the whole world. I may be no better, but at least I am different."[64]

Rousseau's success is legendary. His writings elevated the authorial status to unparalleled heights; his rhetoric seared the hearts of women and men throughout Europe. He was able to speak directly to an absent audience who heard him directly, without mediation. The first writer to be known by his first name, "l'ami Jean-Jacques" was deluged with letters in which his readers bared their very souls. His works were read as programs for moral instruction. He sought to give rein to feeling, not to provide pleasure in the old aristocratic manner, and the force of his personality fueled the power of his works. People remodeled their lives on his characters. His text penetrated into the everyday world of the bourgeois interior. Readers learned a new attitude toward the printed page, an obsessively sentimental, intimate, earnest, and moral one. In the process, Rousseau radically transformed the relationship between writer and reader, and between reader and text.[65] His ideal reader would divest himself or herself of the conventions of literature and the trappings of society — would turn innocent eyes on the text. In this state of natural innocence, far away from the fashionable salons of society, Rousseau promised his readers that they would find truth, for it was this that mattered, not style. Still, they did not need to fear the isolation of being cut off from the institutions of sociability. "Rousseau's rhetoric opened up a new channel of communication between two lonely beings, the writer and the reader, and rearranged their roles. Rousseau would be Jean-Jacques, citizen of Geneva and prophet of virtue. The reader would be a provincial youth, a country gentleman, a woman stifled by the refined conventions of society, an artisan excluded from refinement—it did not matter, provided he or she could love virtue and understand the language of the heart."[66] Rousseau asked his readers to jettison all their old cultural baggage, to join in a journey toward a transcendant truth beyond literature—but also, I argue, beyond the artificiality that women especially represented. Rousseau and reader triumphed together over the artifice of literary communication. By doing so they also triumphed over the artificial, adorned ladies of le monde. They did so, too, by an active textualization of life. "Rousseau taught his readers to 'digest' books so thoroughly that literature became absorbed in life. The Rousseauistic readers fell in love, married, and raised children by steeping themselves in print."[67] Reading—active, not passive—was an element in the process by which life was remade along domestic and virtuous grounds.

## CHAPTER 3

# Rousseau's Reply to Public Women

Elaborating on Michel de Certeau's assertion that "theorizing always needs a Savage," Josette Féral observes that "the Savage in the West has always been the Woman: simultaneously present and absent, present when absent, and all the more absent when she is there." She continues, "His [man's] Savage, The Woman, is here, very close, present and speechless, to take upon herself the full weight of the violence that inhabits such structures as can only exist through her repression."[1] Féral's intuition of the general condition of woman's speechlessness, and woman's positioning as a mirror of male subjectivity, is especially pertinent to a consideration of Rousseau's theory of public life.

Perhaps more than any other writer of the eighteenth century, Rousseau agonized over the appropriate role for women. The woman question is at the center of his critique of the Old Regime and his arguments for a reformed political and social order. Indeed, it could be said that in Rousseau's work Féral's claim about the relationship between theory and the Woman is most convincingly redeemed—for what, after all, is the general will but the effort to construct a theoretical public whose judgment will necessarily be right?[2] A point little noticed in past readings of Rousseau, however, is the extent to which the very generality of the will is predicated on the silent but tacit consent of women. Indeed, Rousseau's argument for the creation of separate

66

sexual spheres is the basis of women's subjection to a rule of silence and to their political quiescence within a reformed republican polity. Nevertheless, Rousseau is far from a pedestrian misogynist. He did not just write about women. He wrote to them. And, by way of this address, he interpellated women as a new kind of political and moral subject. Also, although he denied women a formal public position, he anticipated that they would continue to be active and, in their own sphere, powerful. Indeed, he offered them the opportunity to perform a crucial cultural role on which depended the moral health of the entire polity.[3] In effect, Rousseau extended an invitation to women to join in the creation of his virtuous republic, an invitation that was answered enthusiastically by women of both high and low status.[4]

Rousseau's gender politics has stimulated a wide-ranging discussion among political theorists. The central paradox is easily identified: that the theorist of democratic liberty and the general will has a profound mistrust of women such that he would deny them the most elementary political rights. Among these commentators, Joel Schwartz and Jean Bethke Elshtain take seriously the question of why Rousseau might appeal to feminists and to women. Yet they posit this reception as, for the most part, a hypothetical possibility, although there is massive evidence that Rousseau was read, discussed, appropriated, and resisted by women of his age.[5] With these considerations in mind, I argue that Rousseau ties the subjection of modern women to an implicit opposition between old and new forms of representation, that is, in the terms used here, between the iconic spectacularity of the Old Regime and the textual and legal order of the bourgeois public sphere. Furthermore, his protest against public women cannot be understood apart from the representations of women guiding his writings on family and state. One detects there some interesting parallels to the works of earlier aristocratic reformers in that Rousseau favors many of the same sexualized metaphors of despotism and also yearns for a domestic republic. Yet he rewrites their protest

in a wholly novel fashion, thereby expressing the consciousness of a new age and a new class order.[6]

## Women in the Democratic Public Sphere

In the "Introductory Dedication to the Republic of
Geneva" of his *Second Discourse*, Rousseau makes what
seems at first to be an honorable effort not to forget women,
"the precious half of the Republic" whose gentleness and
wisdom, he says, maintain peace and good morals. He
exhorts women of the Genevan republic and their admirers
elsewhere: "Amiable and virtuous countrywomen, the fate of
your sex will always be to govern ours. It is fortunate when
your chaste power, exercised solely in conjugal union, makes
itself felt only for the glory of the State and public
happiness."[7]

Genevan women are told that their domestic situation is
the very source of their power, a "chaste power" that allows
them to "govern" men, although appearances surely suggest
otherwise. They are reassured that all this is for the greater
public good and happiness of all, not solely for their own
personal well-being. Women, in other words, are encouraged
to find a place in the lawful community. And they are flat-
teringly compared to the greatly esteemed women of ancient
Sparta. Rousseau continues, applauding women's chaste,
familial virtue:

> What barbarous man could resist the voice of honor and rea-
> son in the mouth of a tender wife? And who would not
> despise vain luxury seeing your simple and modest attire. . . .
> It is for you to maintain always, by your amiable and inno-
> cent dominion and by your insinuating wit, love of laws in the
> State and concord among the citizens; to reunite, by happy
> marriages, divided families; and above all to correct, by the
> persuasive sweetness of your lessons and by the modest graces
> of your conversation, the extravagances our young people
> adopt in other countries, whence, instead of the many useful

things from which they could profit, they bring back, with a childish tone and *ridiculous airs adopted among debauched women*, only admiration for I know not what pretended grandeurs, frivolous compensations for servitude, which will never be worth as much as august freedom. Therefore always be what you are, the chaste guardians of morals and the gentle bonds of peace; and continue to exploit on every occasion the rights of the heart and of nature for the benefit of duty and virtue.[8]

The passage contains a truly remarkable blend of the language of domination, exploitation, and servitude with that of sentimental virtues, affections, maternal tenderness, and romantic love.[9] In fact, the latter qualities are made to serve the former, but in a manner that thoroughly confuses the decidedly political (and violent) content of family life. Women and children in Rousseau's discourse are being yoked to a conservative and ultimately passive function — that of serving the state. Woman's duty consists of subordinating her independent aims and interests to a higher goal, the ethical life of the community. But unlike her male companion, of whom Rousseau also demands the sublimation of particular interests on behalf of a desire for the public good, woman is barred completely from active participation in the very sphere that gives purpose to all her actions.

Virtuous republican women, unlike the women whom Rousseau has observed within the absolutist public spheres of his day, are distinguished by their sexual innocence and chastity. His terms of approbation are derived from a strong moral vocabulary, a kind of double standard of female existence: pure or impure, chaste or unchaste, conjugal partner or adultress, domestic or public. As a result, woman's virtue acquires a spatial dimension. Her confinement to the private realm functions as a public sign of her political virtue. This is no small matter. Contradicting all the principles of human virtue he uses to indict the civilized men of his day, Rousseau nevertheless insists that women must always live in the opinion of others, that a woman's reputation weighs as heavily as her deeds. Appearances, therefore, are among the duties of woman. "Opinion," declares Rousseau, "is the grave of virtue among men and its throne among women."[10]

Before exploring further Rousseau's understanding of public and private life, let us consider the fact that it is precisely woman's lack, her absence, that occasions these ruminations. Indeed, the passage cited above begins with a courteous mention of woman's habitual oversight in political discourse, only to find a way of binding her presence to man's project—not least of which is the tension-filled reconciliation of man and society. Much the same structure appears in *Emile,* Rousseau's most extended commentary on female nature and duty. There Sophie (natural Woman) is introduced as an afterthought, but as a necessary requirement for Emile's (natural Man's) completion. Emile's fulfillment as a citizen involves his preparation for the intermeshed roles of husband, citizen, and father—his positioning, therefore, as progenitor of new generations of citizens on which the life of the state depends. Having saluted its mistresses, Rousseau concludes his "Introductory Address" with an image of the happiness of Geneva's citizens and the glory of the republic *of men* to be found therein. He counterposes Geneva to the pomp and dissolute spectacle of Old Regime society; the latter's attraction is said to rest in childish and fatal tastes, a brilliance that dazzles the eyes: "Let dissolute youth go to seek easy pleasures and long tasting repentance elsewhere; let the supposed men of taste admire in other places the grandeur of palaces the beauty of carriages, the superb finishings, the pomp of spectacles, and all the refinements of softness and luxury. In Geneva, one will find only men."[11]

Republican virtue requires that men, too, submit to a reformed canon of masculine behavior. According to Rousseau, man's virility is at risk inside the spectacular settings of the absolutist public sphere, for this sensuously visual universe is an unnaturally feminine one. Thus he interprets the elaborate conventions of sociability of the absolutist state as signs of political decay and effeminacy: the two go hand in hand. "In becoming sociable and a slave he [man] becomes weak, fearful, servile; and his soft and effeminate way of life completes the enervation of both his strength and his courage."[12] Like a woman, the (overly) civilized man is a victim of excessive softness and sensuality.

## Women, Cities, and Spectacles

Rousseau is unconvinced by the mock battle between court and city in the Old Regime. He seems to propose instead "a pox on both your houses." He regards these sorry alternatives as twin aspects of the same decayed civilization, to which he upholds the virtues of a "patriarchal and rustic life, man's first life, which is the most natural, and sweetest life for anyone who does not have a corrupt heart."[13] Indeed, Rousseau is constantly taking leave of the city (and therefore, its women), beginning with his departure from his beloved Geneva, to the figurative journeys of Emile, who flees from the hollow, artificial existence of Paris to discover Sophie and domestic bliss in the countryside.[14] "Cities," Rousseau exclaims, "are the abyss of the human species."[15] But if this is the case, how can we account for Rousseau's unfailing admiration for the ancient republic, also an urban civilization? In his estimation, the two settings are not really comparable. The ancient city-state is the foremost example of a properly ordered republic of (masculine) speech, strictly divided into public and private, male and female, spheres; whereas the despised eighteenth-century cosmopolis is but one face of the (excessively feminized) political spectacle of the absolutist state. In his *Letter to M. d'Alembert on the Theatre*, Rousseau suggests that the corruption of the theater in his time might be "only one manifestation of a deeper or more pervasive state of affairs involving the function of beholding and the condition of being beheld."[16] Moreover, while reproaching the visual spectacle of the theater, he articulates a set of unsettling qualms of a decidedly sexual nature. For example, Rousseau draws a direct comparison between women and the theater:

they are two marks of a peculiarly modern aberration, a narcissistic overinvestment in the image. As Michael Fried observes, the *Letter* "strongly implies that there is no aspect of social life that is not comprised within the dangerous, because readily theatricalized and theatricalizing, realm of the spectacular."[17] Still, it is modern public women—especially speaking women, the actresses of the stage, the salon-going women of the capital cities, and the illicit women of the court—who in their person and their speech best symbolize the evils of an excessively spectacular existence. Unlike the housewife, these vain and independent women show themselves off—tempt the looks of all men—in a public fashion. "Do you want to know men?" Rousseau asks rhetorically:

> Study women. This maxim is general, and up to this point everybody will agree with me. But I add that there are no good morals for women outside of a withdrawn and domestic life; if I say that the peaceful care of the family and the home are their lot, that the dignity of their sex consists in modesty, that shame and chasteness are inseparable from decency for them, that when they seek for men's looks they are already letting themselves be corrupted by them, and that any woman who shows herself off disgraces herself; I will be immediately attacked by this philosophy of a day which is born and dies in the corner of a big city and wishes to smother the cry of nature and the unanimous voice of humankind.[18]

Indeed, Rousseau proposes that the chaste and virtuous woman/wife will be confined to the domestic sphere and controlled by the gaze of just one man, no longer therefore courting the consuming looks of all men. He wards off the anticipated objections of his feminist-leaning contemporaries with the derisive comment: "I will be immediately attacked by this philosophy of a day which is born and dies in the corner of a big city and wishes to smother the cry of nature and the unanimous voice of humankind." The sentence is self-contradictory. How can the *unanimous* voice of humankind be attacked by another voice (the philosophy of the day)? Rousseau asks his reader to follow him into a transparent realm of nature (beyond society) where all claims are unmediated and unproblematic—and where *man*kind owes nothing to the women of the day and *their* philosophy. Also, in opposing women's weakness for self-exhibition, Rousseau does not so much abandon the masculine gaze as attempt to harness it to a system of spectacular controls within the private, domestic sphere. He aspires to control women's narcissism and, at the same time, to eradicate their willful independence. As a consequence, women can neither move nor speak freely among men. This, finally, will abolish the intolerable situation of women in league together, clamoring for their sex, establishing an empire of their sex, or an empire of fashion.[19]

When Rousseau bemoans the theater's capacity to substitute a "theatrical jargon for the practice of virtues," "to turn citizens into wits, housewives into bluestockings, and daughters into sweethearts out of the drama," he expresses a concern about modern woman's intemperate publicness.[20] In contrast to her ancient counterpart's modesty and political silence, she is charged with an excessive use of speech and language. Despite their pleasing talk, "women have flexible tongues."[21] There is always a danger that they will speak nonsense, speak without proper knowledge of a subject as they are wont to do. Rousseau complains that in contemporary plays it is always a woman who knows everything and teaches everything to men. He celebrates the ancients for honoring women's modesty and sheltering women from public judgment and protests against modern women's usurpation of a role in the sphere of critical opinion: "With us, on the contrary, the most esteemed woman is the one who has the greatest renown, about whom the most is said, who is the most often seen in society, at whose home one dines the most, who most imperiously sets the tone, who judges, resolves, decides, pronounces, assigns talents, merit, and virtues their degrees and places, and whose favor is most ignominiously begged for by humble, learned men."[22]

In *Emile*, Rousseau underscores the virtue of cloistering

and silencing adult women through another comparison of ancient and modern. "In France," he bewails, "girls live in convents and women frequent society. With the ancients it was exactly the opposite. Girls, as I have said, had many games and public festivals. Women led retired lives. This practice was more reasonable and maintained morals better."[23] In the topsy-turvy world of the Old Regime, Rousseau discerns an unnatural publicity, penetrating even to the most intimate sphere of life. He links the want of a refuge to the numbers of women who have abandoned their natural role in the family in order to partake of fashionable society: "It is only in the paternal home that one gets the taste for one's own home, and any woman whose mother has not raised her will not like raising her own children. Unfortunately there is no longer private education in the big cities. Society there is so general and so mixed that there is no longer a refuge to which to retire, and a person is in public even in his own home."[24]

Rousseau deplores man's self-contradiction in society. Speaking to his contemporaries, he cautions: "He is one of those men of our days: a Frenchman, an Englishman, a bourgeois. He will be nothing. To be something, to be oneself and always one, a man must act as he speaks."[25] In the theater, however, he finds the most exaggerated instances of the internally divided condition of modern man, split between the requirements of appearance and being.[26] "What is the talent of the actor?" asks Rousseau. "It is the art of counterfeiting himself, of putting on another character than his own, of appearing different than he is, of becoming passionate in cold blood, of saying what he does not think as naturally as if he really did think it, and, finally, of forgetting his own place by dint of taking another's." He continues: "What is the profession of the actor? It is a trade in which he performs for money, submits himself to the disgrace and the affronts that others buy the right to give him, and puts his person publicly on sale. I beg every sincere man to tell if he does not feel in the depths of his soul that there is something servile and base in this traffic of oneself."[27]

Having settled accounts with the acting profession, Rousseau is especially careful to discriminate between the actor's performance and the rhetoric of the ancient orator, a man who is at one with his role and is therefore in his proper place. It is not Rousseau's purpose to castigate all of the speaking arts, only those that function to dissemble, and thereby to intensify, the visual spectacle of a dissolute society:

> When the orator appears in public, it is to speak and not to show himself off; he represents only himself; he fills his own role, speaks only in his own name, says, or ought to say, only what he thinks; the man and the role being the same, he is in his place; he is in the situation of any citizen who fulfills the functions of his estate. But an actor on the stage, displaying other sentiments than his own, saying only what he is made to say, often representing a chimerical being, annihilates himself, as it were, and is lost in his hero. And, in this forgetting of the man, if something remains of him, it is used as the plaything of the spectators.[28]

The actress is considerably more than the actor's female counterpart. She symbolizes all of the evils of a public existence for women (and for men, as well). Yet a stage career was one of the very few professions in which a woman of this era could hope to earn a living, practice a craft, and achieve some measure of social acclaim. Setting all this aside, Rousseau dwells on the actresses' supposedly dissolute character. He even holds them responsible for the general state of bad morals in society, not to mention the fallen morals of actors, by his own definition that least moral group of men. All too innocently, he queries, "How unlikely [is it] that she who sets herself for sale in performance would not soon do the same in person and never let herself be tempted to satisfy desires that she takes so much effort to excite?"[29]

The actress is audacious, and this Rousseau will not permit: "A woman's audacity is the sure sign of her shame," he writes.[30] Even if chasteness were not a natural sentiment in women, he still insists that "in society their [women's] lot ought to be a domestic and retired life, and that they ought to be raised in principles appropriate to it."[31] Women ought to be inculcated, he believes, with the traits of timidity, chastity, and modesty. He applauds the segregated living practices of the ancients, among whom women led "very retired lives; they appeared rarely in public; never with men, they did not go walking with them; they did not have the best places at the theatre; they did not put themselves on display." Rousseau emphasizes this last point in a note: "In the Athenian theatre, the women occupied a high gallery called *Cercis*, neither convenient for *seeing nor being seen*."[32] He congratulates the ancients for their greater domestic peace, and for the fact that they avoided becoming overly "sated" with one another, thus making whatever meetings did occur between the sexes that much more pleasurable.

To be sated is to be glutted, satiated, to have indulged one's appetites and desires to the full, in fact to excess. Rousseau fears the unsettling consequences of unfettered desire in a community of virtuous action. He claims to follow the "maxim of exciting the passions by obstacles."[33] Speaking of love between a man and his appropriately chaste object/partner, Rousseau writes: "The apparent obstacle, which seems to keep this object at a distance, is in reality what brings it nearer. The desires, veiled by shame, become only the more seductive; in hindering them, chasteness inflames them. . . . It is chasteness which lends value to favors granted and sweetness to rejection. True love possesses really what chasteness alone contests with it."[34] The moral element of love, unlike physical desire of one sex for the other, is that which determines desire and fixes it exclusively on a single object.[35] Love, according to Rousseau, is neither forced possession nor immediate, passionate embrace. It is consumed, but paradoxically also fueled, by the obstacles and resistance placed in the way of one's desires. In this cycle of evanescent desire, all women are ultimately substitutable, but no one woman can perfectly satisfy male desire.

Thus Rousseau worries about male sexual appetites. He

seeks to restrain man's excessive, uncontrollable sexual desires, the desires of a beast or a god, not a man.[36] He warns: "To wish to satisy his desires insolently without the consent of the one who gave rise to them, is the audacity of the satyr; that of a man is to know how to give witness to them without displeasing, to make them attractive, to act in such a way that they be shared, to enslave the sentiments before attacking the person. It is not yet enough to be loved; desires shared do not alone give the right to satisfy them; the consent of the will is also needed." He expects the willing participation of both partners, what is after all the lowest common denominator of what has come to be modern sexual love. But Rousseau's continuing comments betray the violence and manipulation at the core of romantic love. In fact, he suggests a less than mutual contract between the man and wife: "The decent man and lover," he writes, " holds back even when he could obtain what he wishes. To win this silent consent is to make use of all the violence permitted in love. To read it in the eyes, to see it in the ways in spite of the mouth's denial, that is the art of he who knows how to love. If he then completes his happiness, he is not brutal, he is decent. He does not insult chasteness; he respects it; he serves it. He leaves it the honor of still defending what it would have perhaps abandoned."[37]

Rousseau insists that the sexual act can never be real violence: "The freest and sweetest of all acts does not admit of real violence. Nature and reason oppose it; nature in that it has provided the weaker with as much strength as is needed to resist when it pleases her; reason, in that real rape is not only the most brutal of acts but the one most contrary to its end."[38] Certainly there is here a problem of figurative language. To great effect, Rousseau masterfully yokes brutality to the cause of sentimental love. But before we excuse his rhetoric as merely self-implicating, it is worth recalling the reason he gives for rejecting physical violence, unbounded by love. He rejects rape, not so much out of respect for woman, but because it would provoke a fight to the death for liberty (anticipations of Hegel's master–slave dialectic), and also because the male's paternity right ultimately would be decided by a woman and threatened by every other man. In other words, Rousseau expounds the principles of sexual coition under patriarchy. The violence inherent in love is permissible under a gender system that refuses to acknowledge the separation of reproduction and sexuality.

*Family Life in the Virtuous Republic*

Rousseau's preferred republic is ascetic in tone. He banishes the spectacle of total luxury, yet visual pleasure does not entirely disappear. Whereas women's ability "to see and be seen" is greatly restricted, men will continue to visualize within the act of reading the tacit (not expressly given) consent of an already textualized woman, one whose desire is authored and authorized by a male, reoriented by her involvement with the printed page, indeed by a certain project of reading (especially, of the romance) that shapes her entire orientation to love, marriage, and childrearing. In the paradigm Rousseau sets forth, women are to become agents and objects of love in something that we might want to call the political semiotics of love. In ruling out rape in favor of love, he necessarily assumes, according to Michael Fried, "that women, in particular beautiful women, traditionally regarded as objects of beholding par excellence, are especially prone to give themselves up to the tainted and debasing pleasures of self-exhibition." But, Fried continues, "the relationship between man and woman remains asymmetrical: the woman, it appears is made a reader and consequently a text only in response to an initial act of textual self-representation on the part of the man; the successful lover is the author, at one remove, of the text the woman becomes. For our purposes, however, the asymmetry is less important than that the woman's innermost being, her very 'self,' is in this way oriented to a textual as opposed to a theatrical paradigm."[39]

Rousseau's carefully constructed romance of Sophie and

Emile illustrates the full measure by which woman's desire comes to be textualized. The meeting of the two lovers within a treatise on education is, to be sure, a fiction—or better, a fiction within a fiction. We have already seen that Rousseau implicates woman in her own conquest; he even charges her with arranging the infamous "other scene." In *Emile*, for example, he puts it this way: "If woman is made to please and to be subjugated, she ought to make herself agreeable to man instead of arousing him. Her own violence is in her charms. It is by these that she ought to constrain him to find his strength and make use of it. The surest art of animating that strength is to make it necessary by resistance. Then amour-propre unites with desire, and the one triumphs in the victory that the other has made him win. From this there arises attack and defense, the audacity of one sex and the timidity of the other, and finally the modesty and the shame with which nature armed the weak in order to enslave the strong."[40]

Woman's role is a contradictory one, to manipulate/seduce and to brake man's unlimited desires. "For the attacker to be victorious, the one who is attacked must permit or arrange it."[41] "Woman's empire" consists in this, according to Rousseau: her greater facility to excite the desires than man has to satisfy them. In this way, "the stronger appears to be master but actually depends on the weaker."[42] Whatever we think of Rousseau's inverted reasoning, it explains a good deal more about man's entrapment than about woman's. The problem remains: Why should Sophie desire Emile—as a future husband, father to her children, and household head? How does she come to participate in Emile's desire to found a family? In fact, Sophie is won over to Emile by an entirely literary device. She takes him to be Telemachus arriving.

Prior to Emile's arrival, Sophie is found suffering from an undiagnosed, disturbing state of languor, a condition so alarming that to her intimates it resembles a state of love. She has already been sent to the city and presented to society, which was made to "see her"; but instead of dutifully choosing among several eligible men as she was expected to do, she rebuffs them all and returns home early to her disappointed parents. Rousseau explains the awful dilemma facing Sophie, the need to choose "a master for the whole of life." He writes, "She needed a lover, but that lover had to be a husband; and given the heart needed to match hers, the former was almost as difficult to find as the latter. . . . She sought a man and found only monkeys; she sought a soul and found none." Sophie is caught unhappily in the grips of an awful dilemma between the duty to love and the lack of a suitable object: "I need to love," she says to her mother, but "I see nothing pleasing to me." She is deterred, she adjudges, by the fact that "the charming model of the man for her is imprinted too deeply on her soul. She can love only him; she can make only him happy; she can be happy with him alone." Her dissatisfaction is so great that she even contemplates death as a way out of her misery. Continuing to speak in the third person about her own state of mind, she says to her mother: "She [Sophie] prefers to pine away and do constant battle; she prefers to die unhappy and free rather than in despair with a man she does not love and whom she would make unhappy. It is better no longer to exist than to exist only to suffer."[43] Romantic heroine that she is, Sophie refuses to compromise, to live without her great love. But in this case the refusal is comic, for her love is excessively absurd, even for one allowed the privilege of romantic folly. Throwing *The Adventures of Telemachus* on the table, she declares to her mother, "Well, here it is." The parents' response, as anticipated, is laughter and disbelief. Indeed, the narrator/tutor Rousseau confesses: "Sophie loved Telemachus and loved him with a passion of which nothing could cure her."[44]

Sophie loves an idealized man, a chimera, even to death. She silences her parents' attempts to bring her to reason by reasoning against them, "by showing them that they had done all the harm themselves: that they had not formed her for a man of her times":

Is it my fault if I love what does not exist? I am not a visionary. I do not want a prince. I do not seek Telemachus. I know that he is only a fiction. I seek someone who resembles him. . . . No, let us not thus dishonor humanity. Let us not think that a lovable and virtuous man is only a chimera. He exists; he lives; perhaps he is seeking me. He seeks a soul that knows how to love him. But what sort of man is he? Where is he? I do not know. He is none of those I have seen. Doubtless he is none of those I shall see. O my mother, why have you made virtue too lovable for me? If I can love nothing but virtue, the fault is less mine than yours?[45]

Sophie is tormented by the fate of all romantic lovers, to love beyond reason. But because of the absurdity of her situation, she must at one and the same time play the roles of victim and observer. She is forced to admit the chimera of her love and to cling to it, all the same—a cruel reward for a girl who has been trained to perfection in the modest and docile vocation of being a woman, which Rousseau believes necessary for one who lives always in the sphere of opinion and can "never cease to be subjected either to a man or to the judgments of men . . . [who can never be] permitted to put . . . [herself] above these judgments."[46] Thus Sophie represents a distorted, almost mocking solution to a dilemma addressed later by Rousseau in his *Confessions*—the problem of growing sensuality without outlet, the excitement of the senses for enjoyment without an object. He, too, used reading materials in order to imagine and therefore fix the object of his desire: "In this strange situation," he muses, "my restless imagination took a hand which saved me from myself and calmed my growing sensuality. What it did was to nourish itself on situations that had interested me in my reading, recalling them, varying them, combining them, and giving me so great a part in them, that I became one of the characters I imagined, and saw myself always in the pleasantest situations of my own choosing. So, in the end, the fictions I succeeded in building up made me forget my real condition, which so dissatisfied me."[47]

Like Sophie, however, Rousseau pays the price of distancing himself from the register of the real in favor of an imaginary universe: "My love for imaginary objects and my facility in lending myself to them ended by disillusioning me with everything around me, and determined that love of solitude which I have retained ever since that time."[48] Any alternative, however, would be terribly flawed. For according to Rousseau the pressing point of fixing the object of desire is to transcend satyriasis for fatherhood, and female license for domesticity. If she is to be not only in this world but of it, Sophie's fate still awaits her.

I said before that Sophie is textualized, but so in a sense is Emile, the author of her fate—or author at one remove. Behind the scenes in this drama are two fathers who contrive to encode the lovers in their respective stories and thus to achieve their union. Of course this all happens in a way that makes the lovers think that they have chosen freely and independently of their parents, as indeed they must if they are to enter into a love match. Sophie's enlightened-sounding father opposes arranged or property marriages and advises his daughter that a self-chosen match in which love unites the spouses is best. But he cautions severely against absolute liberty, preferring a degree of supervision and control. "My daughter," he declares, "*it is to Sophie's reason that I entrust you.* . . . I propose an agreement which is a mark of our esteem for you and re-establishes the natural order among us. Parents choose the husband of their daughter and consult her only for the sake of form. Such is the usual practice. We shall do exactly the opposite. You will choose, and we will be consulted. Use your right, Sophie; use it freely and wisely. The husband who suits you ought to be of your choice and not of ours. *But it is for us to judge whether you are mistaken* concerning this suitability and whether without knowing it, you do something other than what you want."[49]

In fact, the father's words are a bit disingenuous, for he has already selected a mate for Sophie. He welcomes this traveler on foot, this guest with the bearing of an ancient hero, into his home with these words: "Sir, you appear to me to be a likable and wise young man, and that makes me think that

you and your governor have arrived here tired and wet like
Telemachus and Mentor on Calypso's island—to which
Emile answers, "It is true, that we find here the hospitality
of Calypso." His mentor adds, "And the charms of Eucharis."
The last detail, so trivial in appearance, is of course decisive. Emile, it happens, knows his Odyssey but has not read
*Telemachus*. He has missed his cue in this carefully crafted
scene, only to have it redeemed by his tutor, thus stirring a
blush of embarrassment in Sophie. While Emile is entranced
by Sophie's father's story over the dinner table, she has time
to observe the guest who eats at her father's table. "The
young man's naive vivacity enchants everyone," we are told,
"But the girl, more sensitive than anyone to this mark of his
good heart, believes she sees Telemachus affected by Phil-
octetes' misfortunes."[50]

And so it goes, as the youths are enwrapped in each other's desire for the other. Continuing the literary metaphor,
the narrator approvingly writes, "Sophie's mother smiles at
the success of our projects. She reads the hearts of the two
young people. She sees that it is time to captivate the heart
of the new Telemachus. She gets her daughter to speak. Her
daughter responds with her natural gentleness in a timid
voice which makes its effect all the better. At the first sound
of this voice Emile surrenders. It is Sophie. He no longer
doubts it. If it were not she, it would be too late for him to
turn back." The intoxication continues. "Sophie . . . is reassured by Emile's fear. She sees her triumph. She enjoys it:
*Nol mostra già, ben che in suo cor ne rida.* Her countenance
has not changed. But in spite of this modest air and those
lowered eyes, her tender heart palpitates with joy and tells
her that Telemachus has been found."[51] Following this joy-
ous first union, gifts are exchanged—a pleasurable ritual by
which Emile establishes "a sort of connection [*correspondance*] which gives him the right to send things back here
and come back himself."[52] In fact, it is Sophie who is being
exchanged, circulated between the men, the two fathers.

Such is the structure of the textual romance Rousseau has

penned in order to see Emile's passage to manhood, to the status of husband, father, and citizen. The romance allows for conduct to be shaped through love rather than mere discipline. Rousseau is quite emphatic on the subject of romance. Indeed, he intentionally disrupts the narrative line just at this point to defend his chosen literary practice against those who would charge him with an overly naive, too simple history of innocent love. He insists, "If I have said what must be done, I have said what I ought to have said. It makes very little difference to me if I have written a romance. A fair romance it is indeed, the romance of human nature. If it is to be found only in this writing, is that my fault? This ought to be the history of my species. You who deprave it, it is you who make a romance of my book."[53]

Rousseau wishes to generalize the romance, to textualize the entire world. As Fried has noticed regarding the workings of a textual paradigm more generally, Rousseau seeks to rescue women from theatricality (the debasing pleasures of self-exhibition) "by making them at once the agents and the objects (in that order) of two distinct but mutually reinforcing acts of *reading*: that by which the woman first comes to share the feelings which the man expresses; and that by which the man proceeds to discern in the woman's eyes and general demeanor the tacit consent he seeks."[54] Rousseau's rebuke to his imagined critics is sharp. He allows himself to be provoked by the irritating thought of woman's pleasure in ridiculing man's gravely serious discourse: those *femmes ridicules*, to be sure, who confidently stand and speak outside the place of marriage about the chimera of romantic love. Only such as they would deign to mock the proposition that mothers nurse their babies as nothing more than *les vanités de la mamelle* (the conceit of the breasts).[55]

The stakes involved in the textualization of woman are high indeed. They concern the possibility of sexual love and contract, and thus the foundation of society as such. To achieve all this, Rousseau believes it is necessary to overcome the theatrical realm of specular representation in which narcissistic women, pleasuring in the act of self-exhibition, play such a prominent part. Sophie and Emile are united according to their heart's desires but also according to the law of the fathers who have arranged their union.[56] Let us not forget, too, that Emile, who has had the opportunity of meeting women anywhere, finds Sophie not among the fashionable women of Paris but in her father's house. She is in her place, the metaphoric position in which she prepares to assume her "naturally ordained" role as mistress of a virtuous household.[57] Rousseau asks:

> Is there a sight in the world so touching, so respectable, as that of a mother surrounded by her children, directing the work of her domestics, procuring a happy life for her husband and prudently governing the home? . . . A home whose mistress is absent is a body without a soul which soon falls into corruption; a woman outside of her home loses her greatest luster, and, despoiled of her real ornaments, she displays herself indecently. If she has a husband, what is she seeking among men? If she does not, how can she expose herself to putting off, by an immodest bearing, he who might be tempted to become her husband? Whatever she may do, one feels that in public she is not in her place; . . . everywhere [in all the countries of the world], it is seen that, when they take on the masculine and firm assurance of the man and turn it into effrontery, they abase themselves by this odious imitation and dishonor both their sex and ours.[58]

Rousseau is quite certain about the need for boundaries — between men and women, between public and private matters, between nature and culture. The institution of the family is absolutely essential to achieving order and eliminating the chaos that might result from a world without boundaries, a world without law. Moreover, conventional ties (as in the state) require a natural base. Love in the family fosters love of state. A good son, a good husband, and a good father makes a good citizen, despite Plato's famous injunction to the contrary in the *Republic*. The family Rousseau envisions has direct as well as indirect consequences for the state. Rousseau's preferred female figure is the beneficient mother or desexualized bestower of Good, the utopian Maman, Mme de Warens of his *Confessions*. He insists over and over again on the importance of woman's reproductive role. This is the basis, of course, of one of his most searing indictments of the "libertine" women of Paris, those who refuse to bear and rear children in an appropriate fashion. He attacks those unnatural women, "all in league" for having stopped being mothers.[59]

This is more than a casual preference on Rousseau's part, for he links the matter of nursing to morality, natural sentiments, and population. And like other eighteenth-century men of state and of politics, Montesquieu included, Rousseau regards population as a matter of foremost importance. The size of a country's population, and the rate of its increase, are for him indices of its moral virtue, vitality, and good government. But if women are to be mothers, Rousseau is quite emphatic about providing a role in the family for the man as well: "As the true nurse is the mother," he decrees, "the true preceptor is the father."[60] He asks that men take their paternal role seriously. From the institution of fatherhood, too, he derives woman's position: "The austere duties of the woman," he writes, derive "from the single fact that the child must have a father" (that is, one father).[61] In such a world, the greatest crime is woman's infidelity.[62]

Rousseau regards sexual inequality, not just difference, as a *natural* and a *rational* arrangement. And this view extends to democratic political sociability in the virtuous republic, the subject with which this chapter began. In his *Letter to M. d'Alembert on the Theatre*, Rousseau sketches an approving portrait of Genevan social life which illuminates many of his objections to the absolutist public sphere and, at the same time, demonstrates the extent to which gender is a constitutive category of his thought. He observes that Geneva, a city of public liberty without a theater, has nevertheless another kind of spectacle, that is, the total absorption of its occupants. "Everyone is busy, everyone is moving, everyone is about his work and his affairs."[63] Geneva has something else — an active club life. But unlike the salons of the great capital cities, Geneva's clubs—actually called "circles," earlier "societies"—are more modest, sober, and not least, sexually segregated. Men meet mostly in taverns and foster simple amusements suited to republican morals. Like the early English clubs—prior to the "ill-famed" coffeehouses—Geneva's are supportive of the practices of a well-constituted state or government. Genevan girls and women also meet in societies, but at each other's homes rather than in taverns. Still, according to Rousseau, there is a difference. Whereas men amuse themselves and chat, women do the same and indulge in "inexhaustible gossiping."[64]

Rousseau fears that the introduction of a theater in the city of his birth would destroy the cherished circles. He advocates a strong separation between the sexes, believing that from their too intimate commerce women would lose their morals, men their morals and their constitution—forced, as it were, to take on too soft a way of life. In his reverie about the introduction of a theater in the prosperous community of Neufchâtel, he foresees women/wives as the first to collapse into moral decay: "Going first to see and be seen, [they] will want to be dressed and dressed with distinction."[65] Like little girls who prefer ornamentation, or whatever presents itself to the sight as useful to see and be seen, seemingly sober, mature housewives are susceptible to the corrupting influence of their own spectacular senses.[66] Worst of all, Rousseau fears the infectious taint of woman's company: "And, no longer wishing to tolerate separation, unable to make themselves men, the women make us into women." This reminds him, predictably, of the distinction between absolute monarchy and republicanism: a monarch, he insists, is indifferent to whether he governs men or women, "but in a republic, men are needed."[67] Men are unmanned in the absolutist state, a world in which all persons appear to exist, as I have said before, as underlings in the king's household. Moreover, he writes, "every woman at Paris gathers in her apartment a harem of men more womanish than she." Rousseau describes restless men in parlors surrounding a female idol, stretched out motionlessly on her couch, "only her eyes and her tongue active." Such women "take great pains to suffocate their friends in sound rooms well-closed."[68]

Unleashed, free of the constraints of laws, untempered by the proper boundaries, women speak and see. Their loose tongues, particularly, disturb the theorist of democratic liberty. Speech is what Rousseau fears most. In a near frenzy of misogynistic hyperbole, he is driven to embrace the martial aspects of republican liberty in the celebrated Genevan male circles where men exercise, not merely sit and talk, contributing thereby "to making friends, citizens and soldiers out of the same men."[69] Twisting the central Enlightenment metaphor on the status of women and society, Rousseau proclaims that women everywhere debase the level of culture. "Women, in general," he writes, "do not like any art, know nothing about any, and have no genius."[70] Worse yet, "never has a people perished from an excess of wine; all perish from the disorder of women."[71] Women's most disastrous effect is on the order of male speech; grave and serious, it is easily upset by female humor and ridicule: "Our *circles* still preserve some image of ancient morals among us. By themselves, the men, exempted from having to lower their ideas to the range of women and to clothe reason in gallantry, can devote themselves to grave and serious discourse without fear of ridicule. They dare to speak of country and virtue without passing for windbags; they even dare to be themselves without being enslaved to the maxims of a magpie. *If the turn of conversation becomes less polished, reasons take on more weight.*"[72]

But women are necessary, and to some extent so is their speech. There are limits after all on the degree of silence that can be exacted in a human community. The best that can be done is to confine women to the interior. "We need not be much disturbed by the cackle of the women's societies. Let them speak ill of others so long as they like, provided they do so only among themselves."[73] The price of the virtuous republic of laws, and with it the probability that the theoretical public of men will establish principles of general welfare, is the silencing of women, their banishment to the domestic sphere. In that way, women are returned to what is, after all, their proper place. Thus Rousseau objects to women's position in the public sphere in the most uncompromising terms. Like his seventeenth-century forebear Abbé Michel de Pure, he castigates the modern situation in which women participate in the critical functions of the public sphere. Like Montesquieu, he offers women a domestic place in the virtuous republic.

The theoretical public of men must, in a deep sense, keep their own silence, for they share an awful secret about the limits of republican liberty. The story line of Mozart's eighteenth-century fairy tale opera *The Magic Flute* can be viewed as a brilliant gloss on Rousseau's attitude toward women, as emblematic of the gendered composition of the oppositional bourgeois public sphere. After withstanding numerous trials, Pamina is united with Tamino, her virtuous lover. Pamina, who is after all the daughter of the Queen of the Night and has her origin in the realm of darkness, is purified by love to be worthy of her near perfect partner, a man of noble spirit. The high priest Sarastro welcomes the loving couple into the Temple of Wisdom in which the ethical laws of freemasonry are observed. The powers of evil are shattered and cast down into everlasting night. Enlightened, male power reigns supreme. Pamina is resurrected with the destruction of the mother's power: The mother's speech is banished from the public realm of enlightened reason — eerily foreshadowing the fate of women in the revolutionary public sphere, the subject of Part II.

PART II

# WOMEN AND THE
# BOURGEOIS PUBLIC SPHERE

CHAPTER 4

# Women and Revolution

August 8, 1788: the king agrees to convoke the Estates
General, which has not met since 1614. May 5, 1789: the
Estates General opens at Versailles. June 17, 1789: the Third
Estate decides to call itself the National Assembly. July 14,
1789: the fall of the Bastille. October 5–6, 1789: the "October Days"—a large crowd of Parisian market women and
national guardsmen march from Paris to Versailles and bring
the royal family back to the capital.

June 20, 1791: Louis XVI, King of France, hoping to restore
the traditional monarchy, flees Paris in disguise to join with
royalist troops poised on the eastern borders of France. The
royal family is captured at Varennes by the citizenry. This
momentous event destroys the fragile constitutional compromise between monarchy and republicanism which had
obtained since 1789. October 1, 1791: newly elected Legislative Assembly opens. April 20, 1792: declaration of war on
Austria. June 20, 1792: invasion of the Tuileries palace by a
mob. August 10, 1792: insurrection in Paris and attack on
Tuileries leads to suspension of the king. September 21,
1792: the newly elected National Convention meets for the
first time and abolishes the monarchy. January 17, 1793: the
Convention votes the death of Louis XVI. January 21, 1793:
execution of Louis XVI.

February, 1793: founding of the Society of Revolutionary
Republican Women. May 4, 1793: first maximum on grain

93

prices. May 31–June 2, 1793: insurrection leading to arrest of the Girondins in the Convention. July 27, 1793: Maximilien de Robespierre is elected to the Committee of Public Safety. September 5, 1793: adoption of terror as the order of the day. September 9, 1973: creation of the *armée révolutionnaire*. September 17, 1793: Law of Suspects passes. September 21, 1793: the Convention decrees that all women must wear the cockade in public. September 29, 1793: price controls on necessities are established by the Law of the General Maximum. October 16, 1793: execution of Marie Antoinette. October 30, 1793: the government decrees that henceforth all women's clubs and associations are illegal. November 3, 1793: execution of Olympe de Gouges. November 8, 1793: execution of Mme Roland.

February 4, 1794: abolition of slavery in the French colonies. June 8, 1794: Festival of the Supreme Being. July 27, 1794: "The Ninth of Thermidor"—arrest of Robespierre, Louis de Saint-Just, and their supporters (executed July 28–29). November 12, 1794: closing of the Jacobin Club.

### The Collapse of the Absolutist Public Sphere

The king's flight to Varennes undermined the vestiges of Old Regime authority, rapidly accelerating the popular movement for a republican form of government. The arrest of the treasonous royal father spelled his fate—eventual trial and execution by the nation's children. Italian director Ettore Scola has restaged this central episode for a contemporary audience. The action of *La nuit de Varennes* is framed by the king's flight and capture. Scola represents the familiar narrative of the flight to Varennes as a problem of authority and of authorship—that of the king, and also of his subjects. But, as the film reveals, the transfer of legal power from the person to the group is a highly uncertain matter. If "the people" are to inherit power, who are they? Who will speak in their name? What will they say, and how will they say it? Above all, are women, the popular classes, and former slaves to be included in the republican body enshrined by the law?

By highlighting the absence of the (central) male figure, Scola's film exposes the ambivalent implications for women of the dramatic shift in political and cultural life which accompanied the fall of the Old Regime. I begin the discussion of women and feminism in the Revolution with a reading of this stunning film in order to dramatize a basic argument of this book, that the bourgeois republic was constituted in and through a discourse on gender relations. I make no attempt to record the history of the Revolution. My aim is more modest: to relate the political and ideological representations of women to the actions of women in the revolutionary bourgeois public sphere. Like Scola, I am impressed by the fact that the Revolution and the competing representations to which it has given life continues to matter. In a surprising gesture, the film's final scene traces Restif de la Bretonne's climb up the quais of the Seine into the motorized streets of late twentieth-century Paris. We are catapulted out of the past and into the future, our present. By subverting the codes of historical drama, Scola manages to make the familiar strange, to hint that things might have been and could be otherwise, and, finally, to insist that the bourgeois Revolution lives on.

*La nuit de Varennes* is a historical film that employs a resolutely antihistorical method. It is a story about the Old Regime in which the king never appears, a film about a world with a sacred center in which the center is vacant. In its place, we encounter various figures of late Old Regime society: Restif de la Bretonne, a petty provincial noble and Grub Street hack; Giovanni Giacomo Casanova, an aged aristocrat famed for his sexual conquests; Tom Paine, a visiting revolutionary publicist; an opera singer; a widow of the landowning bourgeoisie; a militant student. Alongside them are a magistrate, a wealthy industrialist, and most important, a countess and her two body servants—a gay hairdresser and a black maid. With the exception of Casanova, who for the most part travels in his own conveyance, this odd assortment of people are inhabitants of a public stagecoach. We follow Restif de la Bretonne, the pornographer/journalist, who is pursuing the countess. His suspicions are aroused by a curious package she is carrying and by her departure from the royal palace at an odd hour. Restif guesses that this behavior may have something to do with the king's expected flight, an event already predicted by radical publicists in Paris. Rumors are circulating everywhere, and Restif is a man of the streets. His journey is launched by a key piece of information picked up in a brothel, where he overhears the talk of one of the queen's servants. Restif remains throughout the dispassionate journalistic observer, self-described writer of truth, eyes and ears of the Old Regime. He sees injustice. He warns the nobility and the clergy that they have lost touch with the people. Too late, he pleads with them, "Listen to the voice of a plebian who lives among the people."

Of all the inhabitants of the coach, only the countess has enjoyed continuous access to the concentrated power of the regime. She is the daughter-in-law of a great man of France, a farmer-general and head valet to Louis XV. As the queen's lady-in-waiting, she belongs to the world of the court. Yet, in this highly structured neofeudal world of relations of dependence, it is striking to notice that the countess is also a (maid)servant. Whatever influence she wields derives from her service to the queen, specifically to the queen's body, and through the queen to the monarch. This is not to discount her political importance or her high status; this entire adventure turns on the logistical importance of her actions.

In contrast, the countess's social power is suspended for the moment in this strange venue. As in a salon, coach society exerts a kind of leveling effect. Social hierarchies matter less here than they might otherwise, and individuals are forced back on their talents and personal resources, especially wit, style, and behavior. The countess is a creature of witty discourse. In contrast to the more bourgeois occupants of the coach, she is no prude. She is a devotee of Restif, an admirer of Casanova, an unembarrassed reader of "pornographic" literature. She intercedes ably with the bon mot and a well-placed witticism. She whimsically cuts through the sanctimonious jargon of bourgeois moralizing criticism. She excels at verbal portraiture, especially of her favorite subject, the king. Although she is a lady of the court, not a salonnière, she is quite capable of playing that role, too. The coach becomes a kind of traveling salon; the countess, its substitute hostess.

As in a traditional salon, the participants in this society are both high and low born. Scola plays brilliantly with the ambiguous class distinctions of the Old Regime; even the countess turns out to be an Austrian brewer's daughter, and the shabby Restif carries the title of a provincial noble family. Moreover, the values attached to the older hierarchies are now under attack, and the film constantly poses the question of what is gained, what is lost, and who is the better for it. The turmoil within the class and gender order reasserts itself inside the coach. The stuffy magistrate, himself probably of bourgeois origin, represents the nobility of the Robe. His indignant objection to the pornographic banter of the coach is quickly defused by his opera singer mistress, who insists that it is he who has a filthy mind. The industrialist plays with the two old roués, attempting to provoke yet another episode of Restif's "Revolutionary Nights." He claims simply to be making a study of technique. But it is the countess and the opera singer, not he, who possess the conversational skills to engage the literary men in witty repartee. The countess joins in the game. Why not, she asks, give M. Wendel his pleasure? A stagecoach is far from ideal, but it can be made to do. And, certainly, she tells Restif, you have been in more perilous straits—a confessional, a river barge, in bed beside a snoring husband. The game ends with Casanova's own snores. Restif pronounces dramatically that love requires *le mystère*.

The industrialist's own overriding preoccupation is with the political and economic changes now altering France. He fears the concerted power of workers, especially their new weapon, *la grève*, "the most terrifying sight I ever saw." His traveling companion, the Anglo-American revolutionary Tom Paine, is a sympathizer of the more moderate constitutional forces in France. Nevertheless, Paine is a convinced republican with little patience for aristocracy or monarchy and its pretensions to rule by divine right. But although he quarrels politically with the beautiful countess, he shares a certain affinity for the grace, charm, and style of Old Regime culture. Like several of the men on this coach, he is comfortable in the company of vocal public women. In that respect, he straddles the old world and the new.

In contrast, the widowed winegrower is ill at ease in this society. Dressed all in black, she dutifully plays the role of a grieving wife. She does not join easily into the pleasurable conversation, which spills over from art to life to politics. She is the severe bourgeoise. Her actions are constrained by the pretense of propriety. But in the end she humiliates herself, pleading with Casanova to console her, to make her his one-thousandth conquest. In contrast to the lighthearted *entre deux* between Casanova and the countess, there is a kind of pathos in the widow's encounter with the old nobleman. Despite his gentle and generous refusal, her appeal to Casanova is desperate, slightly embarrassing. With his rejection, however, she steps back across the lines of class and gender she had briefly attempted to cross. Lowering her black veil of mourning, she reaffirms her attachment to rural bourgeois propriety.

Of the female members of the coach, it is the opera singer who is the countess's real ally. But whereas the countess possesses great prestige and position, this woman is a mistress, a fallen, public woman of the stage. She can no longer sing, though she remembers the librettos. Unlike the countess, whose power is a function of her role within the hierarchical order, the singer claims a total independence. At one point she insists on sitting above with the "coachman citizen." Others speak of revolution, she will make one! Moreover, as she exclaims, "art and husbands don't mix." She spurns the magistrate's support and protection. In the face of the frightening popular uprising at Varennes, it is she who consoles the hysterical judge. She sends him back to his wife. Posturing gallantly, he insists that she cannot go on alone. In response, she argues that she has her theater. "Je suis seule," she declares proudly. And when the coach finally catches up with the crowd surrounding the king, it is she who identifies with and welcomes this moment of popular upheaval. "I love disorder," she cries out.

None of the female characters in *La nuit de Varennes* openly advocates revolution. Although the opera singer comes closest to speaking on its behalf, hers is really a rebellious attitude familiar within Old Regime society. She is more at odds with the emerging bourgeois code of virtue than with the older customs. As one who inhabits a sexualized, sinful female body, she can expect small comfort from those who would recast the female as part of a virtuous republican body.

It is not at all clear that the Revolution will bring the countess's two servants personal liberation. Like the sellers of artificial flowers who serve the old aristocracy, the hairdresser has no future in the new order. His sexuality, too, is a sweet residue of the past. Casanova embraces M. Jacob, remarking that it is too bad they did not meet earlier: "I never turn anything down in principle," he admits. Only reluctantly, in the face of the menacing crowd, does M. Jacob accept the protection of Paine and Restif. The beautiful black maidservant, truly at the bottom of this neofeudal hierarchy of service, is valued as nothing more than a piece of property. She is torn between serving her mistress, the countess, and becoming the mistress (another property) of a new master, the middle-class student.

The Old Regime is most poignantly represented in the figure of Casanova; like the world of which he is apart, he is well past his prime. In one dining scene, we witness his revolting gluttony. His enormous appetites symbolize the excess and indulgence of the nation's thousand ruling families, to the absolute ruin of the entire population. Yet, despite his class-specific faults, and even his declining body, Casanova remains irresistible. He refuses the overtures of the women and the male hairdresser, for he knows he can no longer perform; his sexual conquests are a thing of the past. What remains are his reputation as a ladies' man, the talk of others who recount his feats, and his memoirs, to be published posthumously. In one of the film's most intimate scenes, we view the old noble at his toilet in a crude dressing room of a public inn, covering his corrupt body with powder, wig, lipstick, and frilly dress. It turns out that Casanova, like the Grand Seigneur himself, is in flight. He has been reduced to serving a German nobleman as something of a court jester. If he maintains a certain distance from the specific figures of the Old Regime, he can afford to; after all, he knew Louis as a small child. He is quick to perceive that the king's end is near and observes unremarkably, "When a king is captured not by another king but by a postmaster, he's as good as dead."

But Casanova's central convictions are not easily shaken. On events in France since 1789 he merely remarks, "I miss the sweet France of yore . . . dignity . . . respect." He reproves a Parisian national guardsman for his lack of politesse. He rebukes the militant, middle-class student for his poor manners. It is significant that Paine joins Casanova to further chastize the student. For Casanova, "in old France, no one would have forbade me to speak." To Paine, "censorship is the first step to tyranny." But Casanova's allegiance to the Old Regime is to its faded personae, for example, the old and blind composer Goldoni now living impoverished in a Parisian garret, his pension canceled by the new constitutional regime. Casanova's highest attachments are to the theater, the opera, and above all, the old code of honor. These are the values he fears the new order is tearing asunder. Already for Casanova the Old Regime is an object of nostalgia, though in principle the king still rules France.

The countess certainly fears the unknown—the vile drunk (brother-in-law of a Paris executioner) who assaults her in a public courtyard, the people themselves, their speeches, everything unfamiliar. She misses the court, once a cozy nest, and the security of the king's red coat. Heretofore she has been motivated by her faith in a living God. She carries with her the icons of old France, miniature portraits of the king and royal family. She invests her love for the king in a reverent verbal portrait in which she lovingly evokes the good father's unity with his people. For the countess, the French monarch is "my king, my ideal, my religion." She is, however, more than just another faithful servant. On this particular evening she is the custodian of the king's iconic and public body. In her mysterious package are the glorious vestments the king wore while reviewing his troops at Cherbourg. He intends to don them again, this time to lead an *emigré* counterrevolutionary army against the Republic. But without his iconic self, the king is a mere mortal among men.

The countess's mission, then, is to reunite the king's two bodies . But she arrives too late to save her cherished ideal. The king and his family, soon to be delivered to Paris by representatives of the national guard and the masses, are the unwilling guests of the deputy mayor of Varennes, dealer in colonial wares. Disheveled, she peers up a stairwell at the stockinged feet of the monarch, all the audience ever sees of the king's body. She and M. Jacob have to be rescued by Paine and Restif. She is at their mercy. The king's private body is dying, on the way to the block. His public body will never be restored.[1] As Paine remarks, "A king in flight grows less a king by the minute." Disguised as a Russian nobleman, the king is recognized by townsfolk who compare his visage to that on a broadside and on the louis, coin of the regime. They notice the very grossest features of his private body — his big nose, frizzy hair, little braids. A simple postmaster, an insignificant provincial who once served in the guard at Versailles, positively identifies the royal family. They call the king "Big Nose." Indeed, the whole event of the king's capture in the home of a seller of spices appears quite ridiculous. In contrast, we see the grave faces of the revolutionary guards sent by the municipality of Paris. The menacing words of Marat are read to the crowd, demanding that other heads roll, calling for a military tribunal. The farcical denouement of the Old Regime announces the onset of the "tragic" phase of the First Revolution.

In the penultimate scene of the film, the countess and M. Jacob are closeted away with the two men of the press—one a traveling correspondent and revolutionary sympathizer, the other a man of letters, "member of a race of spies." As Restif explains, "We don't participate or form bonds. We're a curious lot. We describe, classify, even confuse things sometimes." Although he is no party man, Restif lives in and for the public sphere of opinion. His curiosity is not satifisfied until he sees the contents of the two packages. While Paine and Restif watch, M. Jacob displays in turn each piece of the king's costume, adorning a dummy as he proceeds. Paine remarks, "It must be exhausting to play king." Restif replies, "To a great task, great honors!" and remarks presciently, "If he'd traveled in that outfit they might not have dared to arrest him!"

The countess looks on, the clothes dummy seems to glow. Slowly, deliberately, she bows to the ground before the absolute fetish of Old Regime power. "Majesty?" she whispers. There is no reply. The body of the king has been reduced to the absurd.

The film begins and ends on the banks of the Seine. A traveling Italian comedic troup performs the great events of history for a sou. A carnival man narrates while the milling crowd of men, women, and children observe the great events of "history" in a miniature mechanical theater. "Look in the keyhole," the carnival man tells the crowd. "See the king and queen. . . . The storming of the Bastille, fortress of tyrants. See the people forge a new destiny . . . the triumph of the Third Estate. . . . Ten thousand starving women, including a few men dressed in women's clothes, march on Versailles and bring the baker, the baker's wife, and the baker's son back to Paris. . . . See the beautiful women. Mme Theroigne de Mericourt—like Mesalina and Joan of Arc. . . . See the Great Harlot. . . . Long live the people!" The magic box offers the crowd a new world with a new perspective. "A new reality becomes fantasy, fantasy becomes reality."

Countess bows before the robes of the king with her hairdresser and Restif de la Bretonne looking on. From *La nuit de Varennes.* Courtesy of Gaumont.

History is framed by popular theater. The narrative of elites is displaced once the people join in. And the people themselves have changed, as everyone learns. To the countess they are distant and hostile—no longer affectionate, pastoral adornments of an aristocratic revel. The people have come to realize that they are poor, humiliated, victims of oppression. Even more terrifying, they have become interested in the "here and now." Still, there is some comfort in the fact that art not only imitates and reflects but also entertains. The people reenact the events of 1789 and 1793. This time, however, as audience, not actors.

*La nuit de Varennes* dramatizes a political turning that also involves a marked shift in both gender and cultural conventions. This traveling salon is the "last" in a mythic "series," in which a Society is first aggregated, then dispersed. The film achieves a fictional condensation of the whole age of the salon.[2] Its high point is represented in the coach, where persons of all social locations are brought together. Gradually, however, a splitting occurs. Characters are lost or captured, until at the end there is no one left but the hairdresser, the countess stripped of her costume and position, and the two ambiguous figures of the emerging bourgeois public sphere, Restif and Paine. As Scola appreciates, the salon's travels end at Varennes. The film celebrates and ridicules the grand artifice of the Old Regime. Above all, the real but fragile power of its representative women is shown to depend on the force of representations—a few portraits, the "inscription of the king's memory," and the emperor's old clothes.

We now know a great deal about the class and political impact of the French Revolution.[3] Attention has recently been called to the symbolic and cultural dimension of revolutionary politics.[4] In light of these contributions, the genius of *La nuit de Varennes* lies in its insistence on the indissoluble character of the revolutionary experience by way of a subtle interweaving of politics, culture, and class—and a disclosure of the gendered nature of the republican political body. It is in this sense that we might understand the complex subject of women and gender relations during the Revolution. First, as the film underscores, the Revolution was a revolt against the traditional patriarchy of the father-king. A discussion of women and feminism in the French Revolution must wrestle with what Lynn Hunt calls "the implicit murder of the symbolic father,"[5] and especially the impact of the fall of the king's iconic body on the constitution of a gendered republican body. From this perspective, we may begin to identify the features that shaped public consciousness toward women and influenced women's social and legal position within the new republic. Because this was a revolution against patriarchy, class issues inevitably became political issues and were argued in gendered terms. For this reason, we would be remiss in restricting the category of gender solely to the problem of women and family life, though it is that as well. Second, women's relationship to the Revolution was determined, in large measure, by their class position. As we see in the film, some women (not all of whom were of the aristocracy) may even have regretted the collapse of the Old Regime. Public women of the stage and opera house, sellers of artificial flowers, servants, and all those employed by the luxury trades had benefited in tangible ways from aristocratic consumption and the corporate privileges of Old Regime society.

Third, the Revolution shattered the privileged, monologic discourse of absolutist France and legitimated the role of public opinion in the nation's political life. Yet the bourgeois emphasis on transparency, nature, and universal reason was at odds with particularistic viewpoints strongly associated in Old Regime life with elite women's language and culture. Moreover, sexual difference was one form of particularism that did not succumb easily to eighteenth-century universalism. The woman question may have been even more irksome to the new proponents of reason than to their Old Regime forerunners. Either women would have to be subsumed within the universal (and effaced) or treated as different by nature but therefore outside the universal (and *its* privileges). Because the rise of opinion unleashed a struggle for authorship, it is important to consider the impact of women's—including feminists'—speech, writing, and political action on the terms of public discourse. Fourth, feminist demands exposed the gap between principles of liberty, equality, and universal law and the revolutionary insistence on preserving—and in some cases, extending—prior inequalities among the sexes. But an examination of feminist discourse reveals the contradictory character for women of the central terms of bourgeois republican discourse. Feminist appeals to nature as the basis for equal rights for women, for example, were offset by claims about the natural grounds of sexual difference. Equality, virtue, transparency, and law meant different things to men and women. Feminists did not always challenge that difference; rather, they attempted to reapply the terms of male discourse for their own purposes, with ambivalent results.

Fifth, our topic requires that we discriminate between the legislative record and the political process, and further between the liberal and republican phases of the Revolution and liberal and republican ideology. In some ways, the National Assembly and the Legislative Assembly were more favorable to women because they were motivated by liberal concerns. The Convention, with its austere republicanism, was less favorable to feminism, though the opening of polit- ical space generally allowed women more room for partici- pation. Finally, however, women's political participation was outlawed and they were returned to the home, deprived of both formal and informal political rights in the new republic. Though silenced, women's role was politicized as women were expected to perform the duties of republican mothers, instilling the home with a powerful political function. Of all the female characters portrayed in *La nuit de Varennes*, it is the widowed winegrower — seemingly the weakest, and surely the least verbal of the women — who typifies best the new era.

### Women's Demands and Revolutionary Activism, 1789

Women were present at the new centers of political com- munication. In a rather characteristic remark, for example, Jules Michelet noticed that on the eve of the Revolution, "the grand club of a hundred clubs, among the cafes, the gaming- houses, and women, is still the Palais Royal."[6] In August 1788, when Louis XVI summoned the Estates General, he directed the population to meet together by order and to draw up a list of grievances and wishes; each estate of the realm was expected to elect its own representatives, who would come to the Estates General with a set of demands. This remarkable directive unleashed the revolutionary process, initially in the sphere of public discourse. Sixty thousand still extant *cahiers de doléances*, compiled by the rural communities and the towns, denote the degree of public speech and the wide circulation of ideas that followed from the monarch's directive. Also, this consultation with the king involved an election, a departure from the traditional scenario whereby the king appointed the "natural" delegates of the various communities.[7] Altogether, the consequences were an unprecedented radicalizing experience for vast numbers of French men and women.[8]

The summoning of the Estates General constituted the opening act in the destruction of the old mode of political sociability, centered on the king, climaxing in the summer months of 1789 with the capitulation of the First and Second Estates, the taking of the Bastille, and the vast popular excitement that exceeded the framework of the old legitimacy. From the outset, women were drawn into the vortex of revolutionary politics. A little noticed fact is that some of the delegates of the Estates General owed their selection to women's votes. Women traditionally could not only vote but were eligible for election to governing bodies.[9] Whereas some women exercised a proxy role, all women were affected by the dramatic alteration of public space which transformed the political geography of power in the French nation.

Women generally did not participate in the officially sanctioned grievance process. Accordingly, the few surviving cahiers de doléances authored by women are from members of religious communities or societies of tradeswomen. Yet even the unofficial protestations in the form of pamphlet literature could be considered cahiers during the Revolution; the very language of rights and liberties was in flux at this time.[10] These early protestations are marked by a divided character. They seem to straddle a desire to restore the old system of moral justice and an impulse to assert women's rights within the new system of legal representation. Not unlike parliamentarians who demand a restoration of their traditional liberties, working women protest the abrogation of their traditional rights in the new political economy.[11] They appeal directly to the king, their traditional benefactor, above his unpopular ministers. The documents also reveal significant competition among women, who sometimes express differences toward others of their own sex in a charged vocabulary of moral sanction and approval. They link poverty and prostitution, economic and moral disorder.

Parisian women who make their living in Paris as flower sellers appeal to the just price and protest the disorder of the market, which they attribute to the abrogation of their corporate privileges by Old Regime laws. They rebuke their unwelcome female competitors for "libertinage" and "shameful debauchery," protesting that "all the unprincipled girls, whom no law, no decency can restrain . . . arbitrarily set the price." They insist on the right to rid the market of malingerers and free traders in order to restore the peace. The petitioners want foremost the reestablishment of their corporation, so that they can police the market for themselves. In the interim, they ask the authorities to cooperate in ridding the market of free traders—that is, other women. "Besides," they protest, "this is a justice that is due them since they paid the king considerable sums for enjoying the advantages of their trade, advantages they are deprived of by too much competition and the disorders it brings with it." Similarly, women of the Third Estate appeal to the king for practical and moral education and for exclusive rights to practice their trades. The *poissardes* (fishwives) compose a song that reflects their confidence that the king will join the Third Estate to protect the interests of his people. Yet they insist that he owes all his power, respect, and esteem to the Third Estate.[12]

The women of the Third Estate and the flower sellers couch their demands in the language of honor. They express concern for the plight of the uneducated, needy girl who easily becomes the prey of a seducer, only to fall into licentious ways. They decry "the difficulty of subsisting [which] forces thousands of them to put themselves up for auction," and they worry that prostitutes can easily pass as virtuous, that they are free to mingle "everywhere in all kinds of clothing." They therefore ask that "this class of women [be made] to wear a mark of identification." They also reassure men that, though asking for enlightenment (that is, free schooling) and for work, they do not do so "in order to usurp men's authority, but in order to be better esteemed by them," so that the most unfortunate among them will not be swept into the streets.[13]

October 1789 was a period of popular mobilization for the women of Paris. By midsummer, women of the people, along with members of the National Guard, were participating in daily processions of thanksgiving, seeming "dress rehearsals for the march to Versailles."[14] Their actions, too, combined old and new forms of protest. Market women were motivated by anxieties about the bread supplies in the capital, but they also bore symbols of hunger and harvest, fallen despotism, and the armed might of a free citizenry. Ritual marches since August had included women's deputations to Versailles. Indeed, the Paris municipal government had been authorizing these processions, and the National Guard accompanied every one of them. These were organized manifestations. Women were grouped by trade, district, and parish; they marched to drumbeat; they were recruited in advance.[15] The marchers asserted their right as women to participate in public affairs. They directed their protest to the very center of municipal, public authority. According to one observer's account, "toward the hour of noon, rioting women went in large numbers to the Hôtel de Ville to complain about the bakers. They were sent for an audience at four in the afternoon and for some kind of answer from the mayor of the city and the representatives of the commune. These women said publicly that 'men didn't understand anything about the matter and that they wanted to play a role in affairs.'"[16]

The momentous march of women to Versailles can be situated within a long tradition of women's participation in popular protest, especially during subsistence crises. There are some additional intimations in this protest of a new political sensibility on the part of the marchers. At the very least, the women's action strengthened the constitutional forces within the nation and prepared the groundwork for the republican movement. The precipitating cause of this particular march to Versailles was the rumor that the Flanders Royal Regiment had at a banquet some days earlier trampled the tricolor cockade, donning in its place not just the white of the Bourbons but the black of the aristocratic counterrevolution and the Austrian Hapsburgs, the queen's family. Many of the marchers were poissardes of the central markets who claimed a special ceremonial relationship to the king. Their traditional right to verify the legitimacy of a newborn heir to the throne linked them logically to the legitimacy of a constitutional monarch. The women obtained a promise of bread from the king and the National Assembly, but in the process they armed themselves, and they brought the king—"the baker and the baker's wife"—and the national government back to Paris.[17] They desired to see the king at Paris, where he would find wise women to give him good counsel. They referred to him as "poor man," "dear man," "good papa." The marchers appealed to the king in a paternalist discourse, yet they cried out for "bread and arms."[18] The market women were joined on their march by a former courtesan and revolutionary activist, the beautiful Théroigne de Méricourt. Descriptions of her figure—"mounted on horseback, in male costume, a scarf fluttering at her neck, a pistol in each hand"—also testify to the recasting of traditional female behavior within a republican mode.[19]

A similar agglomeration of old and new goals emerges in accounts of women's behavior in the National Assembly, which they entered, taking over deliberations for a time, on the evening of October 5; in this they were exercising a popular definition of sovereignty as "the right to legislate directly, backing up the law with armed force if need be."[20] Women from Paris swarmed into the Assembly; they shouted, chanted, interrupted debate, and demanded that the deputies discuss subsistence problems. Notably, the *Journal de Paris* remarks on their odd dress—some of them wore elegant clothing, but with hunting knives or half-swords hanging from their skirts. Although the women relinquished the chair of presiding officer Jean-Joseph Mounier once he returned from his audience with the king, they also mocked him for his support of *ce vilain Veto*. For Mounier, this was evidence of the women's stupidity, ignorance, and lack of gravity.[21] But another journalist reports with sobriety how the women occupying the meeting place of the Assembly voted with the deputies on motions and amendments relating to legislation on the circulation and distribution of grains, and "exercised . . . the function of the legislative power and the executive power."[22]

The October Days provoked ambivalent responses from the outset. Even some radical journalists and polemicists feared that the triumph of the people over reactionaries could result in an uncontrolled explosion of popular, especially women's, energies. Women were being cast as heroines and inspirational symbols, but they were less apt to be counted as people with strong political interests. Applewhite and Levy report that a medal was struck to commemorate the return of the royal family to Paris, showing them led by a female goddess of liberty. Likewise, the unknown author of a polemic, *Les héroïnes de Paris*, ascribed to the marchers a sophisticated political objective to return the king to Paris where he would live under a permanent people's surveillance. But this same author spoke of channeling and reining in the women, warning that they must not model themselves after charlatans, street players, jugglers, magicians, and other uncontrollable popular entertainers. He would restrict them to guarding the tollgates into Paris to prevent the importation of spoiled grains and fruit; in short, he would make them into *bonnes bourgeoises*.[23] The Châtelet inquiry, the government's own investigation of the October Days, worked hard to establish a conspiracy theory, even to discount women's prominence in the events. The questioners suggested that the women were bribed or led by men and even that many were not women, but instead men dressed in women's clothing.[24]

Contemporary and subsequent accounts of the event are marked by a strong ambivalence toward public women (of the court and of the streets). Were they virtuous? Were they really women? The nineteenth-century republican historian Jules Michelet portrays the march as a kind of morality play between virtuous and fallen women. He pronounces, "On the first of October, all was spoiled by the ladies of Versailles: on the sixth, all was repaired by the women of Paris."[25] The imagery of clothes, and attendant moral distinctions among women, appears most emphatically in Edmund Burke's dramatic rendition of the events at Versailles. Burke, an outspoken opponent of the Revolution, is obsessed by two images: one of a beautiful, sexually threatened, passive, and vulnerable queen forced to flee "almost naked" to her husband—an event for which there is no supporting evidence—as the rebellious subjects invade her quarters at Versailles, and one of the procession that carried her to Paris to the accompaniment of vile, abominable women. Of the latter, Burke writes, "The royal captives who followed in the train were slowly moved along, amidst the horrid yells, the shrilling screams, and frantic dances, and infamous contumelies, and all the unutterable abominations of the furies of hell, in the abused shape of the vilest of women."[26] In her first work on the Revolution, Mary Wollstonecraft deflates Burke's hyperbole with a cool appeal to common sense. Quoting this same passage in her text, Wollstonecraft counters with proud understatement: "Probably you mean women who gained a livelihood by selling vegetables or fish, who never had any advantages of education."[27]

## Women's Rights

It was actually a man, the liberal French aristocrat Marquis de Condorcet, member of the Society of 1789 and the Society of the Friends of the Negro, who formulated the most developed, early protest of the revolutionary period on behalf of women's political rights. He boldly submits the topic of women's civil and political inequality to the criteria of the liberal public sphere. His perspective is tempered as well by a favorable disposition toward women and their culture within the official and counterpublic spheres of the Old Regime. Indeed, as Barbara Brookes reports, the salon of Condorcet and his wife, the former Sophie de Grouchy, attracted the survivors of the dwindling philosophe movement and others from outside France so that it rapidly became "le centre de l'Europe éclairée." For her attendance at the lycée where Condorcet and Lacroix taught mathematics and others gave lessons in history and the sciences, Mme Condorcet became known as the Vénus Lycéenne.[28] Condorcet's essay "On the Admission of Women to the Rights of Citizenship"[29] was published in 1790 in the *Journal of the Society of 1789* in an effort to enlighten the representatives of the National Assembly.[30] Yet he was no newcomer to the subject of sexual equality. In 1787 he proposed that women ought to be eligible for election to governing bodies—a forward sounding proposal, it also harkened back to the liberties of women of ancient France, about which this oppositional aristocrat and academician was aware.[31]

In his most famous feminist essay, Condorcet denounces the exclusion of women from the rights of citizenship. Beginning with a remarkably radical interpretation of the principles of equality and rationality, he scorns the train of exception which will inevitably follow if women are barred from political liberties: "It would also be necessary to deprive of the rights of citizenship that portion of the people who, because they are occupied in constant labor, can neither acquire knowledge nor exercise their reason. Soon, little by little, only persons who had taken a course in public law would be permitted to be citizens." "If such principles are admitted," he continues, "we must, as a natural consequence, renounce any idea of a free constitution."[32] In a liberal spirit, then, Condorcet argues that the abridgment of any right risks the foundations of all freedom. "Now the rights of men result simply from the fact that they are sentient beings, capable of acquiring moral ideas and of reasoning concerning those ideas. Women, having these same qualities, must necessarily possess equal rights. Either no individual of the human species has any true rights, or all have the same. And he or she who votes against the rights of another, of whatever religion, colour, or sex, has thereby abjured his own."[33]

Condorcet also ridicules the idea of founding a liberal regime in which women's existing rights and liberties[34] would be undermined: "Several of our noble deputies owe to ladies the honor of sitting among the representatives of the nation. Why, instead of denying this right to women who are owners of noble estates, did we not extend it to all those who possess properties or are heads of households? Why, if it be found absurd to exercise the right of citizenship by proxy, deprive women of this right, rather than leave them the liberty of exercising it in person?"[35]

This defender of the rights of property-owning mulattoes and blacks would extend the right of representation beyond those holding seigneurial fiefs to all holders of landed property and taxable wealth. Qualified bourgeois and noble women, then, would be free to exercise political rights.[36] Yet, although he continues (as in his 1787 essay) to grant women the possibility of serving as representatives in the National Assembly, Condorcet now submits that a liberal, representative form of government already serves as a guarantee against the active participation of all the populace: "There will never be more than a very small number of citizens able to occupy themselves with public affairs."[37] Condorcet believes that women, like agricultural laborers or artisans, will not be torn from their homes by the task of governing the republic. He seems to be arguing that property alone—not race or gender—is a legitimate criterion for citizenship in a liberal polity; but also, because of "representation," limits will be set on widescale, democratic participation.[38]

Condorcet also rejects all prejudicial statements regarding women's inferiority and political incapacity. He wonders why motherhood and "other passing indispositions" ought to be more compelling liabilities than gout or bronchitis. He insists that democratic principles require the extension of rights to all persons irrespective of superior education or genius, and he recalls many superior women from past epochs. As for women's purported lack of reason and their vanity, he observes that there may be two, gender-based, forms of reason: "Women are not governed, it is true, by the reason of men. But they are governed by their own reason." He admits that women's interests may differ from men's, but he attributes this result to legal barriers. Women may, without failing in rational conduct, "govern themselves by different principles" and seek a different goal. "It is as reasonable for a woman to concern herself with her personal attractions as it was for Demosthenes to cultivate his voice and his gestures."[39] Furthermore, Condorcet tackles the persuasive popular conviction that women lack a sentiment of justice—that they obey feelings, not conscience. Again he attributes this difference to women's social situation, not to their nature. In a virtuous state of rights all will expand and uplift their human mental capacities. Condorcet's rationalist feminism, combined with a cultural sensitivity deriving no doubt from his noble background and his marriage to an extremely well educated woman, herself a writer and salonnière, leads him to differ on this crucial issue with the mainstream of the republican movement. He seems less interested in the so-called claims of nature than in the social products of inequality and the means of their eradication. Admitting that women are moved more by feeling than by justice, he declares that "this observation is more correct, but it proves nothing. It is not nature, but education, and social existence, that causes this difference. Neither the one nor the other has accustomed women to the idea of what is just. Instead, they have taught women what is 'proper.' They are excluded from public affairs, from all that is decided according to rigorous ideas of justice or positive laws. The things with which they are occupied and upon which they

act are precisely those which are regulated by natural propriety and sentiment."[40] In other words, Condorcet retains a
measure of respect for the older codes of honor and preciosity. He regards both cultivation and reason as products of
education, not as manifestations of unalterable sexual difference. He repudiates marital subjection as a just cause for
denying women their rights. "The existence of one injustice
can never be grounds for committing another," he writes.[41]
Exhorting the National Assembly to implement fully the
values of a liberal public sphere, Condorcet calls for reform
of the civil law on matters of divorce and marriage, as well
as the outlawing of slavery, press censorship, and the penal
practices of the Old Regime, including torture and the lack
of habeus corpus. As for women's "empire," he states plainly
that "this influence, like any other, is much more to be
feared in secret than in public discussion." Thus he finds the
source of women's power in the traditional order, the abhorrent secret practices of the Old Regime: "Is it not probable,"
he queries, "that this empire would diminish if women had
less interest in preserving it; if it ceased to be their sole
means of defense and of escape from persecution?"[42]
Whereas Rousseau aimed to put women's influence in its
place within the family, Condorcet prophesies the end of
women's empire for want of its causes. He assumes confidently that women's power, along with other superstitions
and evils of the gothic age, will be convicted before the court
of liberal publicity.

Yet even this most impassioned liberal defender of women
worries that, once emancipated, women will neglect their
(feminine) duties. This proves to be the most challenging of
all possible objections to women's cause. Condorcet assuages
his opponents by postulating that representative government can serve as a safeguard against the likelihood that
women will abandon their domestic affairs and aspire to
govern others. At this point in his argument, he appears to
bow to masculinist prejudices of republican doctrine — specifically, to the increasingly popular notion that women's
domesticity can be made to service the wider polity. Used

this way, however, nature is no longer the ground of equality, but of a subtle and pernicious form of inequality. Condorcet promises most emphatically that, although women should be granted political rights, they need not be expected to exercise them fully, surely not to assume political leadership or to wield real power: "And so it is unnecessary to believe that because women could become members of national assemblies, they would immediately abandon their children, their homes, and their needles. They would be only the better fitted to educate their children and to rear men. It is natural for a woman to suckle her children and watch over their early years. Detained in the home by these cares, and less strong than the man, it is also natural that she should lead a more retiring, more domestic life." Still, Condorcet disappoints his most misogynist allies, adding that, although the necessity of performing certain natural duties might be a motive for not giving a woman the preference in an election, it is not a sufficient reason for women's legal exclusion: "Gallantry would doubtless lose by the change, but domestic relations would be improved by equality in this as in other things."[43] But even this vigorous defender of women's liberty subscribes to the republican—ultimately, Rousseauist—demand for a reform of domestic habits, and like the great majority of his compatriots Condorcet is made nervous by overly ambitious public women.

*Women's Struggle for a Liberal Public Sphere*

By the summer of 1791, women were participating avidly in clubs and popular societies, joining fraternal societies for both sexes, and attending as spectators the galleries of section assemblies, the national legislature, and radical clubs professing republican ideas. They were, it could be said, enacting (but also threatening to exceed) the vision of liberal citizenship promoted by Condorcet. Women were attracted to the society wherein Condorcet and other liberal members of the Cercle Social predominated. They joined the

Confédération des amis de la vérité, which, along with the Cordeliers, was the leading club in the movement to establish a democratic republic after the king's flight in June 1917. They signed petitions, including the famous republican petition on the Champs de Mars. Among the women arrested after the demonstration on the Champ de Mars were some leading feminists, notably the Dutch Etta Palm d'Aelders, active member of the Confédération.[44] In this period, too, women studied and sometimes contributed to newspapers and political journals.[45] They formed delegations and deputations and began to actively petition the legislature, a practice that lasted at least until the mid-1790s.

From its establishment in January 1790, the Confédération des amis de la vérité was especially devoted to improving women's condition.[46] During the constitutional monarchy, its members campaigned the National Assembly and published journal articles in support of divorce, for them the crucial feminist issue. Several men (notably Condorcet, Charles-Louis Rousseau, Athanase Auger, and the president of the Confédération, Antoine Mailly) enthusiastically supported women's rights in the sphere of politics and education. Also, it was the first club to admit women as regular members and the first to establish a separate women's section. Certainly not all of the Confédération's members advocated women's rights, but the association of these liberals with feminism earned the Girondin a mixed reputation as supporters of women's rights. The brewing controversy between Jacobins and Girondins, for example, was fought out in decidedly gendered terms. In September 1792, Danton mocked the proposal made to the Convention that Jean-Marie Roland be invited to continue his ministry in these words: "I suggest that if you invite him to be Minister, you should also extend the invitation to Mme Roland, for everyone knows that he was not alone in his department! As for me, I was alone in mine." Marat's assaults on Mme Roland in *L'ami du peuple* were especially notorious: "Tirelessly, he harped on the theme that it was not M. Roland, but rather Mme Roland, who actually ran the Ministry of the Interior.

She was a siren who distributed her favors to her most sub-
missive adorers. Indulging in the coarsest allusions, he compared her to sundry disreputable or unpopular women, from
Lucrezia Borgia to such notorious female poisoners as Brin-
villiers and Voisin and, to make matters complete, to the
hated Marie-Antoinette herself."[47]

A heated debate was provoked by Etta Palm's 1790 speech
to the Confédération on the female condition under the Old
Regime in which she called on men to devote their full
attention to the problem of women's rights, insisting "we are
your companions and not your slaves."[48] Nevertheless, the
Confédération's women's section, which was proposed and
led by Palm, was officially endorsed by the Cercle Social. It
provided the women with a meeting place at its headquar-
ters and one of its leading publications, the *Bouche de fer*,
published announcements and minutes of the women's
meetings. The women's section, as announced by Palm in a
speech to the Confédération on March 18, 1791, was
designed first to lobby for justice for women—for the elimination of primogeniture, protection against wifebeating, a
comprehensive divorce bill, and political equality for
women. Second, Palm conceived of a Parisian and nation-
wide system of affiliated clubs to care for and educate children, especially the offspring of desperate and poor women.
Finally, she planned to establish free clinics for these indigent women and to find work for them.[49]

In a speech of March 23, 1791, Palm again addressed the
society, hoping to increase women's numbers by maximiz-
ing their utility as administrators of welfare within the liberal nation. "In the eighty-three Departments," she recalls,
"armed citizens united to defend the constitution. Do you
not believe, Gentlemen, that these wives and mothers of
families could join together, following their example, to
make it [the constitution] loved? The Société des amis de la
vérité is the first to have admitted us to patriotic session.
Creil, Alas, Bordeaux and several others followed your
example. Would it not be useful to form, in each Section of
the capital, a patriotic society of citoyennes, female friends

of the truth." Palm borrows the republican rhetoric of serving the public good, and of surveilling the nation's enemies. Women, too, she submits, can "supervise efficiently the enemies harbored in the midst of the capital and . . . differentiate the genuinely poor person in need of his brothers' aid from brigands called out by enemies. And the directorate of the central circle, corresponding with patriotic societies in the Departments, would propagate enlightenment and would make it possible to break up more easily the plots hatched by malevolent persons." Women, she insists, need to find a way of "demonstrating that they are worthy of the justice just rendered them by the august representatives of the nation."[50] She skillfully manipulates norms of bourgeois propriety, including fears of moral disorder, on behalf of women's civic involvement in the new polity: "Ah! How urgent that a maternal view be taken of this administration, where a culpable negligence makes nature tremble. Yes, young women from the country, arriving in this huge capital without friends, without acquaintances, abandoned to themselves, without work and wandering around, prey to all kinds of seduction, often return home with their souls debased, their blood polluted."[51]

Palm conceives of these societies of citoyennes as supervisors of public education, teachers of patriotic values, investigators of poor people's conduct and need, and providers for poor unwed mothers. Her vision of welfare work includes "going into humble dwellings to inform themselves concerning morals, conduct or misfortunes of the indigent" in order to guarantee provisions for the deserving poor. Through this disciplinary approach to welfare work by privileged women, Palm would reconcile the opposing classes of the nation. "The morals of both," she projects, "would be purified and egoism destroyed, and the wealthy man, object of jealousy and envy, would become an object of love and veneration to his brother in indigence." Finally, Palm attempts to envelop her republican compatriots in a vision of female citizenship by appealing to their active hostility toward Old Regime society women. Using the Enlightenment metaphor of domestic and political virtue, she speaks on behalf of a reformed notion of female citizenry: "Already they burn to show all Europe that if, when they are degraded under despotism, pleasing frivolity was their lot, then when they are restored to the dignity of their being, they will be the model for all civic virtues." She even conceives of a women's deputation to the National Assembly "to bear respectful and grateful witness before the representatives of France to what they just did for them and to promise these worthy fathers of the people that they will inspire their children with the same respect, the same love, for the constitution and the most ardent zeal in propogating moral and civic virtues."[52]

The women were enjoined by Palm to meet the following Saturday at the printing establishment of the Cercle Social, and thus was formed the Amies de la vérité. The club developed an organizational structure and launched a membership drive. With prohibitive dues for all but the most comfortable and a disciplinary notion of benevolent welfare, the women's section was something between a charitable association of the wealthy for indigent women and a political club on behalf of female rights. In the summer of 1791, however, it was drawn to directly criticize the National Assembly's Constitutional Committee, which recommended passage of Article XIII of its new police code whereby the charge of adultery could be pursued only by the husband. Palm exhorted the National Assembly on behalf of civil equality for men and women, comparing French women to their virtuous Roman forebears: "Will you make slaves those who have contributed with zeal to making you free?" she asks. "Will you stamp a brand on the forehead of a Clelia, a Veturia, a Cornelia? No. No . . . the powers of huband and wife must be equal and separate."[53]

## Feminist Protest in the Liberal Republic

The French Constitution of September 1791, whose preamble was the "Declaration of the Rights of Man and Citizen," divided the populace between active and passive citizens on the basis of wealth, thereby excluding the large majority of male citizens from full political participation. Complicated suffrage provisions restricted popular influence still further. Although the new government remained a monarchy, the document also established the supremacy of the law: "The king reigns only by virtue of the law and . . . it is only in terms of the law that he can demand obedience from his subjects."[54] By virtue of legal authority rather than tradition, the Constitution decreed that only males possessing the appropriate measure of property were eligible to exercise formal political liberties in the new nation. All women were assigned to the category of passive citizens, a departure from Old Regime legal practice whereby women could sometimes vote and act as regents. The systematization of French electoral law eliminated the idiosyncracies that had permitted women to vote. For the first time in centuries, women were completely barred, as a group, from the voting process.[55]

There were, however, some successes. Legal reforms in family life demanded by Palm and other feminists were enacted during the liberal phase of constitutional monarchy. The most dramatic measures were passed in the very last hours of the Legislative Assembly, in the wake of the Revolution of August 10, 1792. Whereas the Constitution of 1791 declared marriage a civil contract, it was legislated along with divorce on an equal basis for both partners only on September 20, 1792. Twenty-one became the age of majority for both men and women, at which point youths of both sexes could marry without parental permission. Perhaps the most important and far-reaching reforms dealt with inheritance. After the abolition of the nobility by decrees following the night of August 4, 1789, the law of March 15, 1790, abolished the right of primogeniture, privileges of masculinity, and all other rules and customs tending to create unequal division of property among formerly noble families. Even greater inequalities among commoners required remedy, however. A proposal of November 21, 1790, called for complete equality in successions, including those between the sexes. Following a heated debate in which Honoré de Mirabeau and Robespierre defended equality of succession rights, the Assembly passed a law in 1791 that insured partial equality, leaving regional differences intact. On March 7, 1793, the National Convention created a uniform rule of equality throughout France. Additional legislation that attempted to correct for the problem of illusory equality between heirs followed.[56]

The passage of the liberal Constitution of 1791 prompted a series of pamphlets and longer treatises on behalf of women's rights authored by Olympe de Gouges, Mary Wollstonecraft, and Theodor Gottlieb von Hippel. Their arguments represent the culmination of rationalist and liberal convictions from the preceding century. Yet their feminism was articulated within the context of the revolutionary movement and bears a republican imprint. Though Jean-Jacques Rousseau was an obvious target of feminist wrath, feminists spoke a language in which Rousseau's virtuous self is the model for political discourse and domestic reform.[57] Ironically, then, feminists adopted many of the contradictory assertions of the republican movement, as between an ideology of rights and a commitment to nature in which women are to be assigned a subordinate place. They sought, of course, to turn the claims of nature to their own advantage. The terms "nature" and "virtue," however, had an ambivalent quality in republican discourse. They functioned to preserve difference and hence guarantee sexual inequality, even as they were yoked to a universalist, egalitarian protest. Moreover, feminists articulated their position in opposition to the cultural styles and influences of elite women in the absolutist public spheres. At the same time, however, they could not help but be inspired by the freedoms enjoyed by Old Regime women at both ends of the social spectrum. Altogether, this conjuncture produced some very odd results. Olympe de Gouges, for example, was a monarchist who at the same time used the language of rights and the principles of republican virtue characteristic of antiaristocratic forces. By the late eighteenth century, feminism was a decidedly cosmopolitan movement, participated in by men and women across national borders. The authors discussed here are French, English, and German. The major impetus to their agitation on behalf of women's cause was the French Revolution, the event that stirred the imagination of an entire age.

Olympe de Gouges, a self-educated butcher's daughter from Montaubon, wrote several plays and a number of pamphlets on the coming Estates General. Yet this woman of the liberal or counterpublic sphere was most often noticed for her "illiteracy" by contemporaries, a sign perhaps of the discomfort with which bourgeois men greeted women's political and cultural intervention in the sphere of opinion as they had in the established venues of court and salon. Gouges is often credited with forming the first women's society during the Revolution. As early as October 1789 she proposed a reform program to the National Assembly which encompassed legal sexual equality, admission for women to all occupations, and the suppression of the dowry system through a state-provided alternative. She was sensitive to racial injustice. Cognizant of the slave uprisings on the Caribbean island of San Domingo (Haiti), she concluded her plea for women's rights with a firm avowal of full equality for all people, even at the cost of the colonies and the French empire.[58] She advocated education for girls, the opening of all careers, which she imagined would acquit women to perform their domestic duties with a wider outlook, and equal political rights. In one important respect her views are exceptional. She envisioned a kind of female-defined public space—the establishment of a national theater in which only plays by women would be acted.[59]

Like the market women who marched to Versailles, Gouges appears in the literature as a person whose allegiances are divided between royalty and a constitutional polity, with a strong preference for the former. One of her most dramatic gestures, prior to her own trial and execution in November 1793, was to offer to defend the king in his trial before the National Convention.[60] Yet even if Gouges was a royalist, she nonetheless appreciated the dramatic possibilities of the revolutionary stage, for how else are we to understand her (predictably futile) effort to insert herself in such a grand theatrical performance as the trial of the king. Moreover, she authored the exceptional document "The Declaration of the Rights of Woman," which appeared in 1791. Gouges addresses the queen, but hardly in the deferential language of an abject subject of the realm. She begins by abjuring the adulatory language of courtiers: "My purpose, Madame, is to speak frankly to you." She declares her loyalty even "when the whole empire accused [the queen] and held [her] responsible for its calamities," but she warns that her allegiance will end abruptly if the queen is found to be plotting with foreigners to bring arms into France. She calls on the queen as a wife and a mother to lend her weight to the rights of woman. In "The Declaration," Gouges insists on the natural, inalienable rights of women. Taking the sexual divide seriously, and replicating within the political sphere her call for a woman's theater, she proposes a national assembly to represent the women of the nation—mothers, daughters, and sisters—and to support "the constitution, good morals, and the happiness of all."[61] With this last purpose in mind, she anticipates no contradiction between the doubled assemblies. She firmly believes that the law should be the expression of the general will. In a wholly moral republic, there must be a singular standard of justice, even if women and men are to be represented separately.

Gouges takes the obvious next step. She makes an immanent critique of the liberal principles of "The Declaration of the Rights of Man and Citizen." By a single standard of justice, she finds it wanting; it excludes people simply by virtue of race and sex, thereby defying the principle of natural equality. As Wollstonecraft exclaims, "The nature of reason must be the same in all."[62] If the grounds for universal human rights are to be meaningful, the republican feminist argues, they must apply to all sentient beings without exception. Thus Gouges organizes her own "Declaration" according to the articles of the original document; women are also entitled to the full exercise of liberty, property, security, justice, political and civil freedom. Among these liberties, Gouges includes the principles of free speech and assembly: "Woman has the right to mount the scaffold; she must equally have the right to mount the rostrum."[63]

Woman must be free, too, to "name" the father of her child; to hold all positions, employment, offices, honors, and jobs (*industrie*). Gouges demands women's rights in the public sphere in yet another sense, that is, their right to an equal share of public administration and a fair measure of taxes. Property, she insists, belongs to both sexes. Her view of marriage is decidedly ambivalent. She calls it the "tomb of trust and love" and she seeks to defend the rights of bastard children of *all* women, irrespective of their marital state. She proposes national education, restoration of morals, conjugal contracts that will eliminate the invidious distinctions of bastardy, and the institution of an equal division of wealth on marital separation. She asks that the rich adopt poor children as a way of equalizing fortune. She envisions a law to assist deceived women, with the responsible man required to pay an indemnity equal to his wealth. Gouges blames "the women of society" for depravity of morals, and she requests that prostitutes be placed in designated quarters. Similarly, she scorns "the nocturnal administration of women" which characterized Old Regime practice. Echoing Condorcet, she prophesies that in the new republic "the powerful empire of nature" will lead women to disavow their former illicit and immoral behavior (their former "empire"). Until that time, there may still have to be distinctions among women. What is remarkable is that this plea for the rights of wives and mothers of the new republic is proferred by a woman whose very occupation and way of being in the (public) world is in tension with the republican code of female domesticity. It is unexpected, too, that she end her tract with a strong familial metaphor in which all political contradictions promise to be resolved. Linking the cause of slaves and women, of the Assembly and the monarchy, she proposes "that these two powers [executive and legislative], like man and woman, should be united but equal in force and virtue to make a good household."[64] Such is the power of republican rhetoric in this period, that the least "domestic" of women is moved to couch her demands in this form.

Mary Wollstonecraft also protests against the architecture of the new political society in France. She dedicates her work *A Vindication of the Rights of Woman* to the French legislator and author of a report on public education to the Constituent Assembly (1791), M. Talleyrand-Périgord. She speaks of influencing the French Constituent Assembly and praises their admirable Constitution. Still, she disassociates herself from France's unconscionable denial of civil and political rights to women: "Consider, I address you as a legislator, whether, when men contend for their freedom, and to be allowed to judge for themselves respecting their own happiness, it be not inconsistent and unjust to subjugate women, even though you firmly believe that you are acting in the manner best calculated to promote their happiness? Who made man the exclusive judge, if woman partake with him the gift of reason?"[65]

Wollstonecraft points out the implicit tyranny behind the act whereby women are to "remain immured in their families groping in the dark." She insists that no duty can be binding which is not founded on reason; that morals must be based on the same immutable principles, for whomever they pertain; and, finally, that if women are to be "convenient slaves," nevertheless "slavery will have its constant effect, degrading the master and the abject dependent." She warns: "But, if women are to be excluded without having a voice, from a participation of the natural rights of mankind, prove first, to ward off the charge of injustice and inconsistency, that they want reason—else this flaw in your NEW CONSTITUTION will ever shew that man must, in some shape, act like a tyrant, and tyranny, in whatever part of society it rears its brazen front, will ever undermine morality."[66]

In these same years, a Prussian civil servant and anonymous writer of sentimental novels produced two anonymous essays concerning women: *Über die Ehe* (On marriage) and the more extensive treatise *On Improving the Status of Women* (1792). Theodor Gottlieb von Hippel condemns the new French constitution "because it has considered it sufficient not to make mention of an entire half of a nation. . . . All human beings have the same rights—all the French, men and women alike, should be free and enjoy citizens' rights." He remarks on a woman's letter to the National Assembly which protested the exclusion of women from citizenship and demanded the right of mothers to take the ceremonious oath of citizenship, and he warns that by March 1792 the situation in France is deteriorating—"the opposite sex is now more urgently demanding these rights."[67] Cognizant of women's participation in the liberal public sphere opened by the Revolution, he cautions men to offer women citizenship rather than risk further sexual strife. Like Gouges and Palm, Hippel advocates women's pursuit of careers in state administration and medicine. He calls for giving women a voice in matters of state, "to which they have an indisputably divine calling."[68] He argues for women's citizenship.

Seeming to invert the liberal relationship between property and rights, Hippel states that, as citizens, women will have legal control over property and wealth. He shares Palm's appreciation for the utility argument of physiocrats, asking "can we then exclude an entire half of the human race from the honor of being citizens—and specifically, that part of the human race which plays the most essential part in its own creation and reproduction?"[69] Finally, Hippel advocates opening the institutions of learning to women. He believes that until age twelve the two sexes ought to be raised and educated in a similar fashion, by an individual of either sex. He conceives of the need to thereafter orient the two sexes to the duties to which they are called by nature. Hippel's contradictory perspective is an excellent index of the extent to which revolutionary concepts of nature served simultaneously the cause of equality and difference. In the area of sexuality, even proponents of female equality allowed the claims of "nature" to erect *barriers* to freedom and equality (though they might not have understood them that way). Both feminists and their adversaries sought to reconcile the strains within bourgeois thought through the category of republican motherhood.

## Republican Motherhood

The feminist writers of 1791 and 1792 insist on a consistent application of the political assumptions of their age, without prejudice of race or sex. They acclaim the role of education in bringing about a progressive future for women and men in society and they support the raising of women's civil and political status. In Hippel's words, "Women, who previously were mere objects without home and rights, would . . . become persons as well as citizens of the state."[70] Because Hippel worries about a possible contradiction between woman's new moral vocation as domestic educator and her inadequate training for that role, he advocates opening the institutions of learning to women. Wollstonecraft goes further, admonishing her readers that if women are not prepared by education to become the companions of men, they will halt the progress of knowledge and virtue. This is her response to Rousseau's influential remarks on female education. As she observes, "If children are to be educated to understand the true principle of patriotism, their mother must be a patriot; and the love of mankind, from which an orderly train of virtues spring, can only be produced by considering the moral and civil interest of mankind; but the education and situation of woman, at present, shuts her out from such investigations."[71] This notion is at the very core of the ideology of republican motherhood Wollstonecraft herself was helping to define. Even as she resists the most inegalitarian implications of republican doctrine, her own rhetoric implies that the home and women's role within it can be given a civic purpose; and, consequently, that women may come to be satisfied with a domestic rather than a public existence. Moreover, in the manner of Rousseau, Wollstonecraft counterposes her project for reformed womanhood to the frivolous ways of women in Old Regime society.

Wollstonecraft also shares Rousseau's ambivalence toward the literary culture of the novel, which she credits with women's false enthrallment and vanity. She attributes their misery and deficiency to a "false system of education, gathered from books written on this subject by men who, considering females rather as women than human creatures, have been more anxious to make them alluring mistresses than affectionate wives and rational mothers." She raises the specter of vain, powerful women, cautioning that force cannot confine women to domestic concerns, "for they will, however ignorant, intermeddle with more weighty affairs, neglecting private duties only to disturb, by cunning tricks, the orderly plans which rise above their comprehension." "Let there be then no coercion *established* in society," she decrees, "and the common law of gravity prevailing, the sexes will fall into their proper places. And, now that more equitable laws are forming your [France's] citizens, marriage may become more sacred: your young men may choose wives from motives of affection, and your maidens allow love to root out vanity."[72]

Wollstonecraft believes that nature will assert itself once force is removed. In its absence, "the sexes will fall into their proper places." Like Hippel, she anticipates that the duty of fatherhood will inspire men to leave their harlots behind and return to the family. In compensation, mothers will "spend their time in the nursery" not "at their glass," and love will "root out vanity." The "exertion of cunning," she writes, "is only an instinct of nature to enable them to obtain indirectly a little of that power of which they are unjustly denied a share: for, if women are not permitted to enjoy legitimate rights, they will render both men and themselves vicious, to obtain illicit privileges."[73]

Wollstonecraft finds it difficult to deny the central presumption of her age, that women possess natures different from men's. She looks to a world in which nature's transparence will accord with human virtue. Then chastity will "more universally prevail," and women's modesty, decency, and cleanliness will reform sexual relations. She refuses to grapple honestly with the limits this may impose on women's public role. Indeed, Wollstonecraft believes that once chastity comes to be respected in the male world, the person of the woman will no longer be idolized. Virtue, mental beauty, even simple affection will supplant the pattern in which sexual relations are sunk. Like Rousseau, she fears the fleetingness of male desire, by which women are turned into "alluring objects for a moment."[74] She assumes that something more permanent can be fashioned. But this will involve men too, for they are the source of cultural values and the more lustful of the two sexes: "Men," she submits, "are certainly more under the influence of their appetites than women; and their appetites are depraved by unbridled indulgence and the fastidious contrivances of satiety."[75]

Mimicking bourgeois male objections to the absolutist public sphere, Wollstonecraft likens women to soldiers and to courtiers. Each inhabits a world of fashion, romantic honor, and gallantry; each lives to please and sacrifices liberty, virtue, and humanity for pleasure and vanity. Gaining only casual knowledge of the world, women and soldiers exhibit no reasoned judgments. Both acquire manners before morals, knowledge of life before "they have, from reflection, any acquaintance with the grand ideal outline of human nature." Indeed, Wollstonecraft sees polished manners—the greatest accomplishment of women under absolutism—as nothing more than a "gay ornamental drapery" that better conceals vice, and she describes fashion as a badge of slavery.[76] In contrast, virtuous women require no costume. They will be dressed in "modesty, the fairest garb of virtue."[77] Wardrobe, speech, and intellectual style are all implicated in her reformist project of virtue.

Wollstonecraft insists that women can be educated rationally, their characters improved, thus profiting human virtue as well. Thereafter, their presumed innate fondness for dress will drop away as an unnecessary affectation. Only women stripped of virtues are decked with artificial graces. Even the art of pleasing is an unneeded liability, good for mistresses, not for wives. A serious mother, with a purified heart, seeks respect, not blind admiration. She is a house manager and friend, not a humble dependent on her husband.[78]

Wollstonecraft's portrait of chaste, virtuous womanhood is certainly austere. A woman's energies are drawn into a constant struggle for self-control. Indeed, Wollstonecraft contends, "to fulfil domestic duties much resolution is necessary, and a serious kind of perseverance that requires a more firm support than emotions. . . . To give an example of order, the soul of virtue, some austerity of behavior must be adopted, scarcely to be expected from a being who, from its infancy, has been the weathercock of its own sensations. Whoever rationally means to be useful must have a plan of conduct; and in the discharge of the simplest duty, we are often obliged to act contrary to the present impulse of tenderness and compassion."[79]

If women are to be good mothers and good household managers, old habits of sensibility must be destroyed. In this respect, Wollstonecraft shares Rousseau's suspicions of women, though she aims to portray women as victims of false education rather than as inferior creatures of nature. But she rails against women and their pleasure-seeking society. In the place of the women of le monde, she would substitute a serene but severe model of female duty: a world populated by rational, self-disciplined individuals, each "content with its own station": "Novels, music, poetry, and gallantry, all tend to make women the creatures of sensation. . . . This overstretched sensibility naturally relaxes the other powers of the mind, and prevents intellect from attaining that sovereignty which it ought to attain to render a rational creature useful to others, and content with its own station: for the exercise of the understanding, as life advances, is the only method pointed out by nature to calm the passions."[80]

Wollstonecraft also employs the metaphor of intoxication

to describe women's overexcited—and unvirtuous—state of false refinement: seduced by the regal homage they receive, they deign to exercise "illegitimate power." It is not, she concludes, a desire to acquire masculine qualities which leads women out of their proper place; nor is it the mannish women or femmes-hommes of conservative nightmares, but rather the overly refined, feminine women, who are the greatest violators of nature and equality. It is they who trade the "placid satisfaction that unsophisticated affections impart" for the heady intoxication of exercising illicit power. Wollstonecraft prescribes a moral renovation, a "revolution in female manners," to precede all efforts to reeducate women.[81] She envisions woman's change as primarily a residual effect of a larger revolution or turning in society.

This is *not* a challenge to women to *act*; rather, as Mary Poovey astutely observes, "women are simply to wait for this revolution to *be* effected, for their dignity to *be* restored, for their reformation to *be* made necessary. The task is primarily men's and it involves not confrontation but self-control."[82] The outcome of all this self-control is to be a very "placid" state of affairs, one in which propriety wins out over artificiality and female despotism, that state in which women exercise more power than they ought to. Like Condorcet, Wollstonecraft reassures her readers that she does not "wish to invert the order of things." She even suggests that, by virtue of the superior physical constitution of their bodies, men may attain a greater degree of virtue.[83] Wollstonecraft argues in a modest, self-effacing manner. Despite the almost unparalleled daring and unconventionality by which she lived her own life, in her literary creations Wollstonecraft challenges women to express themselves through indirection. Everywhere she decries women's influence, their illegitimate use of power. Yet she attempts to influence her audience, and she worries excessively about the manner of her argument.

As we have seen, Wollstonecraft is not alone in her concern about women's public persona and behavior. Even feminists fear misperceptions of their public activities. The women of the Third Estate want assurances of their virtue. They ask for distinctions of dress in the marketplace. Olympe de Gouge proposes placing prostitutes in designated quarters, thereby publicly signifying the differences of character among women. When Wollstonecraft compares marriage to legal prostitution, she is forcefully decrying the state of female dependence and slavery, penetrating the veil of bourgeois hypocrisy. Her remarks also imply, however, that no woman's reputation is safe, especially in a world where, despite appearances, all are in the "situation" of prostitutes. One of her strongest motives for insisting on female employment is to save women from all forms of prostitution, common and legal. In this context, she shudders at the "drapery of situation [which] hides the man, and makes him stalk in masquerade."[84] And she scorns the implicit masquerade that accompanies high fashion. In its place she would put the absolutely transparent, modestly garbed figure of virtuous womanhood.

Above all, Wollstonecraft fears being mistaken by her own readers for a masquerading woman. Her endorsement of the (masculine) values of individualism may derive from an unconscious desire to recuperate the violations of natural order which result from women's artificial tampering with language and thought. She constructs an ideal bourgeois male as the standard against which women are to be measured. Yet she is also discomforted by men and suspicious of male sexual desire. She attempts to resolve her fears about woman's capacity to illegitimately displace power and her ambivalence toward male authority by ceding final responsibility for social change to men rather than women. In effect, she portrays social reform strictly in terms of individual men's acts. Likewise, when she speaks of improvement, rationally planned conduct, order, utility, and self-discipline, she proposes that women incorporate features of male-centered individuality. She ultimately fails to appreciate the contradictions resulting from the applications of masculine ideology to women. Indeed, woman's greatest social contribution turns out to be self-control. It is not surprising, then, that when Wollstonecraft criticizes Rousseau's strangely inverted logic—his claim that if women are educated like men, they will come to resemble men and thus lose what power they have over men, their famous "empire"— she insists, "I do not wish them to have power over men; but over themselves."[85] Woman, it seems, is her own worst enemy.

Wollstonecraft's distrust of her own sexuality has captured the attention of recent feminist critics.[86] Poovey observes that, by affecting an ideal, disembodied state, "Wollstonecraft transcends her femaleness—and with it, presumably, the agitations that make her female heart, now still, cry out."[87] Cora Kaplan is equally persuasive regarding the warring terms of desire and reason which erupt in Wollstonecraft's language throughout this text.[88] But I would argue that Wollstonecraft's absorption in matters of linguistic style is as much a consequence of her stated ambivalence toward words and the women who employ them. She shares the implicitly masculinist values of the bourgeois public sphere, worrying over woman's willful, artificial, and unnatural control over language. Repudiating the female position, she orients herself almost exclusively toward the male logos. She celebrates the virtues of reason and utility over feeling and flowery diction, and of writing over conversation. Thus she announces:

> I shall disdain to cull my phrases or polish my style;—I aim at being useful, and sincerity will render me unaffected; for, wishing rather to persuade by the force of my arguments, than dazzle by the elegance of my language, I shall not waste my time in rounding periods, or in fabricating the turgid bombast of artificial feelings, which, coming from the head, never reach the heart.—I shall be employed about things, not words!—and, anxious to render my sex more respectable members of society, I shall try to avoid that flowery diction which has slided from essays into novels, and from novels into familiar letters and conversation.[89]

Wollstonecraft's discomfort with women's language

extends to her reservations about same-sex fellowship. Her strong views on the subject of female education are especially revealing.[90] She recommends coeducation not simply on the grounds of equality and justice, but for its side advantage: it will promote early marriages![91] Wollstonecraft also objects strenuously to all existing examples of societies of women.[92] She opposes the practice of shutting women up in nurseries, boarding schools, and convents. She especially fears the effects of boarding schools where girls sleep in the same room and wash together, acquiring nasty and immodest habits there or from ignorant servants. She protests: "To say the truth women are, in general, too familiar with each other, which leads to that gross degree of familiarity that so frequently renders the marriage state unhappy." Similarly, she attacks male society for its want of chastity and modesty among men, a situation exacerbated in boarding schools "when a number of them pig together in the same bedchamber not to speak of the vices, which render the body weak, whilst they effectively prevent the acquisition of any delicacy of mind."[93] Her case for coeducation rests on the idea that it will result in sexual fellowship, preparation for marriage, women's fulfillment of the duties of their sex, and, also, enlightened citizenship whereby women are free to earn their own subsistence, independent of men.

Hippel shares Wollstonecraft's appreciation of mixed education, until age twelve. He, too, supports dress reform: the goal of strengthening women's bodies, ridding them of the "tyranny of fashion." In contrast to Wollstonecraft, however, he praises women's facility with language. He finds "purpose, gravity, and vigor in their words." He chastises men for claiming that women talk too much.[94] Yet the difference between these two writers may not be as great as first appears, for neither is an advocate of ornamental speech. Hippel simply praises women for achieving what Rousseau believed impossible and what Wollstonecraft fears is yet to come—grave, improving, rational speech by women. Despite their differing evaluations, all three submit women's speech to the same standard of rationality.

Wollstonecraft wants the virtues of both sexes to be founded in reason. She speaks of the "discharge of mutual duties" in a virtuous society. And although she allows that women and men will be citizens, she firmly redirects women away from the company of their sex toward the fulfillment of their duty in the family. "It is the want of domestic taste," she writes, "and not the acquirement of knowledge, that takes women out of their families, and tears the smiling babe from the breast that ought to afford it nourishment." She appeals directly to the new republican regime in France to grant women the advantages of education and government. Reassuring her audience in the manner of Condorcet, Wollstonecraft avows that only then will women choose—on the basis of reason—to return to their proper place, in the regime of domesticity: "Let an enlightened nation then try what effect reason would have," she prompts, "to bring them back to nature, and their duty." In this context, women will become wiser and free.[95]

Wollstonecraft's vision of "the indispensable duty of a mother" is one all republicans can endorse. Rational motherhood rests on a utilitarian standard of happiness. Wollstonecraft does not mean to eliminate pleasure, only to redirect it toward domestic bliss. Not unlike Rousseau, she savors the portrait of a woman receiving pleasure from nursing her children and celebrates the happy husband who, returning home weary in the evening, finds "smiling babies and a clean hearth."[96] Such a man will not be driven into the amorous arms of a society lady, for in this reconstructed household woman's maternal duty will be enlightened by rational education. But what do the inhabitants of such an insular domestic world have to talk to each other about?[97] Of this we are given only the vaguest intimations. Apart from the presumed beauty and virtue of a well-ordered domestic universe, it seems that the family exists to prepare its members for their role in the state. Like children, women will be educated to a rational affection for their country, founded on knowledge. Private virtues will then emulate public virtues. A universal standard of chastity and modesty will prevail. Then women's difference and her privileges will lose all meaning: "Let women share the rights," Wollstonecraft concludes, "and she will emulate the virtues of man; for she must grow more perfect when emancipated or justify the authority that chains such a weak being to her duty." But lurking uncomfortably in the shadows of enlightened reason is woman's talk, "the language of passion [which] in affected tones slips for ever from their glib tongues . . . [producing] those phosphoric bursts which only mimick in the dark the flame of passion."[98]

According to the logic of republican motherhood, woman's major political task was to instill her children with patriotic duty. It followed, then, that the home could serve as the nursery of the state. As citizens, women would be educated beyond their limited horizons and wholly self-oriented concerns in order to embrace the larger polity, but ultimately in a passive not an active manner. The feminist version of the ideology of republican motherhood was meant to respond to a strictly misogynist construction of the dual spheres of home and state. Feminists strived to alleviate the tensions between a theory of natural rights with egalitarian implications and a gendered construction of sexual difference, but the potential for providing women with a route into the public sphere by way of republican motherhood was undermined by the claims of nature. In the sphere of sexual relations, nature was the guardian of inequality. Thus a demand for citizenship based primarily on woman's performance of her maternal duty was easily refuted. If woman's service to the community was viewed as a function of her mothering role, the most likely consequence was to offer women political representation in a *mediated* fashion.[99] This is ultimately how women's demands for greater participation in the new French republic were greeted. But this outcome was not foreordained. Indeed, the political and legal banishment of women from the public sphere occurred as a response by republican men and other women to the ("disorderly") participation of women of the popular classes in the radical revolution.

*Women and Popular Democracy*

With the establishment in 1792 of the first French Republic, all males were granted universal suffrage, making even
more pronounced the formal political exclusion of women
which appeared in the Constitution of 1791. On the other
hand, women benefited from changes in their legal status
under the Republic. Many of the civil reforms of the Legislative Assembly were extended. Marriage and divorce were
now civil statutes. The aristocratic custom of primogeniture was abrogated and equal inheritance was assured for
women, sons, and illegitimate children. Mothers as well as
their bastard children were protected under the new law,
whereas formerly unwed mothers could lay no claims to
financial support for their children. The Republic softened
the stigma against unwed mothers with promises to establish free rest homes with proper medical care and instruction in breast-feeding.[100] An even more ambitious program
for women's civil and political rights appeared in the never-
implemented Constitution of 1793,[101] which guaranteed the
rights of the populace to work, assistance, and education, as
well as the right to rise in insurrection "when the government violates the rights of the people."[102] Its provisions for
educational reform, public assistance, and jobs might have
enhanced women's opportunities in the new Republic, but
their hopes were largely frustrated.[103] Nevertheless, the
political ferment and reforms accompanying the military
crisis of 1792 to 1795 provided a context that allowed some
women to evolve into participating citizens. Indeed, wom-
en's protest escalated in the radical struggle that followed the
fall of the monarchy. Women exhibited their patriotism in
festivals of support for the war, and support work for the
troops, while continuing to petition for legal reforms. Some
even succeeded in enlisting in the revolutionary army,
sometimes disguised as men; deemed a serious offense, this
practice was finally outlawed by government decree.[104] Furthermore, women were a constant presence at the places of
political decisionmaking, keeping gate at the entrances of

the Convention, determining who would enter; packing the galleries at the Convention or the Jacobin Club, punctuating the debates with loud advice, catcalls, or abuse.[105] Women in one of the Paris sections petitioned the Assembly for the right to bear arms in defense of the city, and women of the popular classes (*femmes sans-culottes*) resorted to *taxation populaire*[106] in the face of speculation and food shortages.

Generally speaking, in the context of increasing democratization, at the peak of the popular revolution during 1792 and 1793, female political involvement increased. Under growing sans-culottic leadership of the sections, the assemblies took on deliberative functions to protect their interests and those of their families. Women were admitted into the spectator galleries, passive citizens were enfranchised, and the national guard was reorganized along sectional lines, strengthening popular control. The fraternal societies also expanded their role and encouraged women's participation. The climax of women's political influence was reached during six months of 1793 when women formed a radical group exclusively for women, the Society of Revolutionary Republican Women.[107] Its two most prominent members were Pauline Léon, an unmarried chocolate maker and Cordeliers Club member, and Claire Lacombe, a provincial actress recently arrived in Paris.

The Society was committed to a radical democratic program and to militant republicanism, its stated purpose being "to be armed to rush to the defense of the Fatherland."[108] It sought to frustrate the schemes of the enemies of the Republic, aristocrats, hoarders, and speculators. During the revolutionary insurrections of May 31 to June 2, 1793, it supported the ejection of the Girondins from the Convention. In association with the enragés and other radical democratic factions, the Society applied enormous pressure to sections, popular societies, Jacobin clubs, and Convention deputies to support a full program of protective and repressive measures for the safety of the people. The Convention legalized the Terror in September and then voted an armée révolutionnaire, a law of suspects, and a law of general maximum providing for uniform price controls on necessities. The Society's members pressured the revolutionary authorities to enforce this legislation energetically. They took to policing the markets to root out hoarders and to insure the passage of grain supplies to the cities. They engaged actively in surveillance, identifying suspects guilty of possible revolutionary infractions to be brought before the revolutionary tribunals.

Inside the club, members made serious efforts to conduct their affairs systematically, much in keeping with the standards of the revolutionary bourgeois public sphere. They applied principles of publicity, codification, and political rotation to ensure against the abuse of authority by the leadership. They established strict procedures for meetings, election of officers, membership, correspondence, and deputations. They printed their regulations and assigned two archivists the task of keeping the Society's papers in order. They received only citoyennes of good habits in their midst, and they specified the wearing of the (male) bonnet rouge, or Phrygian cap of liberty, and a ribbon of the nation by the officers of the Society. In fact, all members of the Society affected a kind of uniform, appearing in public in the red bonnet, with tricolor ribbon, and trousers. They carried arms, usually a pistol and a dagger. In this fashion, the Revolutionary Republicans policed the streets and markets and attended the galleries in the fashion of a revolutionary army, as would a general and her troops.

If feminism is construed only very narrowly to be the organized struggle for women's rights, then it may be that the Society does not fit under this rubric. Women's issues were not foremost on its agenda, and its downfall was precipitated by clashes with market women, religious women, and former servants. Nonetheless, its members were caught up in a scenario of gender politics. At issue were the policies of the Terror and their enforcement by the Society's members, as well as the proper attire for women revolutionaries.

As in the years leading up to the Revolution, political and stylistic questions intersected.

The Society attempted to impose a female version of militant republicanism on other women. In response to rioting during September 1793, the Convention initially responded favorably to the Society's request and voted to require all women to wear the revolutionary tricolor cockade in public. But when the Society also asked the Convention to arrest the wives of émigrés and to confine prostitutes in national homes to be retrained and regenerated for family life and good citizenship, they were greeted with a decree demanding the punishment of prostitutes rather than their redemption.[109] Soon the Society was at odds with its former allies, the Jacobin authorities, whom they accused of compromise with the moderates and failure to fully implement the constitution or to enforce the legislative program of the Terror. Like other radical popular elements in Paris, they questioned the usurpation of authority by the National Convention and suppported a program of sectional autonomy. At a September 16th meeting of the Jacobin Society, the Society was attacked. François Chabot paid the club a backhanded tribute, stating: "It is these counter-revolutionary sluts (*bougresses*) who cause all the riotous outbreaks, above all over bread. They make a revolution over coffee and sugar, and they will make others if we don't watch out."[110] At this same meeting, Revolutionary Republican leader Claire Lacombe and the enragé journalist Théophile Leclerc were denounced. The Jacobins questioned Lacombe's politics and her morals. Chabot "[did] not doubt that she [was] a tool of counterrevolution."[111] They accused her of meddling everywhere, charging that at one assembly meeting "she asked for the constitution, the whole constitution, only the constitution . . . after which she wanted to sap the foundation of the constitution and overturn all kinds of constituted authorities."[112]

The Society's defeat came at the hands of Jacobin authorities and women in the district where the Society was holding its meeting. In October 1793 the Revolutionary

Republicans were attacked by market women in the streets after they attempted to enforce the law of the cockade. At the same time, the Society was escalating its demands for female revolutionary dress. Their campaign for a law to enforce the wearing of the Phrygian bonnet provoked further disturbances among women in the streets of the capital. Encouraged by hostile authorities, the market women stormed a meeting of the Revolutionary Republicans and abused and beat its members.[113] The following day, a delegation of market women filed a formal complaint against the Revolutionary Republican Women with the Convention. After a report from the Committee of General Security, the Convention decreed the prohibition of all clubs and popular societies of women, a first step toward the suppression of all popular societies.[114] Subsequently the Convention outlawed all political association by women. The defeat of the Society marks an important turning point in the Revolution, the growing centralization of power under Jacobin rule and the subsequent period of reaction.

The ruling authorities quickly widened the scope of their investigation beyond the original complaint brought by the market women. Women's rights to govern and to meet in political associations were sharply contested. Fabre d'Eglantine warns the Convention that after the bonnet rouge comes the gun belt, then the gun. He reminds the Convention that women go after bread like pigs at a trough. These are not good mothers and daughters, he adds, but "des filles émancipées, des grenadiers femelles."[115] Speaking on behalf of the Committee of General Security, André Amar reduces women's political rights to meddling and reproaches women for lacking the qualities needed to govern in a commonwealth of laws. Despite the impressive record of women's revolutionary political involvement, he judges women to be lacking in the necessary moral and physical strength required to debate, to draw up resolutions, and to deliberate. Women are to be denied the most elementary political right of meeting in political associations because of the conflicting demands of their nature. The decorum required by an order of nature, a moral imperative he deems necessary to the very fate of the Republic, dictates that women are destined to private functions. The social order results from the differences between the sexes. "Each sex is called to the kind of occupation which is fitting for it." Woman, he concludes, should be confined to the family domain where "morals and even nature have assigned her functions to her. To begin educating men, to prepare children's minds and hearts for public virtues, to direct them early in life toward the good, to elevate their souls, to educate them in the political cult of liberty: such are their functions after household cares. Woman is naturally destined to make virtue loved."[116] Amar also fears women's capacity to bring disorder to the virtuous republic of men; that, too, is in their nature. In an almost perfect inversion of the feminist brief that education, not nature, has produced difference, which in any event ought not to deter men from granting women full citizenship in the Republic, Amar proclaims on the subject of women and politics:

There is another sense in which women's associations seem dangerous. If we consider that the political education of men is at its beginning, that all its principles are not developed, and that we are still stammering the word liberty, then how much more reasonable is it for women, whose moral education is almost nil, to be less enlightened concerning principles? Their presence in popular societies, therefore, would give an active role in government to people more exposed to error and seduction. Let us add that women are disposed by their organization to an over-excitation which would be deadly in public affairs and that interests of state would soon be sacrificed to everything which ardor in passions can generate in the way of error and disorder. Delivered over to the heat of public debate, they would teach their children not love of country but hatreds and suspicions.[117]

There was remarkably little protest against the Convention's decree. When a delegation of women wearing the red caps of the Society of Revolutionary Republican Women appeared before the General Council of the Paris Commune to protest the group's liquidation and the recent banning of all clubs and popular societies of women, they were reminded by Pierre Chaumette, a council member, of their subordinate status: "Be a woman," he scolds: "The tender cares owing to infancy, household details, the sweet anxieties of maternity, these are your labors." Chaumette callously recalls the terrible fate of Mme Roland and "the impudent Olympe de Gouges who was the first to set up women's societies, who abandoned the cares of her household to get mixed up in the republic and whose head fell beneath the avenging knife of the laws." "Is it the place," he demands, "of women to propose motions? Is it the place of women to place themselves at the head of our armies?" Chaumette's proposal that the women's deputation not be heard, that no future female deputation be received, except on an ad hoc basis, was warmly applauded and unanimously adopted by the General Council.[118]

After the defeat of the radicals, other women remained active in the local clubs and section assemblies for a time, continuing to present petitions there and at the National Convention.[119] But the editor of one popular radical newsheet effectively captures the political mood of the day when he observes: "It is no longer permitted to women to organize in clubs; they will be tolerated as spectators, silent and modest, in the patriotic societies; in effect women can no more go searching for news outside their homes; there they will wait and receive it from the mouths of their fathers or their children or from their brothers or husbands."[120] In 1794 all attempts at legal and social reform for women were curtailed. In May 1795 the Convention declared that women were to be kept out of the galleries. Workshops were closed in February. In May 1796 the Council of Five Hundred ruled that "the interests of society and morality" excluded women from senior teaching positions.[121] The Napoleonic Civil Code of 1804 reinforced the authority of husbands and fathers at the expense of wives and children. It resurrected unequal standards of divorce and deprived women of the right to perform as civil witnesses, to plead in court in their own name, or to own property without the husband's consent.[122]

## Rights and Virtues

The changes in the political and cultural orders of representation which accompanied the fall of the Old Regime resulted in a definite realignment of gender relations. Both women and men initially participated in the new public spheres of the Revolution. But as women began to speak and act on their own behalf for the rights of female citizens in the reformed nation, they touched off a virulent debate on representation, eliciting fears that independent, political women might be simply femmes-hommes—women masquerading as men, forsaking their feminine duty, and defying their natural female role. Conservatives and revolutionaries alike recoiled from the unnatural spectacle of political women. A fierce contest was waged within the Revolution over how women would be represented and by whom. This, in turn, provoked powerful anxieties about women's speech, action, and attire. At issue were the questions of which women would symbolize free womanhood in the new order—the public women of the street and theaters, the austere female goddesses of the ancient republic, or the privatized housewife-companions of the ideal republican family? And for whom would women speak? For themselves, for particular female interests, or on behalf of a transparent, noncontradictory set of civic values?

It is striking that women's presence in demonstrations during the critical summer months of 1789 did not elicit a torrent of comment from male observers of the period; but then in 1789 women were not yet operating from a set of independent motives, and their behavior could still be interpreted within the traditional motives of a bread riot.[123] Initially, too, feminist protest won favor with many in the liberal clubs and societies of the constitutional monarchy. Women's involvement accelerated in the democratic popular movement of the first republic. In the interim, their participation increased dramatically. Their revolutionary activities combined old and new goals. They joined subsistence demands to constitutional objectives, ritual drama to the demand to exercise legislative power. Most significant, they enacted the programs and institutional practices, first, of the liberal, then, of the republican public sphere—not realizing that women's exposure to public view was beginning to be seen by men as a violation of virtuous, republican conduct. Arguments for gender propriety surfaced in the language of duty, conduct, and costume, as they had earlier in the century. But they seem to have intensified precisely when men determined to *outlaw* women's political life. By doing so, men upheld the *political* complement of bourgeois rights in private property. By 1793 women were banned from active *and* passive participation in the political sphere.

In the minds of its advocates, the Revolution was to be much more than a simple change of government. At stake was nothing less than a total recasting of the relationships between citizens and their government, between citizen and citizen, and between the individual and the general will. Authenticity required that there be no artificial manners or conventions separating men from one another.[124] Revolutionary transparency was harnessed to a belief in the moral regeneration of the people, that is, to the possibility of their return from vice to natural virtue. The claims of nature were reflected everywhere in the political discourse and symbols of the new republic. Yet, according to the symbolic discourse of the radical bourgeois revolution, public women of the absolutist public sphere were virtually synonymous with artificiality, ornamentation, and disguise. Thus, while the norms of publicity, authenticity, transparency, and universal reason may have affirmed men's participation in the public realm, an emerging code of gender propriety prescribed that women were most in conformity with these norms when their behavior and conduct were least public. Republican motherhood proved to be insufficiently supple to allow women to join on equal terms the armed and virtuous citizenry of the militant republic. Nor did this doctrine combat the increasingly common association—which we see expressed by Amar—of mobs out of control with the female. If anything, republican motherhood was a solution for the problem.

The language of transparent, democratic revolution represented women as most virtuous while performing private duties as mothers, sisters, and wives. Once silenced and domesticated, women were to be represented in the public realm by men, predictably their male kin. Having revolted against the older patriarchy of the father-king, then, fraternal men imposed on women a legally secured definition of politics—this time, the patriarchy of brothers and honorable husband-fathers. The contradiction between political democracy and private virtue was resolved in favor of a mediated existence for women in the reformed republic. Women were deprived of access to the public sphere at the very height of the popular revolution, foretelling women's fate in nineteenth-century bourgeois society—and also, as it turned out, the fate of the democratic revolution itself.

Feminism, too, bore the stamp of ambivalence toward public woman. As feminists attempted to negotiate the terrain opened up between the language of rights and the republic of virtue, they opted for a definition of republican womanhood which functioned to inscribe women within the domestic sphere. There is no question that feminists of the 1790s were vigilant in their defense of universal rights. Taking the metaphor of slavery seriously, they struggled to free women from male tyranny. But one wonders whether they, too, were not troubled by the examples of female impropriety posed by radical women of the popular classes.

Condorcet relies on the crutch of representative government to temper his liberal feminist vision. Olympe de Gouges distinguishes women with morals from those without. The Girondin feminists of the Cercle Social attempt to bring a virtuous offering to poor, unwed mothers. In her 1794 history of the French Revolution, Mary Wollstonecraft distances herself from those women who marched to Versailles in 1789. Her estimation of this event and of the public women who had won her reasoned sympathy in 1790 changed markedly in four years. Writing now in the shadow of the Jacobin Terror, and manifesting a strong disillusionment with all forms of popular mobilization, Wollstonecraft dismisses the march to Versailles in an almost Burkean fashion. She now credits the Châtelet investigator's charges of bribery and cross-dressing as evidence of a likely plot by the duke of Orleans to kill the king and queen and capture the throne for himself. She writes of the mob as a "rabble," as being showered with gold, and of its "barbarity." She describes the multitude of Parisian women gathered at the Hotel de Ville as "the lowest refuse of the streets, women who had thrown off the virtues of one sex without having power to assume more than the vices of the other," concluding that "such a rabble has seldom been gathered together; and they quickly showed, that their movement was not the effect of public spirit."[125] As for the arrival of "the tumultuous concourse of women" at Versailles, she notices that "there was a number of men with them, disguised in women's clothes; which proves, that this was not, as has been asserted, a sudden impulse of necessity." She speaks of "the brutal violation of the apartment of the queen" as certain proof that there was a design against the lives of her and the king.[126] She even sums up the occasion with a great measure of sympathy for the queen:

> The laws had been trampled on by a gang of banditti the most desperate—The altar of humanity has been profaned—The dignity of freedom had been tarnished—The sanctuary of repose, the asylum of care and fatigue, the chaste temple of a woman, I consider the queen only as one, the apartment where she consigns her senses to the bosom of sleep, folded in it's arms forgetful of the world, was violated with murderous fury—The life of the king was assailed, when he had acceded to all their demands—And, when their plunder was snatched from them, they massacred the guards, who were doing their duty.—Yet these brutes were permitted triumphantly to escape—and dignified with the appellation of the

people, their outrage was in a great measure attempted to be excused by those deputies, who sometimes endeavoured to gain an undue influence through the interposition of the mob.[127]

Most disturbing of all, Wollstonecraft dismisses as incredulous the notion that women, by their own initiative, could have instigated this event:

That a body of women should put themselves in motion to demand relief of the king, or to remonstrate with the assembly respecting their tardy manner of forming the constitution, is scarcely probable; and that they should have undertaken the business, without being instigated by designing persons, when all Paris was dissatisfied with the conduct and the procrastination of the assembly, is a belief which the most credulous will hardly swallow, unless they take into their view, that the want of bread was the bye word used by those, who in a great measure produced it.[128]

Finally, Wollstonecraft spares nothing in her description of the duke of Orleans, who she holds most responsible for this sorry episode. Most interesting, however, is the way she tars this libertine with the smut of prostituted females:

Having taken up his abode in the centre of the palais royal, a very superb square, yet the last in which a person of any delicacy, not to mention decorum, or morality, would choose to reside; because, excepting the people in trade, who found it convenient, it was entirely occupied by the most shameless girls of the town, their hectoring protectors, gamesters, and sharpers of every denomination. In short by the vilest of women; by wretches who lived in houses from which the stript bodies, often found in the Seine, were supposed to be thrown—and he was considered as the grand sultan of this den of iniquity.[129]

The paradoxes of feminist thought do reflect the extent of class divisions among women in late eighteenth-century France, but they are not only attributable to class factors.

Market women's resistance to the imposition of the program of the Terror by radical republicans surely reflected differing property concerns, but also at stake was a conflict over codes of dress and the norms of publicity appropriate to women and family life in the new republic. Militant women's very "publicness" worked against them. And, although the rhetoric of free womanhood pronounced by the Society of Revolutionary Republican Women was a fair and logical extrapolation of republican virtue, it was at variance with the dominant standards of sexuality and respectability within bourgeois republican discourse. While the Society is not mentioned in her 1794 history of the Revolution, Mary Wollstonecraft could not have failed to notice its rise and banishment—coming as it did directly upon the guillotining of the queen and Mme Roland, whose circle Wollstonecraft joined—and perhaps to have been repulsed by the women's public impropriety and their militant politics. It is difficult to conclude otherwise once we read her revised estimation of the market women's march on Versailles and her strong reservations about political initiatives by women of the popular classes. Wollstonecraft's reserve speaks as well to the restrictions placed on the liberal program for women. Proposals to extend bourgeois liberties to women were intended in practice only for women of the propertied classes. Feminists of this era had difficulty reconciling women's liberties and their virtues. Finally, notwithstanding the Society of Revolutionary Republican Women's efforts at surveillance, women of the revolutionary bourgeois public sphere discovered that for them "publicity" and "propriety" proved to be irreconcilable goals.

CHAPTER 5

# Republican Bodies

In 1785, four years before the outbreak of the Revolution, Jacques-Louis David's masterpiece *The Oath of the Horatii* was shown before the Parisian public to great acclaim at the biennial Salon exhibition of the Royal Academy of Painting and Sculpture.[1] David fashions an image of exquisite visual simplicity and power which foreshadows the gender outcomes of the political revolution. In the atrium of a Roman household, three youths are depicted swearing allegiance to their father. The men's metallic dress is accented by swatches of bright red cloth. The brothers' outstretched, tensile arms point outward and upward to the sword-bearing, raised hands of their father—the compositional and narrative center of the work. In his left hand, the father holds three swords that symbolizes the uniting of three wills. His brilliantly lit open right hand conveys the potentially sacrificial outcome of this event. Indeed, the action represented here is a strangely solemn and verbal one. The men's taut bodies are straining to become instruments of the Word.

In the painting's right foreground, David groups three seated women and two children dressed in muted, earthy colors. Their drooping, soft, sensual bodies evoke an atmosphere of deep sorrow. The women's heads are bent, their eyes closed, even though they are surely witnesses to this dramatic *mise-en-scène*. In the shadowy rear of the group,

152

Jacques-Louis David, *The Oath of the Horatii*, 1785. Louvre. Photograph courtesy of Réunion des Musées Nationaux, Paris.

the mother attempts to shield the children's eyes, though one small boy forces open her fingers to gaze at the swords. Of the entire group on the right, only this child truly sees. In contrast, the women seem not to see. They are present but strangely passive—even to the point of lacking vision. Their knowledge is one of intuition. They feel the gravity of the moment, symbolized by the grave deed of creating a political future, one in which they will not participate.

Owing to the popularity of Pierre Corneille's drama *Horace*, as well as various classical accounts by Livy, Dionysius of Halicarnassus, and Plutarch, David's audience would have been quite familiar with the Horatii saga. In the reign of Tullus Hostilius (672–640 B.C.), the neighboring kingdoms of Rome and Alba had sunk into a state of war. Each people selected three heroes to do battle for it; the Horatii would represent Rome and the Curiatii Alba. Yet these two groups were joined by marriage as well as feud. One of the Horatii was married to Sabina, sister to the Curiatii (the second of two grieving women in the right foreground), and Camilla, sister to the Horatii (the other woman of this sorrowful pair), was betrothed to one of the Curiatii. Thus, cruel bereavement within the family would result from any of the possible outcomes to this battle. The battle was won by the Horatii. When the eldest brother announced the victory, his sister cursed him for the loss of her lover, whereupon he drew his sword and killed her. After an appeal by the father of the Horatii, the people acquitted the brother of the charge of murder.

David seems to have invented the subject of the oath for this pictorial account, there being no precedents for its inclusion in the Horatii story. By borrowing the oath motif, he is able to depict a moment of unvacillating will, where personal determination passes over into impersonal commitment. He captures the men's momentous resolve to act for a higher duty than self-interest. The men's raised swords communicate the gravity of their deed, the implied violence bound up with this awesome act of political allegiance. Not death but liberty, however, inspires their action, a liberty predicated on this willingness to defy or risk death itself. This is what the state asks of its sons.

David's painting conflates the representation of family or paternal authority with that of the state. The three brothers are actually portrayed as taking an oath to the father. Moreover, David figures the entire political drama in and through the family and he represents political space in the restricted domestic arena. But this is a supremely austere family compound. David complicates our reading by making the space in which the action occurs a decidedly ambivalent one, at once public and private. The seated women appear to reinforce the scene's familial dimension, but the strong verticality of the half-seen Doric columns and the play of light in the stony atrium suggest a more public locale. There is a grandeur to the picture's dimensions. The high arches and antique columns imply that we may be outside as well as inside. The lack of furnishings, combined with the absence of sensuous and subtle shadings associated with the eighteenth-century rococo painting David opposed, works to extirpate any sentimentalizing or domestic interpretation of this scene. In effect, the work's most forthright political or public implications virtually empty out the painting's domestic content. The grieving women are almost beside the point—that is, of oath taking and political allegiance, which is man's duty alone. They are merely there to suffer; they represent the consequences of political deeds, not the deed itself. The painting's imposed ambiguity between public and private, state and family, is to that extent recuperated. David merely depicts the uncontestable fixing of sexual boundaries.

Insofar as David represents the oath as one between father and sons, there exists a possibility that he means to invoke for his audience the privileged status of the highest earthly father within the French kingdom. Moreover, the work was done on a royal commission. The painting's narrative, however, disrupts any comfortable affirmation of monarchical authority, for oath taking violates the traditionalist practices of Old Regime life. It is an act of contract, of foundation, of commitment and recommitment to eternal values— the point at which a common utterance arises that will be "the source of future law, at once impersonal and human."[2] The oath, then, is at odds with both the pleasurable fetes of the aristocracy and the traditional ceremony of the *sacre*, the annointing of the kings of France. Stylistically, too, the painting undercuts any simple traditionalist reading. David introduces no emotional or dramatic nuance, no painterly complexity, no imaginative play or erotic suggestion. For all that, he substitutes a harsh, even dissonant, abstract, and geometric conception. The painting's oppositions—between masculine strength and feminine weakness, rationality and passion, verticality and slackness—are never modulated.[3]

Thomas Crow speaks of a hallucinatory vision that leads the viewer almost disruptively into "another space," far from the fictional and pleasurable outlook of the imagination. David substitutes for the world of art an immutable order of nature whose principles are "already-seen and already known."[4] The strange, translucent lighting makes the truth of nature and its representations appear absolutely transparent to the viewer's eye.

The repudiation of the perfumed, stylized, theatrical, ultimately feminine atmosphere of the Old Regime court and society by writers and artists of the oppositional bourgeois public sphere, such as David, gives to this implied order of nature an undeniable gender complexion. The painting constructs a world without artifice, disguise, or erotic pleasure. The groupings of male and female actors signify a space in which the sexes are in their proper place — proper in that nature, working with a mathematical rigor, distributes life in this way. Thus, by opposing nature to art, David also succeeds in naturalizing the image of sexuality. And the results are far from equal. David's masculine figures are self-determined, metallically rigid, vibrantly rectilinear. The women are limp, malleable, fluent in contour, slack, strangely diminished.

I have referred to the violence underwriting the moment of political foundation represented here by the oath. Yet it seems that the violence that sharpens the men's iron determination also threatens them. And so it is if their lives are to be sacrificed to an idea, to the state. The story's classical elements, however, speak of a conflict between love and duty. When the victorious Horatius is accused by his sister Camilla of murder, he slays her for lack of devotion. Only women experience so dramatic a conflict between family duty and loyalty to the state. Only women are traded between the two communities. Even fidelity to the family, woman's highest duty, is complicated by the choice she must make between father and brothers, on the one hand, and husband, on the other. Males experience no such conflict between political and familial duty. For them, the state wholly encompasses, indeed rests on, the bond that joins father to son. On this score, the republic merely recapitulates monarchy. Moreover, the ambiguous space of the painting reinforces the idea that family life is the ground of the state—it is both premise and outcome of political existence. The two spheres are joined by a unitary principle, one that ultimately favors only males. The truly tragic element in David's *Oath*, then, turns out to be the impending sacrifice of the daughter.

David's painting departs from Corneille's *Horace* in an important respect. In the climax to the play, Camilla denounces not only her murderous brother but the whole Roman cult of military valor, which she sees as brutal and inhuman. Her betrothed is the only male character in the play whose feelings are not centered exclusively on glory. The play ends with the grief-stricken father's appeal to the king for clemency for his son, which is granted, thus recuperating Camilla's challenge. Still, as Norman Bryson observes, Corneille's Camille is part of the same order of language and of signs, of *gloire*, as the men, capable of projecting the most heroic and defiant image of the play: "The men may have the sword, but Camille has the Word, and she uses it to full effect, as a weapon directed at the Roman state." In contrast, "David's Camilla and the women around her are placed *outside* the register of speech, which belongs exclusively to the males: drained, exhausted, hardly capable of sustaining the weight of their own bodies, the women are unable to mobilise any resource of language or image that might challenge the males. . . . The women cannot produce an image of *acting* within male vision; all they can do is become the site of a male look that apprehends the female as passive before vision, the object of and for the male gaze."[5] Even those women who survive the blade meet a tragic fate. David's painting points to an unavoidable feature of bourgeois representation. Whether in shadow or light, women are truly off stage to the central drama of political life. To swear an oath is to dedicate oneself *publicly*, to speak one's duty in words that can be heard and witnessed by others.

Who, then, are witnesses to men's deeds? In *The Oath of the Horatii*, it is the grieving, muted women who affirm and witness men's act of oath taking. Women are spectators, not actors, a speechless audience at the scene of men's duty. Paradoxically, too, these witnesses are virtually blinded by their own grief and foreboding. Two key senses required by the modern polity, vision and speech, are impaired. The place of women in the Republic is marked by these multiple erasures. In this context, it is interesting to recall the small boy's look. However unbearable the consequences, he must be made to see the duty of men, for unlike the women he will assume his place as a citizen among men. He, too, will swear an oath of allegiance to the state.

Behind the moment of contract and law lie the fears of the male subjects of the republican state. From somewhat different perspectives, both Crow and Bryson use psychological vocabulary in describing David's near paranoid state and the painting's nervous mood and hysterical effects. Similarly, in the Revolution itself one discovers traces of hysterical fear of female subjectivity on the part of the male leadership.[6] The sons' revolt against the father was not just a quarrel among men. Indeed, the Revolution's phallic quality was a product of the way political legitimacy and individual rights were predicated on the entitlement of men alone. The universal bourgeois subject was from the outset a gendered subject. Only male rights to full individuality were protected. The revolt against the father was also a revolt against women as free and equal public and private beings. Undeniably, then, liberty and equality came to be overshadowed by fraternity (the brotherhood of men) within the new order produced by the Revolution.

*Symbolic Politics and Political Women*

David removes his dutiful Roman matrons to the sidelines of political life; still, they are there. Similarly, even as women were being silenced and domesticated, representations of women were featured prominently in the new state. The revolutionaries traded the old iconography of monarchical France for one of nature and abstract, civic virtues typified by three women—Liberty (carrying a pike capped with a red bonnet), Equality (carrying a level), and Fraternity (carrying the fasces).[7] When Liberty, a young woman draped in a Roman tunic, was chosen for the first seal of the Republic in September 1792, she replaced the single paternal figure of the king, whose seal or portrait personified the royal state, "by a visual symbol of the Republic, a State that was anonymous and abstract." She was, states Maurice Agulhon, an obvious choice; there could be no risk of her cap being confused for a crown.[8]

The symbolism of a female representation suggests the repudiation of male authority. But, in practice, the assault on patriarchalism was limited both by force (as in the banning of the Society of Revolutionary Republican Women and the denial of women's political rights) and by the redirection of women's public and sentimental existence into a new allegory of republican, virtuous family life. Liberty herself is a profoundly ironic symbol, a public representation of a polity that sanctioned a limited domestic role for women. Marina Warner has explored this paradox in light of "a recurrent motif in allegory, the female form as an expression of desiderata and virtues [and] the plural significations of women's bodies and their volatile connections with changing conceptions of female nature." She cautions against a too easy elision of sign and signified, declaring, "Justice is not spoken of as a woman, nor does she speak as a woman . . . because women were thought to be just, any more than they were considered capable of dispensing justice. Liberty is not represented as a woman . . . because women were or are free." She continues: "Often the recognition of a difference between the symbolic order, inhabited by ideal, allegorical figures, and the actual order, of judges, statesmen, soldiers, philosophers, inventors, depends on the unlikelihood of women practising the concepts they represent."[9] Like David's Camilla, Liberty is sister (not equal partner) to reason and nature, equality and fraternity. Freed by her brothers from the paternal tyranny and the threat of royal rape, she is ensconced by them within the family for safe keeping. Over time, the representations of Liberty became more sedate and tranquil, reiterating on the symbolic plane the defeat of women's independent, radical political initiatives within the Revolution.

Before the Convention's ban on women's societies, the Revolutionary Republican Women's performance was in the streets. They made revolution their stage.[10] And when these "disorderly viragos" appeared as a revolutionary army led by a chief of staff, they pursued a practice of absolute and total disruption—of the grain markets, the Convention, political meetings, and the streets. The women's revolutionary army aimed to create chaos in order to push the Revolution forward. Like the enragés, the Revolutionary Republicans were committed to a politics of participatory democracy. They worried not about the suffrage but about the source and locus of revolutionary power, and they contested the claims of legislators to represent the nation. They criticized the distance that separated the National Convention from the section assemblies and their members. When accused by the Jacobins of meddling in politics and practicing disruption, Claire Lacombe insisted on due process, justice, moral virtue, law, and the right of her group to keep watch over all public figures.[11] Similarly, the Society opposed the Jacobin emergency, demanding instead the implementation of the Constitution of 1793, which also guaranteed the right of insurrection. Pauline Léon proposed that the Paris sections ask for new elections to the Convention, seeing like Rousseau that "the prolongation of power was often the tomb of liberty."[12]

It can be argued that Liberty functioned as a representation of the extent to which gender relations were submitted to republican order. Lynn Hunt makes a striking point about the feminine allegorizations favored by the Revolution, of which Liberty was initially only one until her elevation in September 1792 to the seal of the Republic. "These female figures," she writes, "whether living women or statues, always sat or stood alone, surrounded most often by abstract emblems of authority and power." Liberty's poised demeanor on the Republic's seal "evoked little of the frantic violence of the various revolutionary 'days' of popular mobilization. Like a Counter-Reformation saint, she represented the virtues so desired by the new order: the transcendence of localism, superstition, and particularity in the name of a more disciplined and universalistic worship. Liberty was an abstract quality based on reason. She belonged to no group, to no particular place."[13] If Liberty represented woman, surely it was as an abstract emblem of male power and authority.

A glance at nineteenth-century republican historian Jules Michelet's description of the Festival of the Confederation in 1790 is revealing of the doubts registered from the 1790s onward about the inadequacy of a purely rational representation of the new Republic. Amid altars either of the holy sacrament or "the new cold abstract image of Liberty," Michelet is comforted by the discovery of the true (masculine) symbol of the new order. Barely noticing the implicit subordination of women his remarks convey, he pronounces that "the noble relations of family, nature, and country were sufficient to give these fêtes a touching and religious interest. Everywhere the old man was found sitting in the first place, far above the crowd. He was surrounded with young girls, as with a crown of flowers."[14] Michelet praises women's great ardor to take the civic oath, expressing some regret about their withdrawal from public life. With unintended irony, he writes that during the great festivals of this early euphoric stage of the Revolution there were no spectators, only actors: men, women, old people, and children — infants brought to be blessed at the altar of their country, devoted by their tearful, but resigned and heroic mothers, given by them to France."[15] But the female role whose supposed passing he laments is the public ceremonial one of matrons of the Republic. At this point in his text, the historian of the Revolution erupts in a near hymnal to Liberty, mothers, and women, all symbols of the new religion. He rapturously celebrates women's naturally assigned place in the new order: "The Revolution, returning to nature, to the happy and naive sentiments of antiquity, did not hesitate in confiding its most sacred functions to woman, who, as the solace of the heart, the soul of the family, the perpetuator of mankind, was herself the living altar."[16]

But women's return to the hearth was not so easily achieved, nor were all women satisfied with an entirely ceremonial role. Liberty did not simply appear on the seal of the Republic, nor did she remain fixed on canvas or carved in stone. She went into the public forum: "She was all over the place: in Paris and in the provinces, in open public places and in private ones, in fixed edifices and in transient settings; not to mention the paintings and engravings of popular appeal . . . or the ceramic works which reproduced themes taken from prints, or the imagery of public monuments."[17] In the great fetes of the Revolution, women played Liberty before vast crowds of people.[18] This practice seems to have resulted from a desire by the organizers to achieve a transparent representation, "one that would be so close to nature that it would evoke none of the old fanatical strivings after false images."[19]

Leaving aside the question of whether pure "transparency" can ever be achieved, one thing is certain. Neither Revolutionary Republican Women nor bourgeois feminists could fulfill the expectations set by the goddess Liberty, who was chaste, pure, self-sacrificing, and wholly dedicated to the universal aims of the Republic. For who were these women? Among the most prominent were single women (Wollstonecraft, Lacombe, Léon), widows (Gouges), actresses and women of the theater (Lacombe, Gouges), former courtesans (Théroigne de Méricourt), women of the literary public sphere (Wollstonecraft, Gouges), a chocolate maker (Léon), educators (Wollstonecraft, Palm), and women of questionable morals (Wollstonecraft, Gouges, Lacombe, Léon, Méricourt, and, increasingly, all "public" women): all of them poor candidates to represent Liberty or to symbolize the virtuous republican mother of the bourgeois public sphere.[20] They placed themselves in jeopardy by their political participation, their extremism, their association with the stage, their literary careers and other questionable professions. The reigning atmosphere may help to explain why a profound anxiety surfaces in the writings and demands of these same women about prostitutes and prostitution. As Mary Durham Johnson observes, in eighteenth-century Paris "the term prostitute loosely designated any woman who did not appear to have a permanent abode or a respectable occupation. Even if women claimed to be seamstress-workers, actresses, dancers, or domestic servants, the police were likely to presume they were *filles publiques* and treat them accordingly."[21]

It is noteworthy that perhaps the strongest challenge to Liberty's place in the iconography of republican France occurred during the summer and fall of 1793 from within the ranks of the republicans themselves. Concurrent with the arrest of Girondin deputies (who opposed the growing power of the Parisian sections and their Jacobin leaders), the adoption of the Terror, the executions of the queen, Olympe de Gouges, Mme Roland, and countless others, and the banning of women's clubs, the Convention voted to make the statue of Hercules proposed by the artist-deputy David the subject of the seal of state. In the choice between Marianne and Hercules posed in the 1790s, Lynn Hunt argues, "the colossal male figure represented more than just a repudiation of the moderate, feminine civic image; it reminded its beholders that radical revolution, like industrial labor . . . was 'man's work.'" In the festival of August 10, 1793, planned by David, just preceding the executions of leading women and the outlawing of women's activities, the terrifying monster of federalism (the great crime of the feminist-leaning Girondin) is crushed by Hercules. The monster itself was reported to be half woman, half serpent.[22] There is no doubt, then, that in this context the deputies of the Convention were attracted to the masculinity of the Hercules figure when they chose him to replace the goddess of Liberty on the state seal. In Hunt's estimation, the decision was in the first instance political: choosing Hercules enabled the Jacobins to distance themselves iconographically from their opponents, the Girondins. Hercules stood for the people on whom the Jacobins were dependent for their precarious superiority in national politics.

More was involved here, however, than just a straightforward political message. David's Hercules recaptured and rehabilitated the distinctly virile representation of sovereignty, a concept that had connotations of domination and supremacy in any case. Yet Hercules was not a paternal emblem of authority; in the David-Dupré figuration he was a powerful brother protecting the sister figures of Liberty and Equality. The masculinity of Hercules reflected indirectly on the deputies themselves; through him they reaffirmed the image of themselves as the band of brothers that had replaced the father-king. In addition to supplanting the king, Hercules dwarfed his female companions. In this way, the introduction of Hercules served to distance the deputies from the growing mobilization of women into active politics. On the grounds that women's active participation in politics could lead to "the kinds of disruption and disorder that hysteria can produce," the Convention had outlawed all women's clubs at the end of October 1793. That action preceded David's proposal for a gargantuan statue by only a few days. In the eyes of the Jacobin leadership, women were threatening to take Marianne as a metaphor for their own active participation; in this situation, no female figure, however fierce and radical, could possibly appeal to them. Hercules put the women back into perspective, in their place and relationship of dependency. The monumental male was now the only active figure.[23]

Surely the Revolutionary Republicans shared a political discourse with their radical male associates. They, too, evinced an aversion to appearances, a desire to root out conspiracy, to ensure publicity and transparency. By wearing the male bonnet rouge—the Phrygian cap, ancient symbol of the freed slave—they asked to be treated as (equally) virtuous and vigilant republicans.[24] But they failed to see that their dress signified to men a mere performance of citizenship—ultimately, a terrifying spectacle in which cross-dressing and masquerade could become routine occurrences. Women's dress and conduct signaled to their adversaries an irreversible process in which women would demand and concentrate power at men's expense. So deeply inflected by gender was republicanism that, when women attempted to enact openly its program of political virtue, they were accused of violating nature, propriety, and decency. In effect, there was no way women's behavior could be absolutely transparent without simultaneously transgressing the worst of all prohibitions—that there be no particular interests within or especially against the community as a whole. What ought to have been a symbol of patriotism—women dressed in the tricolor cockade, trousers, red bonnets, and donning swords—became instead a public statement of women's collective interest against the harmonious familial symbolism and masculinist practice of the virtuous republic. It is no coincidence that, as Mary Johnson reports, disorderly women of the popular classes were regularly treated more leniently than men by the revolutionary courts and, most significant, were usually remanded to the care (and discipline) of fathers or husbands in lieu of a prison term.[25]

Whereas Liberty figured the harmonious achievement of political community, "unrestrained" public women and their sexuality threatened its very foundation. The goddess Liberty increasingly offered not an active image of women in struggle but rather what the repudiated Christian kingdom had failed to achieve—an imaginary point in past and future time where women are in their proper place. One cannot overlook the fact that society women best typified the evils of artificial conduct, dress, speech and masquerade which the revolutionaries sought to exorcise. All women, but especially those who ventured into the sphere of political action and particularly those who made claims for women against the universal (male) community, were tarnished by association with women of the aristocratic public spheres. "Reputation" was the price to be paid for unacceptable conduct. In the eyes of male radicals, "impudent" revolutionary women were often indistinguishable from the queen, aristocratic émigrés, or Girondin intriguers. Rather than guaranteeing universal liberty, publicity functioned first to expose, and ultimately to remove, women from the bourgeois public sphere.

The point about Liberty, then, is that the stage on which she appeared was a profoundly theological one. Her audience was increasingly divorced from the text of the republic of which they were purportedly the authors. Women attended the revolutionary festivals, but they were there to be instructed by a script whose purpose was entirely didactic. The play told a tale of republican virtue, and although Liberty embodied the Republic, her posture became more and more passive. She needed the protection of her male defenders. Women in the audience became spectators, readers and listeners—rather than agents, of the Revolution. Lynn Hunt reminds us of the extent to which this didacticism was challenged and sometimes inverted by the people, but in the end independent popular initiatives by women and men were defeated. Moreover, she observes, after the fall of the radicals the deputies turned away from Hercules to more abstract symbols. Liberty returned, but as an abstract female bearing little resemblance to living women. In Hunt's words, "The people were no longer directly represented in imagery; the republic might be for the people, but it was neither by nor of them."[26]

In another vein, Marie-Hélène Huet is surely right to insist that the alienation between participant and spectator in all forms of public spectacle is never perfect. The possibility always exists that the spectator retell or reenact the drama, that she transmute her role from that of a receiver to that of an actor. As Huet observes, the spectator's justification may be her rehearsal to become an actor. But Huet insists that the revolutionary public sphere is unique in the form surveillance takes: repression occurs by means of the spectacle. So female actresses and audiences were necessarily present, not only because of their intense interest and commitment to the process, but in order to learn a message—that of their acceptable place in the revolutionary bourgeois public sphere. Women's presence, then, affirms what Huet believes to be the essence of revolutionary power: "To make a spectator of the people, while making sure that the possibility of spectator-actor reversibility remains carefully controlled, is to maintain an alienation that is the real form of power."[27]

Women's presence in the galleries was at first welcomed, but eventually even a spectatorial position was denied them. By assigning women wholly and entirely to the family, the possibility of women's independent participation must have appeared to contemporaries to have been permanently suppressed. But just as every spectator takes her place and derives her significance from a set of beliefs that involves acceptance of a power — that of the father, order, the word, or the law,[28] so, too, the successful taboo on women's public and political performance was made possible not strictly by coercion but through some measure of consent as well. In November 1793, after the suppression of the Society of Revolutionary Republican Women, Pauline Léon — a "loose" woman and revolutionary militant — married enragé Théophile Leclerc, who had also had a liaison with Claire Lacombe. Léon and Leclerc were arrested in April 1794 and served terms until August 19, 1794. In pleading the Committee of General Security for her release, Léon spoke the language of virtuous womanhood. "I have entirely devoted my attention to my household," she vowed, "and given proof of conjugal love and domestic virtues which are the basis of love for the country."[29]

We can afford to be suspicious about the truth value of Léon's "confession." But it would be a mistake to exaggerate the degree of possible resistance to the triumphant ideology of female virtue. Sexual love and domesticity did prove to be successful mechanisms for "rescuing" women from theatricality, the condition of being objects of public acts of beholding. If Léon's speech is rhetorical, it is by the same token neither entirely false nor illusionary. While her motives were coerced, her words are also a fine measure of the altered reality for women. Between 1791 to 1793 there had been competing discourses of virtue and liberty—that is, to the extent that republican women expanded on the form and style of participation in the new republic and challenged an overly restrictive definition of rights. Yet the militant participation of women provoked a violent and fearful response on the part of most men. After the fall of 1793, as Léon's statement reveals, the range of legitimate politics and discourse had narrowed decisively. Thereafter, republican women were expected to express their patriotism and their (personal) virtue in the language and practice of republican motherhood.

The rhetoric of republican virtue was not something that could be worn or set aside at will; rather, language was one of the most central instruments whereby a people fashioned itself. Republican women—whether of a liberal feminist bent or a radical Jacobin spirit—were important participants in this process. They were not innocent bystanders to the making of the republican body politic. The female spectators described by Michelet entered into this process of cultural formation, even as "ordinary" housewives. Through language and a vast lexicon of symbolic behavior, women, like men, engaged in the invention of a modern political identity. It is paradoxical that even those women who fought for female rights were seduced by a version of equality that privileged fraternity and domesticated women. Although protestations about "conjugal love" and "attention to my household" by a female militant must at some level ring false, Léon's words do testify to the fact that politics was not a separate realm from culture. She, too, subscribed to an ideology of virtue, one inflected through and through by gender distinctions. As we have discovered, the body politic produced by the bourgeois revolution was a gendered body. To the extent that feminism and women's protest arose out of the contradiction between women's position and the principles of rights, popular sovereignty, and democratic rule, it was doubtless bound to reproduce as well something of the gendered imagery of bourgeois republicanism.

CHAPTER 6

# The Gendered Republic

Following the Revolution, nearly three decades passed
before feminists again achieved a public outlet. Beginning in
the 1830s, women organized collectively to demand redress
from patriarchal institutions. Despite the public silencing of
women during the Revolution, however, it was then that
feminism acquired its modern shape and consciousness — as
a reply to the refusal of both liberals and republicans to
resolve the problem of women's civil and political subordination, and as an effort by women of diverse social backgrounds to participate in and to claim for their own the
literary and political institutions of the revolutionary bourgeois public sphere. In Claire Moses' estimation,

> for the long-term development of feminism, these Revolu-
> tionary years proved extremely important. Before 1789, advo-
> cacy of the emancipation of women — or at the least, for
> greater opportunities for women — had been restricted to the
> upper classes, and support was usually in the form of approv-
> ing women's desire for a better education. With the revolu-
> tionary upheaval came the rise of a feminism more sweeping
> in its scope and more inclusive in its following. Feminists not
> only added new demands to the "program" — the rights of full
> citizen participation in politics and government; the right to
> work; the right to equality in marriage; and even the right to
> share the burdens of a nation at war — but they also adopted
> new methods to obtain their goals. They comprehended that

169

political action was more than a "demand"; it was a means to
achieve their demands. They had grasped the potential
strength of collective female action. This was an invaluable
legacy to the nineteenth-century.[1]

All women, not just feminists, were affected by the fall of
the absolutist public sphere. New representations of women
emerged in post-revolutionary culture. In the past, women
were faulted for their lesser and weaker characters, which
were variously attributed to their lack of adequate education or to their baser natures. Now, however, women's nature
began to be credited as a source of difference *and* as the
cause of their superiority, a superiority that was nonetheless reckoned only in the moral and spiritual domain. In
their civil and political existence, nineteenth-century
women were seriously disadvantaged. The subordination of
women to men and a rigid sexual differentiation were
encapsulated in the uniform body of laws codified by Napoleon during the first decade of the century. The Civil Code
excluded women from the definition of citizenship even as
it recognized the equal rights of all citizens. This paradox
carried with it a series of loaded implications. As Moses
observes, "Women had been reduced to the status of a legal
caste at the same time that the *ancien régime* legal class
system was abolished for men. Women's status had wors-
ened, if not in absolute, then in relative terms. The code
would serve as a rallying point for feminist protest not only
because it discriminated against women but also because it
intensified women's sense of sex identification. By pro-
claiming the political significance of sex, the code helped
shape a feminist consciousness."[2]

Although women failed to achieve political emancipation, the Revolution bequeathed them a moral identity and
a political constitution. Gender became a socially relevant
category in post-revolutionary political and civil life in a way
that it would not have mattered formerly, for Old Regime
France was a class society wherein masculinity in and of
itself carried some but not vast privileges. To their dismay,

many men found themselves outmaneuvered and out-ranked by women, and women's inequality was tempered legally and socially by the privileges enjoyed and disabilities suffered by all persons depending on their class position. In bourgeois society, class continued to be a dominant struc-turing factor, even when—as occurred at various points of revolutionary upheaval and republican success—constitu-tional guarantees of rights and universal male suffrage were established. But, in addition, sexual difference was force-fully underscored by law. Consequently, gender conscious-ness was a paramount feature of post-revolutionary life, all the more so since bourgeois claims to universality raised hopes for the elimination of all social distinctions before the law. Viewed from women's perspective, then, the Revolu-tion's most important legacy may well have been the cul-tural inscription of gender in social life. Domesticity, including republican motherhood, and feminism can be viewed as the two variant outcomes of the transformation of the absolutist public sphere.

I have titled this chapter "The Gendered Republic" in order to denote the enormous force and protean character of republican ideology throughout the nineteenth century. During these years, of course, French state structure vacil-lated between dictatorship, constitutional monarchy, and republicanism, interspersed by moments of revolutionary upheaval and defeat. In a narrow sense, then, republicanism was just one of several oppositional movements, including socialism and feminism, and the links among all three were simultaneously firm and complicated. Indeed, nineteenth-century French feminism was both republican and socialist, and its fate was tied to the fortunes of the political Left. Yet radical republicans from Rousseau to the Jacobins upheld a sexually differentiated standard of virtue (citizenship for men, motherhood for women), and in the Revolution repub-lican men displayed outright hostility toward feminist ini-tiatives. The Republic was constructed against women, not just without them, and nineteenth-century republicans did not actively counteract this masculinist heritage of republicanism. Even those who subscribed to feminist aims often did so on the basis of a culturally gendered doctrine of separate spheres. Moreover, the royalist Right, restored to power in 1815, also moved closer to republican dictums. Such major thinkers as Louis de Bonald and Joseph de Maistre blamed aristocrats for their own defeats, arguing that women's visible role in aristocratic institutions sapped virtue and contributed to the aristocracy's old sinful ways. They favored a strong aristocratic state buttressed by the husband's authority and a subordinate, domestic role for the wife.[3] To be sure, nineteenth-century feminists faced a formidable enemy that transcended the usual divisions between Left and Right.

With regard to its ideology of womanhood, then, republican doctrine succeeded enormously. From divergent routes, post-absolutist French society carried on the Jacobin task of remaking the sinful female body into a virtuous republican body.[4] Whereas liberal individualism held all reasoning, sentient beings to be equal and free in principle (if not in practice), republicanism seemed to build difference into the very heart of its worldview. In addition, liberalism never conquered more than a minority position in post-revolutionary France. Certainly, it was not aided by the fact that there was a pervasive distrust of the individual and of individualism across the political spectrum. On the other hand, as K. Steven Vincent notices, there was a prevalent desire to foster solidarity and to promote some form of "universal association" which would lead away from the social evils of the contemporary world. There was also wide support in France for the conviction that society ought to be guided by a sense of morality. This politicization of virtue was, of course, tied to the strong influence of republican ideas and, especially, republican notions of civic virtue and civil religion.[5]

My aim is not to rehearse the general and feminist history of the nineteenth century, nor to document the position of working-class and bourgeois women. Instead, I propose to explore something of the range of gender representations characteristic of this world in which images had been decentered, released from the iconography of kingship. Adherence to and struggle for the "Rights of Man"—depersonalized principles of law, universality, equality, and contract—characterized the political terrain of the nineteenth century. Images were everywhere, but in the new symbolic order wrought by the bourgeois revolution the old hierarchy between icon and sign was reversed. Even visual images were textualized, increasingly responsive to legal forms of public discourse. I weigh the power of language and images within the bourgeois republican lexicon in the early nineteenth century by way of an examination of the discourse of two contrasting figures, the "anticipatory conservative" Auguste Comte and the utopian socialist feminist Flora Tristan.[6] Despite their antagonistic politics, Comte and Tristan shared a critical posture toward post-revolutionary bourgeois society as well as a common influence from the Saint-Simonian movement, whose impact on romantic views of womanhood and on feminism has been traced elsewhere.[7] By this focus, therefore, I hope to identify the positivist and socialist imprint on nineteenth-century republican and feminist discourse.

## Women in the Positive Society

Auguste Comte lived from 1798 to 1857. He was a secretary and one-time disciple of Claude Henri de Saint-Simon. In post-revolutionary France, no one approached the task of articulating a discourse capable of regulating the understanding of the social world and of guiding social action more seriously than did Comte, self-proclaimed creator of positivism, the new religion of society. Comte's Second System, *Système de politique positive* (1851–1854), is the most explicit of his writings in its concern with gender relations, marking, too, a subtle shift in attitude from his earlier work, *Cours de philosophie positive* (1830–1842). Appealing now directly to women, he titles an important chapter of the Second System "The Feminine Influence of Positivism."[8] Indeed, he celebrates women, along with the new philosophers and the working class, as one of three major social groups in the coming positivist republic. It is noteworthy, then, that Comte published the Second System in the aftermath of a revolutionary uprising.

Ostensibly, Comte is not troubled by these events. He recalls "the memorable crisis of 1830, by which the system of reaction, introduced thirty-six years previously, was brought to an end." And he adds: "Thanks to the instinctive sense and vigour of our working classes the reactionist leanings of the Orleanist government, which had become hostile to the purpose for which it was originally instituted, have at last brought about the final abolition of monarchy in France." Still, he regards this republican achievement as merely the culmination of the first or negative phase of the revolution in society. He prefaces his applause for the changes of 1830 to 1848—which he insists have accomplished politically "all that is required"—by recalling that "it was impossible for the regenerating doctrine to spread more widely and to be accepted as the peaceful solution of social problems, until a distinct refutation had been given of the false assertion so authoritatively made that the parliamentary system was the ultimate issue of the Revolution. This notion once destroyed, the work of spiritual reorganisation should be left entirely to the free efforts of independent thinkers."[9]

In France, the February Revolution of 1848 unloosed an era of "association par excellence."[10] Feminists were caught up in this swarm of activity, attending mixed-gender political meetings and also organizing autonomously. The declaration of universal male suffrage at the outset of the Revolution, however, magnified rather than resolved women's political subordination. With the failure of the working-class insurrection and the bourgeoisie's return to power, the government banned all participation of women and minors in the revolutionary clubs. The clubs were dissolved and restricted suffrage returned. Once again, revolution failed to secure women's rights.

Comte responds to the altered situation. Registering women's revolutionary role, he shrewdly designs a plan to contain their further political movement. He praises women as the vehicles of feeling over reason, morality over politics. Like Rousseau, he abhors the corrosive impact of unleashed egoistic, self-interest on society. In many respects, Comte appears to be Rousseau's post-revolutionary counterpart. But, unlike his predecessor, Comte celebrates women's emotional character, about which Rousseau remained deeply suspicious, as the foundation of a new morality. He looks to women as a natural source of social feeling, cooperation, and universal love. Along with praise, however, one discovers in Comte's writings a discomfort, perfectly familiar to readers of Rousseau, toward public women. Comte affirms the masculinist bourgeois revolutionary project (although for politicians, he would substitute social engineers of a kind to guide the ideal order in the principles of positive philosophy). Comte also aims to silence women's public speech, to deny them access to the public sphere by imprisoning them in the realm of feeling and domesticity.

Comte thereby extends Rousseau's argument that order within the ideal republic cannot be achieved unless women are accorded a proper place. He tempers the suppression of women's (particularistic) interests under positivism by appealing to them to be matrons of a new, superior civilization. He even proposes a Cult of Woman, her worship to occur in a series of public festivals — not unlike those during the years 1789–1794. The adoration of women, then, will be an element of the new Religion of Humanity, the cornerstone of the entire positivist system.[11] This bid did not go unanswered. Comte won a following among reformers, including women's advocates inside and outside France. Feminist positivist circles existed in North America and England, where John Stuart Mill (who in 1847 fell out with Comte) and Harriet Martineau can be counted among his followers.[12]

The father of modern positivism is best regarded as an anticipatory or progressive conservative, a tenacious but sometimes critical defender of the gendered bourgeois order. Comte affirms that the alteration of the old society is permanent; there can be no return to a simple pre-revolutionary past. Conservatism in his thought is not an effort to restore Old Regime life. Instead, he proposes a new role for science, one that preserves the birth of the new order while containing its most radical implications — among which must be counted the "uncontrolled" participation of public women. He would perfect the world born of change. In this project, women figure importantly as spiritual guardians of a stable social universe. Whereas in the Jacobin imagination domestic virtue was the flip side of active, political virtue, Comte presents domesticity as a solution to politics — which by definition he regards as leading to anarchy.

Beginning from the premise that the time is ripe for the first negative phase of the Revolution to be transcended, Comte aims to redirect the Revolution in a more positive direction. Claiming the Revolution for positivism, he writes, "The direct tendency, then, of the French Republic is to sanction the fundamental principle of Positivism, the preponderance, namely, of Feeling over Intellect and Activity." He adds, "To set up any permanent institution in a society which has no fixed opinions or principles of life, would be hopeless. . . . Inevitable as this consequence of our revolutionary position is, it has never been understood, except by the great leaders of the republican movement in 1793. Of the various governments that we have had during the last two generations, all except the Convention have fallen into the vain delusion of attempting to found permanent institutions, without waiting for any intellectual or moral basis."[13]

On the one hand, Comte seeks to extend what he believes to be the inherent rationality of the new symbolic order to all institutions, including the family. But having learned from Rousseau and the Jacobins something about the limits of pure reason, he makes a place beside reason for emotions and feelings — indeed, for "civil religion" itself. He states, "The moral constitution of man consists of something more than Intellect and Activity. . . . besides these there is feeling, which, [is] the predominating principle, the motive power of our being, the only basis upon which the various parts of our nature can be brought into unity." What is needed, he urges, is a source of "emotions of a gentler and less transient kind" than can be provided by men, even those of the working class who provide activity, not intellect, to society. This source is women, whom Comte associates with the indispensable "work of regeneration."[14]

Comte's overriding aim is to transform politics into a "positive" science. He would thwart any recurrence of a revolutionary public sphere, especially one in which women might once again be politically active. Extrapolating from the Jacobin episode, he favors the mutual containment of revolutionary and feminist politics. Applying the lessons of the Saint-Simonians, Comte celebrates sexual difference: "The social mission of Woman in the Positive system follows as a natural consequence from the qualities peculiar to her nature." He proposes that the noblest power, spiritual power, belongs to woman, not man: "In the most essential attribute of the human race, the tendency to place social above personal feeling, she is undoubtly superior to man." Yet, while Comte applauds women's superior moral powers, in reality he robs them of all political efficacy. Women's natural preeminence does not involve their social ascendance, Comte retorts (presumably to feminists and Saint-Simonians), "which some visionaries have dared to claim for them, though without their consent."[15] The paradox is stunning: woman's intellectual inferiority is presented as the basis of her superiority in spirituality or love; sexual equality is redefined as a radical differentiation of functions and natures. As he observes, "Equality in the position of the two sexes is contrary to their nature, and no tendency to it has at any time been exhibited."[16]

Comte offers women multiple assurances for the losses they are invited to suffer. He ingeniously posits a version of republican motherhood in which moral aims still predominate but the goal of citizenship is eliminated. Yet, since Comte's two other substantive societal elements (the proletariat or people and the philosophers or New Priests) are also assigned a nonpolitical role, women's domestic seclusion appears unremarkable: "The fact is, that although the people constitute the basis on which all political power rests, yet they have as little to do directly with the administration of power as philosophers or women."[17] Furthermore, positivism dispenses with classical definitions of virtue. Exhibiting the prejudice of a wide range of nineteenth-century French opinion, Comte explicitly demotes politics as an arena of human activity, equating it with physical force. He advocates an uncompromising rupture with all classical notions of the good life that take the state or the polis as their object. Rather, he discovers within civil society—the new division of labor, the market, and the administration of justice confirmed by the bourgeois revolution—the principles of a new positive entity, a method of organizing social activity. He postulates that science and administration will supplant political action; that the institution of the state will succumb to new local and international forms of association; and that domination—hitherto identified with the violent and forceful organization of political life—will be eliminated within a cooperative commonwealth oriented by scientific-rational principles, whose aim is harmony and efficiency. In other words, Comte intends to break the tie between virtue and political action, transferring the responsibility for social goals to an administrative apparatus. Politics, whether of the battlefield or the assembly, will have been made superfluous in the domesticated society of the future. All this, he tells his readers, will be the coming age of woman.[18]

There seem to be no positive uses to which politics may be put. Yet Comte enjoins his followers to tolerate its continued existence since administrative goals cannot be met in the absence of the practical organization of society, and hence the necessary application of force. In this contradictory situation, those who are confined to the apolitical spheres of life are well placed to contribute to the positivist goal of the ultimate depoliticization of society. Women ought not to regret their exclusion from politics, the unfortunate residue of an older order of society. They, like living deities, embody and prefigure the future moral state of humanity. Their weakness is also their strength, and this requires that they always remain as they are, for to participate actively in the public sphere would be to lose their special advantage. Comte appoints women to a special mission, that of the moralization of society, a carryover of their moral influence and a sign of their strict place in the sexual division of labor.

The division of labor is a necessary feature of society, but Comte insists that the differentiation of activities will result in cooperation, not antagonism. He therefore binds women firmly to the domestic sphere, where they will perform the work of regeneration by promoting universal love, "the final object of moral education."[19] Men may occupy different functional strata within society, but women are excluded by a castelike principle from ever acquiring political power or entering the governing class. By nature, women are deemed unsuited to any but a domestic role. Comte justifies women's seclusion through a naturalistic reading of history: "Hence we find that it is the case in every phase of human society that woman's life is essentially domestic, public life being confined to men. Civilization, so far from effacing this natural distinction, tends . . . to develop it, while remedying its abuses."[20] In a more perfect formulation, he proposes that human progress is bound up with the deepening association of women with the family:

The continuous progress of Humanity in this respect, as in every other, is but a more complete development of the preexisting order. Equality in the position of the two sexes is contrary to their nature, and no tendency to it has at any time been exhibited. All history assures us that with the growth of society the peculiar features of each sex have become not less but more distinct. Catholic Feudalism, while raising the social condition of women in Western Europe to a far higher level, took away from them the priestly functions which they had held under Polytheism; a religion in which the priesthood was more occupied with art than science. So too, with the gradual decline of the principle of caste, women have been excluded more and more rigidly from royalty and from every other kind of political authority. Again, there is a visible tendency towards the removal of women from all industrial occupations, even from those which might seem best suited to them. And thus female life, instead of becoming independent of the Family, is being more and more concentrated in it; while at the same time their proper sphere of moral influence is constantly extending. The two tendencies, so far from being opposed, are on the contrary inseparably connected.[21]

Comte easily disposes with the feminist hope for women's emancipation through the law. Far from regretting their domestication, women are advised to rejoice in it. Borrowing from the Civil Code—even though he regards the Napoleonic period as one of counterrevolution and reaction—Comte freely injects the social division of labor directly into the universe of law. As is not surprising, he is completely indifferent to woman's demand for subjecthood. Only men, he implies, could have invented such a preposterous—because unnatural—set of claims. "Morally, therefore, and apart from all material consideration, she merits always our loving veneration, as the purest and simplest impersonation of Humanity, who can *never be adequately represented in any masculine form.*"[22]

Comte appreciates the link between symbolic and political representation. What he refuses to represent is woman insofar as she is independent of man's desires and the purposes of the whole. Because woman cannot be represented as a legal and moral subject, her exclusion from political and civil liberties requires no further basis of legitimation. By tying woman's political subordination to her sexual nature, then, Comte is able to dispense with liberal individualist claims for universal rights. Indeed, all rights will be eradicated in the positivist order:

The most important object of this regenerated polity will be the substitution of Duties for Rights; thus subordinating personal to social considerations. The word *Right* should be excluded from political language, as the word *Cause* from the language of philosophy. Both are theological and metaphysical concepts; and the former is as immoral and subversive as the latter is unmeaning and sophistical. . . . Rights, in the strict sense of the word, are possible only so long as power is considered as emanating from a superhuman will. In their opposition to these theocratic rights, the metaphysicians of the last centuries introduced what they called the rights of Man; a conception the value of which consisted simply in its destructive effects. Whenever it has been taken as the basis of a constructive policy, its anti-social character and its tendency to strengthen individualism have always been apparent. In the Positive state, where no supernatural claims are admissible, the idea of *Right* will entirely disappear. Every one has duties, duties towards all; but rights in the ordinary sense will be claimed by none.[23]

Comte also has little use for the revolutionary slogan of equality. Reviving Old Regime arguments about woman's empire formerly disputed by Condorcet, he yokes women's civil and political inequality to their greater spiritual power:

In that which is the greatest object of human life, they are superior to men, but in the various means of attaining that object they are undoubtedly inferior. In all kinds of force, whether physical, intellectual, or practical, it is certain that Man surpasses Woman, in accordance with the general law prevailing throughout the animal kingdom. Now, practical life is necessarily governed by force rather than by affection. . . . If there were nothing else to do but to love, as in the Christian utopia of a future life in which there are no material wants, Woman would be supreme. But we have above everything else to think and to act, in order to carry on the struggle against a rigorous destiny; therefore man takes the command, notwithstanding his inferiority in goodness.[24]

Woman is entirely selfless, a pure and simple approximation of humanity. It would appear as if Comte's desire to subordinate women to the other-serving goal of universal love confirms his overall effort to suppress individuality.[25] But Comte never aims, nor deems it possible, to eradicate thoroughly (male) individual motives in the economic or political spheres of practical activity. He grounds women's subordination in a strict functional differentiation of society. He refers to "a universal tendency, confirmed by careful study of the whole past history of Man. The principle is, that *Man should provide for Woman*. It is a natural law of the human race; a law connected with the essentially domestic character of female life."[26] Furthermore, he argues for "the separation of the two elementary powers of society: the moral power of counsel and the political power of command," on the grounds that: "the necessary preponderance of the latter, which rests upon material force, corresponds to the fact that our imperfect nature, where the coarser wants are the most pressing and the most continuously felt, the selfish instincts are naturally stronger than the unselfish. Without this compulsory pressure, even our individual action would be feeble and purposeless, and social life still more certainly would lose its character and its energy. Moral force, therefore, resting on conviction and persuasion, should remain simply a modifying influence, never assuming imperative authority."[27]

Insofar as women speak and act, they must do so in a wholly self-denying manner. Even so, they can only modify, never initiate, action. They, not men, speak with authority on matters of social improvement. But what if women's goodness merely serves as a reminder of the most degrading features of a market-driven society of competitive individualists (which Comte hopes to contain without eliminating its capitalist source)? In any event, women seem powerless to affect this altruistic behavior in others. At most, they have their children as pupils in the school of universal love. But, since on maturity their sons will need to struggle against destiny, to resist and intermingle with the material conditions of existence, it is daughters who are really the best novitiates for the Religion of Humanity, which, Comte hopes, "will teach the conservatives of the West how revolutionary they are."[28]

In his first systematic effort to define positive philosophy, the *Cours de philosophie*, Comte emphasizes the need to regenerate education in order to orient it toward positivism and away from theological, metaphysical, or literary modes of training. He desires to replace intellectual anarchy with a universal agreement on first principles, conceiving of a new unity of method rather than a homogeneous doctrine among all the sciences, of man and the natural world.[29] Comte argues that human social behavior operates according to lawlike regularities, knowledge of which is the task of the positivist scientist cum philosopher. Social scientific understanding offers man the possibility of technical control of social circumstances, just as control has already yielded beneficial results in the natural sciences. Comte therefore prophesies a period in which positivist philosophy and science will provide the normative and intellectual integument of a well-ordered, harmonious society. Education stands to positivism as one, if not its most, elementary goal. The regeneration of education and the reorganization of society are really the same objective. As he states:

> The Positive Philosophy offers the only solid basis for that Social Reorganization which must succeed the critical conditions in which most civilized nations are now living. . . . Ideas govern the world, or throw it into chaos; in other words, . . . all social mechanism rests upon Opinions. The great political and moral crisis that societies are now undergoing is shown by a rigid analysis to arise out of intellectual anarchy. While stability in fundamental maxims is the first condition of genuine social order, we are suffering under an utter disagreement which may be called universal. Till a certain number of general ideas can be acknowledged as a rallying-point of social doctrine, the nations will remain in a revolutionary state . . . and their institutions can only be provisional. But whenever the necessary agreement on first principles can be obtained, appropriate institutions will issue from them, without shock or resistance; for the causes of disorder will

have been arrested by the mere fact of the agreement. It is in this direction that those must look who desire a natural and regular, a normal state of society.[30]

If the *Cours* offers a diagnosis of societal malaise, then the Second System is Comte's attempt to redirect society's moral education in a way that underscores woman's educative role. But Comte appreciates that women will first need to be won over to positivism from their traditional loyalties—to the church and medieval institutions. How can this be achieved? By making apparent "the true connection of the Revolution with the Middle Ages," Comte answers. "Women will feel enthusiasm for the second phase of the Revolution, when they see republicanism in the light in which Positivism presents it, modified by the spirit of ancient chivalry."[31] Whereas women's religiosity led other republicans to repudiate them as full partners in their cause, Comte attempts to reorient women toward a new secular religion, one in which they (not some abstract and transcendant God) will be the objects of worship. Thus he argues for the restoration of chivalry, faith in a future utopia, and universal love. He offers women religion without priests and without church. As teachers of social feeling rather than self-love, however, they will need to be carefully educated. Again, like all republicans, Comte is careful to supervise the content of that education—to make certain that women will learn to serve the whole. Dismissing the idea of coeducation, he nevertheless intends to introduce women to the same curriculum as men at the most rudimentary level, after which their education will halt and they will return to the family to preside over the first principles of moral education in the home.

Comte does permit some very circumscribed forms of social participation by women. As already mentioned, women are present at the positivist festivals. In addition, he advocates the recuperation of an often maligned—because Old Regime—female institution, the salon. But even here, in this demipublic sphere, he qualifies women's opportunities for public speech, subtly suggesting that in this sphere (and only here), the most meritorious (male or female) will take the lead. In other words, he would have women suppress their own particular interests in order to serve as better facilitators of intercourse among (men of) different classes. Women may also appear in two other important public spaces — clubs and temples. But, like women during the Revolution, they are to be there as silent spectators. Comte writes of the positivist salon,

> this is, then, the mode in which women can with propriety participate in public life. Here all classes will recognise their authority as paramount. Under the new system these meetings will entirely lose their old aristocratic character, which is now simply obstructive. The Positivist *salon* placed under feminine influence completes the series of social meetings, in which the three elements of the spiritual power will be able to act in concert. First, there is the religious assemblage in the Temple of Humanity. Here the philosopher will naturally preside, the other two classes taking only a secondary part. In the Club again it is the people who will take the active part; women and philosophers supporting them by their presence, but not joining in the debate. Lastly, women in their *salons* will promote active and friendly intercourse between all three classes; and here all who may be qualified to take a leading part will find their influence cordially accepted.[32]

But, Comte continues, "however important the public duties that women will ultimately be called upon to perform, the Family is after all their highest and most distinctive sphere of work."[33] Under positivism, the most important aspect of the family is its moral dimension, particularly its ability to restrain the effects of naked individual self-interest and to teach the value of universal love. Although this vision of the family is thoroughly patriarchal, it is distinguished from other conservative views, such as that of the church, by an interest in women's moral activities rather than their pro-creative or reproductive functions. Comte insists firmly that women lack independent interests; they are destined for marriage, "the most elementary and perfect mode of social life," "the only association in which entire identity of interests is possible."[34]

The positivist requirements for marriage are exacting, and they accord well with the post-revolutionary legal reversals women suffered under the Napoleonic Civil Code. Virtually every feminist demand for marital reform is repudiated here, for Comte believes that the marriage union aims at moral completeness, which he defines as the subjection of self-interest to social feeling. Marriage ought to be exclusive (monogamous) and indissoluble, sexual love ought to be placed under rigorous and permanent discipline, divorce outlawed, widowhood made a state in perpetuity, and marital partners laid to rest in the same grave. These conditions describe woman's lot as a wife. Furthermore, says Comte, "maternity, while it extends her sphere of moral influence, does not alter its nature. As a mother, no less than as a wife, her position will be improved by Positivism. She will have, almost exclusively, the direction of household education. Public education given subsequently will be . . . little but a systematic development of that which has been previously given at home." In other words, woman completes man's moral education. Man, in fact, is said to submit voluntarily to woman's authority in the family sphere: "By marriage he enters into a voluntary engagement of subordination to Woman for the rest of his life. Thus he completes his moral education. Destined himself for action, he finds his highest happiness in honorable submission to the ennobling influence of one in whom the dominant principle is affection."[35]

Public and private duties affirm male and female natures. As woman by nature lacks the ability to exert physical force in the material world, she is destined to be divorced from labor just as she is divorced from all other public functions such as thought and governance. In a farsighted fashion, Comte scolds the capitalists of his day for failing to recognize that the family wage is a necessary requirement of a society of order and progress; men must be paid earnings sufficient to support a nonworking wife. Indeed, Comte's rebuke of industrial practices occurs at the moment when increasing numbers of women and children are being drawn into industry as wage laborers—when mere survival for working-class people requires the economic contribution of all household members. Cognizant of these facts, Comte forecasts a higher stage of capitalism in which males alone will endure economic responsibility for all family members through the introduction of a "family wage system." He aspires not to the abolition of wage labor but to its masculinization.

Comte begins his influential Second System with a sentimental invocation of women's impact on his thought. Sainte-Clothilde, his lover of one year before her early death, his mother, and Sophie Bliot, a working-class assistant, are all petitioned. Through worship of Clothilde, Comte claims to have learned to venerate his mother and to have been taught the religion of feeling. He celebrates the moral influence of all three of his angels, implying that the lessons of social hierarchy learned in the sphere of intimacy may later be applied to public life in its entirety: "The combination of these three beautiful womanly types is a special incentive to the culture of the three sympathetic instincts, attachment between equals, veneration for superiors, kindness to inferiors. Thus the affections of my daily life are a strong confirmation of my conception of the true confirmation of society, in which the maintenance of order depends on the twofold relations of philosophers with women and proletarians."[36]

Sentimental love, purportedly woman's natural feeling, infuses Comte's entire system with a false aroma of saintliness. Like the priest of the new order, woman is made to serve the whole. Preparation for her social role begins in the family, only to continue there throughout her life. Comte offers women a way of integrating their private duties within a social context. Their assignment to the tasks of socializing children and wifely responsibility is compensated for by a relationship to the totality and by their domestic power, to which men are expected to submit themselves willingly.

Women become moral authorities in the positivist society, even though they do not possess any power short of moral influence to impress their claims on the public world of material affairs. Comte hopes to win women's approval for his social project by invoking their sense of moral self-importance within the given order of male domination. Whereas Mary Wollstonecraft acknowledged women's weaknesses in order to remold them through a project of rational education, Comte utilizes women's supposed flaws for the purposes of social order and control. He positions them as central conveyors or communicators, as mothers of a cultural project they can never author. Women are not merely unsuited to perform the roles of philosopher, worker, or governor, they wholly lack any degree of autonomy. In a sense, they are the perfect political subjects for a positivist society; even more than men, women are individuals manqué.

In Comte's sociology: Woman lacks/ Woman occupies the position of truth, as figure of the Religion of Humanity. This oxymoron is at the heart of the positivist project. Woman's moral stature is the consequence of woman's low material status. In that respect, Comte understands and articulates well the gender oppositions of public and private life in the post-revolutionary, capitalist order. In a recent article, "Is There a Woman in This Text?," Mary Jacobus speculates that the function of women in theory is "to provide the mute sacrifice on which theory itself may be founded; the woman is silenced so that the theorist can make the truth come out of her mouth."[37] Comte speaks directly of and to women, dedicating his system to three female angels and eliciting all women's support and involvement in the new symbolic order. Yet the institution that matters most is the family. Outside its walls, women have no rightful place; their only legitimate speech is family discourse. Positivism, then, is one more version of the male republican response to women's political activism, especially to the effort of revolutionary republican women and nineteenth-century feminists to enact a female version of republicanism in which women are guaranteed an authentic public place.

As for the question "Is there a woman in this text?" Jacobus replies that we ought instead to be asking "Is there a text in this woman?" The problem is one of the conditions of woman's representability. If "shutting-up a female 'victim' can open theoretical discourse," what the preceding examination shows is that premise's political corollary.[38] Once yoked to family duty and to the identity of the universal, the possibility of women's representation is seemingly solved. If women speak for the universal against all particular interests, or at least for others against their own interests, then one of the most egregious political facts of early nineteenth-century society—that women as a class are denied political rights and equality—is masked. Women's self-sacrifice in the family is transposed to the political arena, but women themselves are absent. Thus Comte reverses Rousseau's indictment of women as self-absorbed, narcissistic, and particularistic by making women's narcissism serve the whole. He carries forward the eighteenth-century bourgeois ambition to textualize women's lives within a narrative of family romance—but with this difference: he offers women a place, even a voice, in the new order on the condition that they suppress their independent speech, power, and activity.

### Flora Tristan and the Promise of a Feminist Public Sphere

Flora Tristan's life and writings stand as a compelling example of one woman's refusal of republican designs to silence women. She was born in 1803, just five years after Comte, the daughter of a French émigrée and a Spanish-Peruvian nobleman. Because of the French state's unwillingness to recognize her parents' religious marriage, which had occurred in Spain, Tristan was technically illegitimate, unable to inherit her father's property. Her father's sudden death in 1807 resulted in the confiscation of his property by the French government, which was then at war with Spain.

She grew up in poverty in the French countryside and returned to Paris in 1818 with her mother. An unfortunate marriage in 1821 only compounded her troubles. At seventeen she learned the lithographic coloring trade and married her employer, the engraver André Chazal, with whom she quickly had three children. After an extremely unhappy, abusive relationship, she left Chazal in 1825, embarking on journeys to England as a "ladies' companion" and to Peru to reestablish ties to her father's family. Her earliest writings, which succeeded in winning her literary fame, are about these experiences. During these same years, she was absorbed in a battle for a legal separation from Chazal and for custody of her children. She also intensified her involvement in feminist and socialist activities. By 1835 Tristan was in contact with Fourierists, and during 1836–37 she attended the weekly meetings of the feminist *Gazette des femmes* group. She also encountered Robert Owen on one of her journeys to England. She published a pamphlet, "On the Necessity of Welcoming Foreign Women," and she petitioned the Chamber of Deputies for the right to divorce, which was abolished in 1816 (and not restored until 1884), and to abolish capital punishment. Her personal torment climaxed in 1838 when she was shot and seriously wounded by Chazal. Although she did finally win a legal separation from her husband and the right to take back the name Tristan, she was forbidden by law to remarry.

In 1839 Tristan journeyed again to England. In 1840 she published her observations on British life and society, *Promenades dans Londres*. She expanded on the theme of working-class poverty in her most ambitious work, *Union ouvrière* (The workers' union), which appeared in 1843.[39] Tristan died in Bordeaux in 1844 from typhoid fever, exhausted by an ambitious mission to carry her program to the French working class. Perhaps her greatest success was in Lyons, where the workers raised enough money to pay for a third edition of *Union ouvrière*. In Marseilles, Carcassonne, Avignon, and Bordeaux branches of the Worker's Union were formed, and the press in many towns published articles by workers supporting her efforts. A memorial was placed at her grave in 1848 in a ceremony attended by eight thousand people. Though her social background was aristocratic, not working class, Tristan certainly experienced poverty. She knew firsthand of women's legal inferiority. As a writer, traveler, legal petitioner, and political activist, she was well acquainted with the impoverished state of women's rights in post-revolutionary France. Rather than shunning the notoriety that she earned because of her struggles for legal, political, and domestic rights, Tristan chose instead to label herself a "social pariah," boldly defying the double moral standard of bourgeois society.[40]

Tristan wholly embraces the proposition put forward by Fourierists, Saint-Simonians, and Owenites that sexual equality would be achieved through the emancipation of the working class. She signs herself "your sister in humanity" in the "Dedication to the Working Classes" of the 1842 edition of *The London Journal*, self-consciously adopting the fraternal rhetoric of the republican movement.[41] She is convinced that the time has come for the working class and women to make their own "1789"; together they will complete the unfinished work of the Revolution. Happily, she is willing to be a "sister" in the cause of freedom. Tristan similarly exhorts the working class in her 1843 manifesto: "Workers, for more than two hundred years the bourgeois have fought courageously and ardently against the privileges of the nobility and for the victory of their rights. But when the day of victory came, and though they recognized de facto equal rights for all, they seized all the gains and advantages of the conquest for themselves alone."[42]

Tristan is the first to conceive of the need for workers to organize themselves into a class, which she deems a necessary step toward self-emancipation. She regards the working class as the world-historical successor to the bourgeoisie and expands the Saint-Simonian principle of association by advocating the internationalization of the working class. Her plea includes women—not as an afterthought but as a basic element of the movement for human liberation.

"Workers," she declares, "in 1791, your fathers proclaimed the immortal declaration of the *rights of man*, and it is to that solemn declaration that you owe your being free and equal men before the law. May your fathers be honored for this great work! But, proletarians, there remains for you men of 1843 a no less great work to finish. In your turn, emancipate the last slaves still remaining in French society; proclaim the *rights of woman*, in the same terms your fathers proclaimed yours."[43]

Tristan proposes a practical program for the achievement of these goals, calling for the creation of "worker's palaces" in all localities, organizational centers for the achievement of true equality, and forums for the common education of the two sexes—a kind of proletarian public sphere, supported by workers' self-taxation, in which women will occupy a central place. She envisions a series of democratic institutions that, on a much wider scale, will perform the functions of the elitist academies and salons of the eighteenth-century oppositional public sphere. Like Comte and so many of her republican contemporaries, Tristan places a very high priority on education. Yet she regards education as more than an affair of the classroom, or of the family. She believes that merely to publish a plan for reform is not sufficient. Gathering direct inspiration from the first Christian apostles, Tristan deems it necessary to go forth in the world with the word, "to preach fraternity and unity." She prophesies the establishment of a wholly new communication structure, predicated on the liberation of working-class speech. She states, "The workers have often been spoken *of* in the legislature, from the Christian pulpit, in society gatherings, on the stage, and especially in the courts." Yet Tristan's mission is also didactic. She appreciates the need for pedagogical work in the task of building class consciousness. Speaking from a position of divinely sanctioned authority, Tristan justifies her apostolic mission: "No one has yet tried to speak *to* them. This had to be attempted. The Lord tells me it will succeed. That is why I am so confidently embarking on a new path. Yes, I shall go and find them in their workshops, in their attic rooms, and even in their taverns, if necessary. And amidst their very misery. I shall convince them about their own fate and force them, in spite of themselves, to escape the terror of that degrading and fatal poverty."[44]

Tristan rejects the surrounding forms of association, corporation, and organization. Borrowing very likely from Fourier's notion of the phalanstery, Tristan proposes the building of palaces. These will serve as combination workshops, farms, and residences for two to three thousand members, and persons of all ages will be admitted. There will be places of study, recreation, and nursing for the very young and the very old. Like Fourier, Tristan is committed to overcoming the division of labor. Work within the palaces will proceed according to its essential worth and necessity. She refuses to elevate mental over manual labor. Both have their place in the new world. If anything, it is the latter that is privileged.

Tristan bases her plan on the self-activity of the working class, and on the basic human right to work. She wants nothing of the old system of charity and social dependence, scorning welfare societies, guilds, and hospices. She sees universal union as an opportunity for the working class to leave "its precarious state gradually and nonviolently."[45] Because political action risks fueling individualist motives, Tristan (like Comte and the Saint-Simonians) conceives of a nonviolent, apolitical strategy for realizing the universal content of a future republic. Necessarily, however, this inclination toward harmony shapes her ambivalent approach to women's liberation. Although Tristan openly endorses the goal of freedom, she repeatedly positions women in an uncomfortably passive role as the recipients, not the initiators, of their freedom. In *Union ouvrière* she implies that women must wait to be emancipated by the organized working class.

Still, Tristan calls for women's equality in the home and in the union. She appeals to working men's sense of justice as well as to their self-interest. She forthrightly protests woman's position as the slave of a slave, proletariat of the proletariat. She calls, not for a Comtean celebration of women's superiority, but for a repartition of existing roles. She asks working-class men to admit women of their class to full and equal membership, the first step toward the future evolution of society's morals. She believes that divorce and the reform of monogamous marriage will bring into existence a natural and moral state of sexual equality. But, because she deems marriage to be women's overriding goal, she searches for "alternatives within, rather than to, its structure."[46]

Tristan justifies her pleas for women's education according to sound republican principles. She ties female education to family life and the requirements of citizenship in a democratic republic. Like Mary Wollstonecraft, Tristan perceives that instruction will enhance women's natural talents, and that mothers require education to properly train their children. But by framing her argument this way, Tristan admits to many of the standard male criticisms of women. She adopts many of the bourgeois republican complaints about women: that they stand in need of reform; that they need to be raised up to nature; that they lack a proper model of motherhood. What Tristan adds is an explicit concern for *non*-bourgeois women. She cautions working-class women directly, asking their forbearance: "Working-class women, take note, I beg you, that by mentioning your ignorance and incapacity to raise your children, I have no intention in the least of accusing *you* or *your nature*. No, I am accusing society of leaving you uneducated—you, women and mothers, who actually need so much to be instructed and formed in order to be able to instruct and develop the men and children entrusted to your care."[47] Like Wollstonecraft, Tristan appeals to men's want of domestic peace. Moral improvement, she submits, will be a further benefit resulting from the education of their wives and daughters.

> I call for woman's rights because it is the only way to have her educated, and woman's education depends upon man's in gen-

eral, and particularly the working-class man's. I call for woman's rights because it is the only way to obtain her rehabilitation before the church, the law, and society, and this rehabilitation is necessary before working men themselves can be rehabilitated. All working-class ills can be summed up in two words: poverty and ignorance. Now in order to get out of this maze, I see only one way: begin by educating women, because the women are in charge of instructing boys and girls.[48]

Even as she struggles to defend women's social, economic, and political equality, Tristan remains bound to the dominant forms of representation of the female in postrevolutionary bourgeois society. She speaks of women's backwardness, their need for rehabilitation. She positions them, as mothers, wives, sisters, to be responsible for the moral standing of their men. Perhaps she fears another masculine backlash against powerful, independent women. She pays society women a backhanded compliment, recalling their "useful role" in preparing noble and bourgeois men for their privileged station in life. Yet she insists that her aim is not to point to woman's superiority but to recognize her social individuality and to advance the universal well-being of all men and women. She writes:

To be raised, educated, and taught the science of the world, the son of the wealthy has governesses and knowledgeable teachers, able advisers and finally, beautiful marquises, elegant, witty women whose functions in high society consist in taking over the son's education after he leaves school. It's a very useful role for the well-being of those gentlemen of high nobility. These ladies teach them to have proper manners, tact, finesse, wit; in a word, they make them into men who *know how to live*, the right kind of men. . . . While you, poor workers, to rear and teach you, you have only your mother; to make you into civilized men, you only have women of your class, your companions in ignorance and misery.[49]

Tristan follows Fourier and other utopians in arguing for

economic equality. For women to be free from prostitution—a situation she fears desperately, and one she discerns, on the basis of personal experience, is easily the fate
of even so-called respectable women in bourgeois society
who are forced to sell themselves on the marriage market—
they must achieve material independence. She is firm on the
need for employment for professional and working-class
women. She outpaces Comte by making women's moral
superiority the basis for their future engagement in the public sphere rather than a reason for their imprisonment in the
private domain. Thus Tristan does insist that women are
also by nature workers. Yet she ties this conviction to the
dominant bourgeois ideology of domesticity. At one point
she proclaims, "Let the women of the people receive from
infancy a rational, solid education fit to develop all their
good tendencies, so that they may become able workers in
their crafts, good mothers capable of raising and guiding
their children . . . and so that they may serve as moralizing
agents for men on whom they exercise influence from birth
to death."[50]

It seems that Tristan's arguments do reflect something of
the defeated version of republican womanhood attempted by
militants during the Revolution. She, too, is struggling to
define an authentic—not just a symbolic—public role for
women. She is persuaded that women can only achieve freedom and dignity on the basis of economic independence, a
conviction shared by Mary Wollstonecraft. Indeed, Tristan's
real inspiration comes directly from Wollstonecraft, a
kindred spirit who also knew the hardships of constructing
for herself a viable independent professional existence, and
who suffered, too, as a public woman and an unmarried
mother, the price of her sexual reputation. Tristan's tribute
to Wollstonecraft—whose name at the time of her writing
was anathema even among seemingly progressive English-
women and whose writings were censored—is truly stirring:

> Mary Wollstonecraft was already publishing in 1792 the self-
> same principles that Saint-Simon was to disseminate later,

and which spread so rapidly after the Revolution of 1830. Her criticism is admirable: she reveals in their true colours all the evils arising from the organisation of the family, and her powerful logic is irrefutable. She boldly undermines the mass of prejudices which envelope our society; she demands equal civil and political rights for both sexes, equal admission to employment, professional education for all, and divorce by mutual consent. Without these fundamental principles, she says, any social system which promises universal happiness will only betray its promises.

Mary Wollstonecraft's book is an *imperishable* work: imperishable because the happiness of the human race is bound up with the cause which *A Vindication of the Rights of Woman* defends. Yet this book has been in existence for half a century and nobody has ever heard of it![51]

Tristan's admirable summary of Wollstonecraft's position is especially revealing. She chooses to emphasize civil rather than political liberties for women. Likewise, nowhere in her writings does she appear especially concerned with the issue of female suffrage, an issue of increasing importance in the 1840s. Tristan shares the republican feminist outlook that women must be perfected, educated to their true moral role in society; *pace* Comte, goodness is not their natural state. Even though she, like the Society of Revolutionary Republican Women, attempts to articulate a nonbourgeois position on women's rights, their positions are really very different. While the militant women of the Society were wholly impressed with the need to educate the citizenry in republican values, they chose an active, political route. For them, there could be no separation between education and revolutionary action. Education was their politics, and, in their eyes, the Terror was the most perfect way of bringing about a virtuous republic of women and men. In contrast, Tristan fears "brute force" and violence. She regards politics as leading inevitably to individualism and away from collective goals and social cooperation. She therefore hopes to substitute education for political revolution. Challenged and harrassed by the state authorities during her 1843 tour of

France, Tristan retorted to one officious police chief, "I'm here to prevent a revolution, not to start one!"[52]

Tristan firmly believes that women's fulfillment depends on a total transformation of the social order. Only if the working man's emancipation succeeds can women be free. In large measure, she looks to him to emancipate his sisters and wives.[53] But woman's chance for subjecthood is ultimately jeopardized by her maternal role. In that sense, Tristan incorporates into her theory of society a version of female morality that reproduces many of the most conservative features of the sexual division of labor she tries so desperately to overturn. She, too, is attached to the dominant republican version of female morality in which women's spiritual influence, rather than their political existence, holds sway. Tristan fashions for the working class something like the program for rational domesticity that Wollstonecraft articulated for the bourgeois family. She asks both men and women to subordinate their own happiness to the goals of family love, well-being, order, and harmony. Once properly educated, women will be able to introduce the new morality to their children and husbands. Working-class women are thus offered a program for emancipation which subordinates their independence to family harmony and invites them to order their own behavior as a way of improving the behavior of their closest kin.

### Intersections

Flora Tristan died before Comte authored his influential Second System. Nevertheless, her life testifies to the failure of domesticity to contain women entirely within the family sphere. Even domestic impulses might lead women out into public life, if for no other reason than to extend their spiritual influence to the wider world. Tristan calls willingly upon women's domestic inclinations to enhance the cause of social cooperation. Still, her own infusion of feminism with spiritual and domestic values is not unproblematic; if women are always to exemplify human values, to suppress their particular interest, they are likely to be burdened forever with an apolitical (and subsidiary) role within the movement for social emancipation. In this regard, it is interesting to compare the religious dimension in Comte's and Tristan's writings. Both look to a future cult of woman to anchor the cooperative society of the future. For the sake of consistency, Comte (the man) is obliged to pay homage to his cherished female ideal. Tristan can afford to take the religious imagery even further, fashioning herself as a female messiah whose mission it is to spread the new social gospel to the workers of France. She compares herself with St. Theresa of Avila and likens her role to that of Christ himself: "The Jewish people had died in abjection, and Jesus raised them up again. The Christian people are dead today in degradation and Flora Tristan, the first strong woman, will raise them up again."[54] Thus, rather than containing her activism, Tristan's humanitarian or Christian socialist motivations led her to pursue an active campaign throughout the nation. Her "martyrdom" in the cause of social emancipation also produced a following among French workers. Her friends even hoped that her tomb would become a place of pilgrimage for workers all over the world. But Tristan's cult was short lived. Her mission failed to achieve its desired results. Nor could it have, for her message wavered between a call for change and a promise to forestall revolution, between the demand for female emancipation and the celebration of republican motherhood.

I began by noting the curious fact that both domesticity and feminism resulted from the fall of the absolutist public sphere. It is striking that both Auguste Comte and Flora Tristan speak the language of revolution. Republican domesticity and socialist feminism are articulated in the context of republican ideology. They therefore cannot be taken as simple opposites. They represent two intersecting, if different, responses to the problem of women's subjectivity within the gendered republic. Domesticity and socialist feminism are features of a cultural conjuncture that privileged a highly gendered, bourgeois male discourse, one dependent on women's domesticity and the silencing of public women. Neither the feminist advocate of sexual equality nor the proponent of domesticity cares to redeem the negative evaluation of aristocratic women produced in the Revolution. More surprising, however, each also veers away from images of disorderly women. Even Tristan seeks to align women's body and women's speech to the requirements of order within a harmonious, democratic, social republic of the future age. Her defense of women's rights implies a defense of the family and a repudiation of the forms of publicity in which women engaged during the Old Regime and during the Revolution. Thus we are left to ponder the paradox that, in more respects than either would have liked, Comte and Tristan stand on common ground in the manner in which they choose to represent Woman.

# Conclusion

This book has arrived at an introduction, not a conclusion. I end with some beginnings of modern feminism, insofar as feminism's tasks and dilemmas have been shaped by changing configurations of politics and culture in the era of the French Revolution. The treatment accorded these matters here has necessarily been selective, incomplete, and localized. Regional pride aside, however, so was the Revolution and its effects. Indeed, this study has had to challenge the Revolution's claim to universality at its *political* core, to display the posturings of the particular behind the veil of the universal. From the point of view of a retrospective feminist criticism, the masquerade performed by the society women of the Old Regime, and condemned by the Revolution's masculinist leadership, is that of the Revolution itself.

Nevertheless, I have not been primarily concerned to unmask, to repeat the very gesture of the Revolution in its critique. Although the Revolution's *universal* political significance is contested, its *general* importance for feminist modernity has been underscored. For women today, the revolutionary era has not yet ended, even though the conditions under which specific feminisms have emerged will be seen to have varied. The prospects were by no means the same for all women in Europe, not to speak of the rest of the world. But as contemporaries rightly sensed, what happened in France during these years would throw events elsewhere into sharp relief.

Wherein does this general importance of the Revolution and its outcomes reside *for us*? I have sought to show how the political relations of representation en-gendered by the Revolution might still figure for today's feminist movement. In light of those struggles brought to a crest by the latest wave of feminism, the ongoing celebration of "post-modernity" is premature. Yet the claim that the "modernity" inaugurated in part by the French Revolution has "not yet" exhausted its liberatory potential is equally suspect. In the historically oriented critique of the public sphere here projected, this claim can never be redeemed, for the women's movement cannot "take possession" of a public sphere that has been enduringly reconstructed along masculinist lines. Accordingly, neither side in the debate between the partisans of a post- or an unfulfilled modernity can be unequivocally joined by feminists. To paraphrase Walter Benjamin on another occasion, the conflict is not between two forms of the modernist Spirit, but of women against still-powerful structures of political representation (and the representation of "the political"). Allow me, then, by way of conclusion to offer general reflections on some enduring, but hardly timeless, generalities.

We were in the habit of thinking that politics has always been the province of men, private life that of women—and that women's silence in public reflected their natural condition of domestication. Now, however, we are supposed to be authenticating a comprehensive, if belated, participation of women in the political public sphere. Even those who have decried women's exclusion from this sphere have sought to explain it with reference to a universal (or nearly so) patriarchal impulse. Some feminists have proposed that the entire symbolic order (of language and culture) is a masculine construct. For good or ill, women have been confined largely to the presymbolic world of the "Imaginary" and to their locus within the familial triangle of Daddy, Mommy, and Me.[1]

There is merit in these arguments insofar as they deepen our appreciation for the relationship between culture, discourse, and gender relations. But I wish to question the negative universalism of some theorists of patriarchy. I have tried to show that women's public silence in the post-revolutionary West is an imposed condition of relatively recent origin. Certainly I do not argue that other cultures and periods were gender blind. Considerable evidence testifies to the preponderance of women's oppression in most societies. But the patterns, scope, and intensity of such oppression are not uniform or easily transferable across cultural-historical divisions. I hope the reader will have appreciated the extent to which the changes in one regional culture, within a fairly concentrated time span, produced important differences in the quality of women's involvement in political life.

I have tried to show how the relationship of women to the post-absolutist public sphere was produced by a historically specific reconstruction of the category of the "public" as a category of bourgeois society. Those who have addressed the question of legality in a Freudian perspective may have arrived at related conclusions. Norman O. Brown's radicalization of Freud's theory of civilization captures the hidden content of bourgeois law as a revolt of the "sons" against the patriarchy of the father-king. Or, to employ a more Lacanian formulation, one might say that bourgeois society substitutes the Law of the Father for the father's rule.[2] Such arguments still imply that women are always dominated. But does it make a difference that women in the past have enjoyed a certain measure of power? that they spoke publicly on matters of policy and shaped public (and not just "interpersonal") speech and manners? By answering these questions in the affirmative, I do not merely deny that silence and domesticity are the inescapable state of womankind. At the very least, the post-revolutionary identification of masculine speech with truth, objectivity, and reason has worked to devalue women's contribution to public life to a degree rarely matched in earlier periods. More interesting, the structures of modern republican politics can be construed as part of an elaborate defense against women's power and public presence.

The shift from the iconic imagery of the Old Regime to the symbolic structure of bourgeois representation was constitutive of modern politics *as* a relation of gender. Women's absence from the bourgeois political sphere has not been a chance occurrence, nor merely a symptom of the regrettable persistence of archaic patriarchies. From the standpoint of women and their interests, enlightenment looks suspiciously like counterenlightenment, and revolution like counterrevolution—all the more reason not to identify these processes with a local male conspiracy, even though there is much to suggest that men in politics consciously combined to drive women from their midst. These politicians by no means mastered the course of history, and we have seen how the discourse of the victims served to perpetuate their victimization. Women and feminists adopted the republican project of political, moral, and social reform that was nonetheless predicated on removing women, and women's speech, from the public sphere. This is not intended as another stale confirmation of the irony of history. Instead, this paradox demands that we continue a detailed exploration of the intersection of patterns of cultural representation with forms of public and private life.

An investigation of how gender was inscribed in language at the onset, and in the aftermath, of the revolutionary era leads to surprising results. On the one side, elite women of the salons were scorned for their overly stylized discourses and artificial manners. What, then, of the "common" presumption that women's speech is more natural than that of men, that it is tied to the (allegedly) universal facts of domesticity, natality, and sexuality? Against the "artificial" practices of some women, "nature" would have to be administratively enforced. On the other side, feminist writers such as Mary Wollstonecraft joined the assault on female preciosity—and women revolutionaries, then and afterward, were caught in the contradiction between republican virtue and female propriety. Women who attempted to fashion new public languages or personae in the post-revolutionary age violated the symbolic code of bourgeois representation, which dictated a more "natural," transparent mode of female gender behavior. Those who aimed to *represent* women's interests violated norms of universal reason and appeared symbolically aligned with the corruption of the defeated regime. The critique of the gendered (masculinist) public sphere cannot overlook the problematic character of the new, feminist discourse that was engendered in and through that sphere.

Representation is a plurivocal concept. But in one prominent meaning, to represent is to re-present, to make present again. Additionally, power is (among other things) a relation of representation, one in which something is "presented" to something else. In her study of political representation, Hanna Fenichel Pitkin notes the paradoxical character of representation so conceived: "Representation, taken generally, means the making present *in some sense* of something which is nevertheless *not* present literally or in fact. Now, to say something is simultaneously both present and not present is to utter a paradox, and thus a fundamental dualism is built into the meaning of representation."[3]

In the present context, I am less concerned with the general duality, or duplicity, of "representation," in which everything to be (re)presented must be absent, than with the senses in which the representation of women in modern public life seem to require their exclusion. This exclusion does not automatically "depoliticize" women but rather transforms them into the political *subjects* par excellence of the modern system of representation. In other words, the system requires the production of a subject who complies in becoming the *object* of an act of political representation. Only those who embody the principle of a disinterested, rational discussion, free from external coercion, within which the claims of particular interests can be subsumed, are so entitled to act (for themselves and for others). This principle of reason, which was from the outset coordinated with the organization of the bourgeois public sphere, and not just "representative" government, barely conceals its essential antipathy to the "feminine." Accordingly, the transformation of modern modes of discursivity becomes a fundamental task for feminists. This most obviously involves the authorization, through language, of women's legitimate participation in the public realm and their status as political actors in their own right. As a practical measure, women have had to acquire the power to represent other women, and men as well; women's "rights" are also figured in how they are seen, and by whom. This is a cultural question of primary political importance, and it has by no means been resolved—all the more reason to honor the contributions of those women and men who first attempted to open a discursive space for women *within* the modern public sphere.

Their efforts have not gone unrewarded. Yet it is perhaps less clear than at any time in the past that women can simply "occupy" a domain so enduringly grounded in their non-residence. Once the young Habermas quoted the young Hegel to this effect, that "it has been reserved for our times above all to vindicate, at least in theory, those treasures which were formerly wasted by relegating them to the heavens; but which age will have the strength to enforce this right, and to take possession of it?"[4] By performing our own critique of the French Revolution, I have been prompted to raise another set of questions. Which age will it be, then, that will put paid to the enforcement of right and the strength of possession? Will this still be the age of the masculinist public and of the feminisms that addressed its problems? These questions must remain unanswered until the women's movement more fully engages its symbolic determinations as a practical, political task. Or, to paraphrase Habermas in a related context,[5] on the level of self-reflection about its commitments to a political practice operating under the obligation of fundamental rights, feminism cannot remain content with the postulate of universal liberation or with the critique of domesticity. Instead, it will have to understand itself as a component of all the practical interrelationships of life—as an agent within them.

# Notes

## Introduction

1. The term "feminism" is not known until the nineteenth century. Its invention is usually attributed to Charles Fourier, although even this claim is open to dispute. At that time, the eighteenth-century "woman question" gave way to "women's emancipation movements." I have, however, taken the liberty throughout this work to use the term broadly, in order to make sense of a set of convictions and principles which we now identify as feminist.

2. As Sigmund Freud comments in a footnote to his famous case study, "The question whether a woman is 'open' or 'shut' can naturally not be a matter of indifference"; see Freud, *Dora: An Analysis of a Case of Hysteria,* ed. Philip Rief, p. 84.

3. See J. G. A. Pocock, *The Machiavellian Moment: Florentine Political Thought and the Atlantic Republican Tradition.* For a recent feminist discussion, see Hanna Fenichel Pitkin, *Fortune Is a Woman: Gender and Politics in the Thought of Niccolò Machiavelli.*

4. In its elitist and democratic versions, American political thought appears wedded to a nostalgic romanticization of the ancient polis. Compare Leo Strauss and Alan Bloom to Hannah Arendt and Sheldon Wolin. Pocock, whose method is decidedly more historical than philosophical, seems to favor the Roman over the Greek model.

5. See Susan Moller Okin, *Women in Western Political Thought;* Jean Bethke Elshtain, *Public Man, Private Woman: Women in Social and Political Thought;* Lorenne M. G. Clark and Lynda Lange, eds.,*The Sexism of Social and Political Theory:*

*Women and Reproduction from Plato to Nietzsche*; Zillah Eisenstein, *The Radical Future of Liberal Feminism*; Judith Hicks Stiehm, ed., *Women's Views of the Political World of Men*.

6. I have already mentioned Hanna Fenichel Pitkin's contribution (note 3 above). See also Jean Elshtain, *Public Man, Private Woman*; Nancy Hartsock, "Prologue to a Feminist Critique of War and Politics," in *Women's Views*, ed. Stiehm. Finally, for a revisionist work by a feminist classicist, see Eva C. Keuls, *The Reign of the Phallus: Sexual Politics in Ancient Athens*.

7. Jürgen Habermas, *Strukturwandel der Öffentlichkeit: Untersuchungen zu einer Kategorie der bürgerlichen Gesellschaft*. The book appeared in a French translation some years later, and it is only now scheduled to appear in an English language version (forthcoming, M.I.T. Press). My own citations are to the French version of Habermas' study, *L'espace public: Archéologie de la publicité comme dimension constitutive de la société bourgeoise*. In the United States, the journal *New German Critique* made available selections and summaries of Habermas' argument and translated contributions to the literature it provoked. Additionally, Peter Uwe Hohendahl, a German literary critic influenced by Habermas, published a book in English that summarized the debate and also expanded on the "literary" dimensions of Habermas' thesis; Peter Uwe Hohendahl, *The Institution of Criticism*. These contributions helped to inspire the present study, but they did not make up for this lacuna in the work of Habermas in translation. Even as his reputation among American and English readers grew, Habermas' work on the public sphere remained terra incognita.

8. Habermas draws his argument from the Frankfurt School, as well as certain American theorists of the "public and its problems." See Max Horkheimer and Theodor Adorno, *Dialectic of Enlightenment*; John Dewey, *The Public and Its Problems*; C. Wright Mills, *The Power Elite*; Hannah Arendt, *The Human Condition*; idem, *On Revolution*.

9. It may be that the long-delayed publication of the English translation of this book will favor its reception, for we have seen the revival of historicist methods among political theorists; and, in the cognate field of literary criticism, New Critical approaches to the text have been subjected to the searing questions of reader reception, deconstructive, and new historicist readings.

10. With one exception: no R. H. Tawney or Christopher Hill stepped forward to introduce Habermas' ideas to an Anglo-American audience. This was doubly peculiar. Habermas was hardly the first

twentieth-century author to reflect at length on the fate of the liberal democratic "public" and its "structural transformation" during the nineteenth century. At the time, he acknowledged his indebtedness to John Dewey, C. Wright Mills, and Hannah Arendt, in her English-language writings. These theorists of the public and its problems either had, or were having, a considerable impact on political discussion in the United States. It is sad, therefore, that Habermas on the public remained outside the scope of Anglo-American discussion; he could have helped considerably to advance this debate.

11. Jürgen Habermas, *The Theory of Communicative Action*, vol. 1: *Reason and the Rationalization of Society*.

12. For a short bibliography of public sphere literature, see Theodore Mills Norton, "The Public Sphere: A Workshop," *New Political Science* 11 (Spring 1983).

13. See, especially, Michel Foucault, *The Birth of the Clinic: An Archaeology of Medical Perception*; idem, *Discipline and Punish: The Birth of the Prison*; idem, *The Order of Things: An Archaeology of the Human Sciences*; François Furet, *Interpreting the French Revolution*; Marie-Hélène Huet, *Rehearsing the Revolution: The Staging of Marat's Death, 1793–1797*; Mona Ozouf, *La fête révolutionnaire, 1789–1799*; Louis Marin, "The Inscription of the King's Memory: On the Metallic History of Louis XIV," *Yale French Studies* 59 (1980); idem, *Le portrait du roi*; Jean-Marie Apostolidès, *Le roi-machine: Spectacle et politique au temps de Louis XIV*. See also two recent studies by American scholars of eighteenth-century French politics and the public sphere: Lynn Hunt, *Politics, Culture, and Class in the French Revolution*; Thomas Crow, *Painters and Public Life in Eighteenth-Century Paris*.

14. See Karl Marx, *The Eighteenth Brumaire of Louis Bonaparte*.

15. See, especially, Huet, *Rehearsing the Revolution*; Hunt, *Politics, Culture and Class*; Furet, *Interpreting the French Revolution*.

16. See Marshall Sahlins, *Historical Metaphors and Mythical Realities*; and *Islands of History*.

17. As the reader may infer, I take issue on this point with feminist political theorists who have applied the traditional methods of theory or adopted the canonic definitions of who or what counts as theory. Entire books have been authored on images of women in political texts without considering any feminist theorists, without appreciating how the figuration of women may reflect larger historical circumstances, or, finally, without accounting for the

way men and women in society appropriate and resist dominant ideological conventions.

## Chapter 1

1. Ernst Kantorowicz, *The King's Two Bodies: A Study in Medieval Political Theology.* For an excellent recent study of the political philosophy of early modern France, see Nannerl Keohane, *Philosophy and the State in France: The Renaissance to the Enlightenment.*

2. These aspects of absolutism have been brilliantly set forth in the recent works of Louis Marin and Jean-Marie Apostilidès; see Apostilidès, *Le roi-machine*; Marin, "The Inscription of the King's Memory; idem, *Le portrait du roi.* See also Foucault, *Discipline and Punish*; Lynn Hunt, "Hercules and the Radical Image in the French Revolution," *Representations* 1:2 (Spring 1983).

3. See Marc Bloch, *The Royal Touch: Sacred Monarchy and Scrofula in England and France.*

4. Habermas, *L'espace public*, chaps. 1 and 2. See also Norbert Elias, *The Court Society*; and *The Civilizing Process.*

5. Erica Harth has produced an extraordinarily rich account of the mechanisms and content of representation in seventeenth-century France; see *Ideology and Culture in Seventeenth-Century France.*

6. Joseph Klaits, *Printed Propaganda under Louis XIV: Absolute Monarchy and Public Opinion*, p. 13.

7. Emmanuel Le Roy Ladurie, "Versailles Observed: The Court of Louis XIV in 1709," in *The Mind and Method of the Historian*, pp. 149–174.

8. I am arguing here for the iconic or visual structure of the absolutist public sphere. Nevertheless, Klaits has demonstrated the use of printed propaganda alongside censorship and court spectacle to support absolutist rule. Elizabeth L. Eisenstein has argued for what might appear to be a competing thesis regarding the emerging role of the printed medium. Following Huet, I situate the break between a visually oriented and a textually oriented or print culture somewhat later. I would not, however, want to dismiss the cultural renovations that accompanied the print revolution—several of which are discussed later in this chapter. Also, as recent studies by Erica Harth and Chandra Mukerji demonstrate, the new technologies associated with printing were applied in a more general fashion to a wide range of cultural commodities and artistic

representations. See Klaits, *Printed Propaganda;* Huet, *Rehearsing the Revolution;* Elizabeth L. Eisenstein, *The Printing Press as an Agent of Change: Communications and Cultural Transformations in Early Modern Europe,* vols. 1 and 2; Harth, *Ideology and Culture;* Chandra Mukerji, *From Graven Images: Patterns of Modern Materialism.*

9. For a very general statement of the problem, not tied to the European case, see Sherry Ortner's wide-ranging speculative essay, "The Virgin and the State," *Feminist Studies* 4:3 (October 1978)

10. Davis examines the contradictory appeal of early Protestantism to sixteenth-century French urban women. She concludes that women already independent in the street and market were summoned to intellectual activity and self-control, called to a new relation to church theology. But it seems that Protestantism had a more diminished appeal for literate women than it did for those less privileged. Davis notes that literary woman, already admitted to the castle of learning, did not seem to need the Religion of the Book. Also, nuns were less attracted than the male religious to the Reformation movements; they were always the strong holdouts. Not only did theological doctrine and familial practice now uphold a singular patriarchal standard, but the women who joined the new reformed communities were less inclined than Catholic city women to participate in organized group action among women, whether in the female orders or in all-female Catholic crowds. Davis' point is not that Catholic women were more liberated than their Protestant counterparts; rather, she urges us to reappraise the ways the new "this-worldly asceticism denied laymen and laywomen much of the shared recreational festive life allowed them by Catholicism. It closed off an institutionalized and respectable alternative to private family life: the communal living of the monastery. By destroying the female saints as exemplars for both sexes, it cut off a wide range of affect and activity. And by eliminating a separate identity and separate organization for women in religious life, it may have made them a little more vulnerable to subjection in all spheres"; Natalie Zemon Davis, "City Women and Religious Change," in *Society and Culture in Early Modern France,* pp. 65–96, 94.

11. Perhaps more important than religion in accounting for the loss of women's status in the first centuries of the modern era was the changing structure of property, marriage laws, and above all the shift in the organization of productive activity within commerce and agriculture which differentially altered men and women's lives. On the impact of capitalism, see Roberta Hamilton, *The Lib-*

*eration of Women: A Study of Patriarchy and Capitalism;* Alice Clark, *The Working Life of Women in the Seventeenth Century;* Ivy Pinchbeck, *Women Workers and the Industrial Revolution, 1750–1850;* Louise A. Tilly and Joan W. Scott, *Women, Work, and Family;* Natalie Zemon Davis, "Women in the Crafts in Sixteenth-Century Lyon," *Feminist Studies* 8:1 (Spring 1982).

12. Joan Kelly, "Early Feminist Theory and the Querelle des Femmes, 1400–1789," *Signs* 8:1 (Autumn 1982), p. 23. See also Joan Kelly-Gadol, "Did Women Have a Renaissance?" in *Becoming Visible: Women in European History,* ed. Renate Bridenthal and Claudia Koonz.

13. See Barbara Pope Corrado, "Revolution and Retreat: Upper-Class French Women after 1789," in *Women, War and Revolution,* ed. Carol R. Berkin and Clara M. Lovett, p. 216.

14. The opposition between city and court in France was dramatically sharpened by Louis XIV's decision to remove the court from Paris, the national capital and focal center of all national economic and political life, to Versailles, an estate on the environs of Paris.

15. Amelia Gere Mason, *The Women of the French Salons,* p. 124.

16. See, for example, Norbert Elias' high estimation of women's power at court; *The Court Society,* p. 243.

17. See Carolyn Lougee, *Le paradis des femmes: Women, Salons, and Social Stratification in Seventeenth-Century France,* for an excellent discussion of the wider social implications of the woman question of the seventeenth-century. Lougee demonstrates the extent to which this issue was interwoven with the question of the proper stratification of society. The ensuing discussion is indebted to Lougee's pathbreaking analysis.

18. Simultaneously, the king, Louis XIV after 1680, gradually succeeded in taming the feudal nobility, demanding that they disarm and live at court. These two processes are related only imperfectly. The sale of venal offices from the early seventeenth-century onward made social mobility for non-nobles possible. But, in part as a consequence of this, the old nobility also revolted between 1648 and 1654 in the Fronde—its final, violent rebellion against the absolutist order—making its taming even more necessary, and bringing about a royal attempt to curtail the expansion of office-holders. To be sure, the sale of venal offices continued and was decried by reformers of varying stripes into the eighteenth century.

19. On the last point, the materials on Germany are most compelling; see Hannah Arendt, *Rahel Varnhagen: The Life of a Jewish*

*Woman.* The best recent analytical work on the cultural assimilation of Jews in German salon society has been done by Deborah Hertz, *Jewish High Society in Old Regime Berlin;* and "Salonières and Literary Women in Late Eighteenth-Century Berlin," *New German Critique* 14 (Spring 1978).

20. Lougee, *Le paradis des femmes*, p. 48.

21. See Anne Liot Backer, *Precious Women: A Feminist Phenomenon in the Age of Louis XIV.*

22. Lougee, *Le paradis des femmes*, p. 52.

23. See the "Plaintes des dames de la cour contre les marchandes ou bourgeoises de Paris: Requeste des dames de la cour présentée à Monsieur Colbert Superintendant de la réforme du royaume de France sur le luxe des bourgeoises de Paris," in Lougee, *Le paradis des femmes*, p. 73.

24. Backer, *Precious Women*, p. 16. See also Harth, *Ideology and Culture*, pp. 37–40.

25. Both cited in Lougee, *Le paradis des femmes*, p. 71.

26. Ibid., p. 81.

27. Ibid., p. 84.

28. For example, see Philippe Ariès, *Centuries of Childhood: A Social History of Family Life;* Elinor Barber, *The Bourgeoisie in Eighteenth Century France.* The Marxist view, which attributes these changes to the rise of capitalism and hence the dominance of the bourgeoisie, could be considered another version of this general argument. Lougee's work is a refreshing alternative to the predominant emphasis in the historical literature on family reorganization.

29. Fénelon has often been credited as an early feminist for his views on female education, but those who hold to this estimation overlook the fact that he was advocating education for domesticity.

30. See Lougee, *Le paradis des femmes*, p. 186.

31. Another element to be considered is the so-called civilization of a brute, martial nobility by conventions of courtliness, associated with the Italian Renaissance court. In this sense, courtly etiquette, which was inseparable from the presence and sway of women at court, was regarded as a repudiation of masculine values—this despite the undeniable fact that the French monarchy remained a war machine of the first order. Of course, another change involved the monarch's centralization of war-making powers, so that even serving in the military was not sufficient compensation for a nobility that had lost its control over the means of violence. On this last insight into the character of the modern state, see Max Weber, "Politics as a Vocation," in *From Max Weber: Essays in Sociology.*

32. Harth, *Ideology and Culture*, p. 26.

33. Ibid., p. 105. For the argument that preciosity actually contributed to the growth of classicism through its attention to language (as that which gives pleasure) and to form, see David Maland, *Culture and Society in Seventeenth-Century France*.

34. Domna Stanton, "The Fiction of Préciosité and the Fear of Women," *Yale French Studies* 62 (1981), p. 129.

35. Cited in ibid., p. 130.

36. Charles-Louis de Secondat, Baron de Montesquieu, *Persian Letters*; idem, "Lettres persanes," in *Oeuvres complètes*, vol. 1, ed. Roger Caillois. For two recent feminist treatments of this work, see Mary Lyndon Shanley and Peter G. Stillman, "Political and Marital Despotism: Montesquieu's *Persian Letters*," in *The Family in Political Thought*, ed. Jean Bethke Elshtain; and Anna Yeatman, "Despotism and Civil Society: The Limits of Patriarchal Citizenship," in *Women's Views*, ed. Stiehm.

37. In the symbolic structure of eighteenth-century representation, a discursive appeal is made to a normal, normative, and natural order that has somehow been violated. Woman is the figure of that violation and displacement. She signals the very possibility of (social) disorder. She might be compared to the metaphor through which her cause is identified. Woman and metaphor are both transfer terms; each is in the position of being out of its proper place. The dictionary defines "metaphor" as that figure of speech in which a name or a descriptive term is transferred to some object different from, but analogous to, that to which it is properly applicable. Similarly, writers and rhetoricians of a classicizing disposition in the late early-modern period (whether noble or bourgeois, traditionalist or revolutionary) seem obsessed with the problem of woman's proper place. I address this issue in more detail in the following two chapters. On the general point, see Larysa Myktyka, "Lacan, Literature and the Look: Woman in the Eye of Psychoanalysis," *Sub-Stance* 39 (1983); Jacques Derrida, "Le Retrait of Metaphor," *Enclitic* 2:2 (Fall 1978).

38. Keith Michael Baker makes a similar point, in this case regarding the eighteenth-century French, but also Montesquieu's measured view of English liberty. He argues that Montesquieu's "adumbration of a theory of the separation and balance of powers, understood as the essential condition of English liberty, did not entirely erase from his work the evidence of hesitations and ambivalences in the face of the English system of government. To many of his contemporaries, he still seemed to be describing an ambiguous, disturbing, and even dangerous phenomenon—a phe-

nomenon to be understood and marveled at — rather than a model to be imitated"; see "Politics and Public Opinion under the Old Regime: Some Reflections," in *Press and Politics in Pre-Revolutionary France*, ed. Jack R. Censer and Jeremy D. Popkin, p. 215.

39. Montesquieu, *The Spirit of Laws: A Compendium of the First English Edition*, ed. David Wallace Carrithers, bk. 7, chap. 9, p. 168; idem, "De l'esprit des lois," in *Oeuvres complètes*, vol. 2, p. 341.

40. Ibid., bk. 7, chap. 9, p. 168; *Oeuvres complètes*, vol. 2, p. 341.

41. Ibid., bk. 19, chap. 15, p. 294; *Oeuvres complètes*, vol. 2, p. 565. Montesquieu means something like the ancient constitution in which monarchy and noble rule are appropriately balanced, rather than despotic, absolutist rule by an all-powerful, central monarch. As he states elsewhere, "Monarchy is a state of tension, which always degenerates into despotism or republicanism"; *Persian Letters*, letter 102.

42. Ibid., bk. 7, chap. 16, p. 169; *Oeuvres complètes*, vol. 2, p. 348.

43. Joan Kelly observes that "republicans, bourgeois by class and outlook (as in Renaissance Florence and Venice, Calvinist Geneva, and Puritan England), had no question about the domestic and subordinate nature of women"; "Early Feminist Theory," p. 23. Similarly, William E. Monter finds that, whereas the religious institutions of Calvinist Geneva worked positively for women, its republican institutions sorely restricted them; see E. William Monter, "Women in Calvinist Geneva (1555–1800)," *Signs* 6:2 (Winter 1980).

44. Montesquieu, *Spirit of Laws*, bk. 8, chap. 2, p. 171; *Oeuvres complètes*, vol. 2, p. 350.

45. Georges Bataille, "The Enigma of Incest," in *Erotism: Death and Sensuality*, pp. 218–219.

*Chapter 2*

1. François Furet and Jacques Ozouf, *Reading and Writing: Literacy in France from Calvin to Jules Ferry*, p.197. The argument in this chapter, with additions and revisions, is indebted to Habermas, *L'espace public*, chaps. 1 and 2. For an extension of Habermas' perspective on the literary public sphere, see the excellent study by Hohendahl, *The Institution of Criticism*.

2. Richard Sennett, *The Fall of Public Man: On the Social Psychology of Capitalism*, p. 17.

3. See Thomas Crow, "The Oath of the Horatii in 1785: Painting and Pre-Revolutionary Radicalism in France," *Art History* 1:4 (December 1978); and *Painters and Public Life*. I am not speaking here of the old burgher class of the medieval towns. Whereas such institutions as the guild were part and parcel of the structures of corporate privilege within absolutist society, the new institutions of the bourgeois public sphere were in principle distinguished by their market character and their openness.

4. Robert Darnton, *The Literary Underground of the Old Regime*, p. 16.

5. An important clarification is in order. I am certainly not arguing that words were unimportant in Old Regime society (as I well appreciate, Old Regime France was a society of letters). Nor do I imply that visual images were effaced by the new regime of words. Elizabeth L. Eisenstein insists that the cultural metamorphosis produced by printing was much more complicated than any single formula can capture. She points out that engraved images became more, rather than less, abundant after the establishment of print shops in Western Europe; that Protestant propaganda exploited the printed image as much as the word; and that printed picture books were newly designed by educational reformers for the purpose of instructing children. Her point, then, is well taken. Surely images did not simply disappear in the new symbolic universe opened by print culture. On the other hand, as Eisenstein herself intimates, pictures may convey a pedagogical, moral message; images may be textualized. Accordingly, Eisenstein's study provides ample evidence that the image did not vanish; rather it was reframed and textualized. Moreover, as Norman Bryson argues in his important account of French painting, paintings may be organized narratively; the image may serve to communicate information. See Elizabeth L. Eisenstein, *The Printing Revolution in Early Modern Europe*, pp. 35–37; Norman Bryson, *Word and Image: French Painting of the Ancien Régime*.

6. Huet, *Rehearsing the Revolution*; Furet, *Interpreting the Revolution*; Baker, "Politics and Public Opinion."

7. Terry Eagleton, *The Function of Criticism: From "The Spectator" to Post-Structuralism*, p. 9.

8. Jürgen Habermas, "The Public Sphere: An Encyclopedia Article (1964)," *New German Critique* 3 (Fall 1974), p. 49.

9. Jürgen Habermas, *Theory and Practice*, p. 4.

10. Eagleton, *The Function of Criticism*, p. 15.

11. Habermas, "The Public Sphere," p. 49.

12. Eagleton, *The Function of Criticism*, p. 16.

13. Ibid.

14. This criticism of Habermas' argument has been made by Habermas' leading German critics, Oskar Negt and Alexander Kluge. See their *Öffentlichkeit und Erfahrung: Zur Organisations analyse von bürgerlicher und proletarischer Öffentlichkeit* (Frankfurt: Suhrkamp, 1972); Eberhard Köndler-Bunte, "The Proletarian Public Sphere and Political Organization: An Analysis of Oskar Negt and Alexander Kluge's *The Public Sphere and Experience*," *New German Critique* 4 (Winter 1975); C. Wright Mills, *The Power Elite*, esp. chap. 13.

15. Habermas, "The Public Sphere," p. 50.

16. In the often recounted, romantic estimation of the nineteenth-century writers the brothers Goncourt: "The soul of this age, the center of this world, the point from which all things radiate, the summit from which all things descend, the image upon which all things are modeled, is Woman. Woman was the governing principle, the directing reason and the commanding voice of the eighteenth century. She was the universal and fatal cause, the origin of events, the source of things. She presided over Time, like the Fortune of her history. Nothing escaped her; within her grasp she held the King and France, the will of the sovereign and the authority of public opinion—everything! She gave orders at court, she was mistress in her home. She held the revolutions of alliances and political systems, peace and war, the literature, the arts and the fashions of the eighteenth century, as well as its destinies, in the folds of her gown; she bent them to her whim or to her passions. She could exalt and lay low. . . . From one end of the century to the other, government by woman was the only visible and appreciable government." Edmond and Jules de Goncourt, *The Woman of the Eighteenth Century: Her Life, from Birth to Death, Her Love and Her Philosophy in the Worlds of Salon, Shop and Street*, pp. 243–244; idem, *La femme au dix-huitième siècle*.

17. Condorcet, to be discussed in Chapter 4, is perhaps the most notable exception. As Barbara Brookes observes, "Prominent philosophes such as Montesquieu, Thomas, Diderot and d'Alembert were tentative in their claims and they did not present a sustained argument to counter the prevailing ideas of woman's assumed biological, and therefore, social, inferiority. Condorcet, part of the later Enlightenment, met the question of woman's inferiority directly and argued in favour of complete equality for women before the publication of Mary Wollstonecraft's well-known work, *A Vindication of the Rights of Woman*; Barbara Brookes, "The Feminism of Condorcet and Sophie de Grouchy," *Studies on Voltaire and the Eighteenth Century 189*, p. 297.

18. Denis Diderot, "On Women," in *Dialogues*, p. 196, emphasis added; idem., "Sur les femmes," pp. 28–53, in *Oeuvres complètes*, vol. 10, introd. Roger Lewinter, p. 53. Thus the modern "style versus substance" dichotomy carries a freight of gender associations from this period on.

19. See Judith Shklar, *Men and Citizens*. See also Jean-Jacques Rousseau, "Essay on the Origin of Languages," in *On The Origin of Language*; idem, "Essai sur l'origine des langues," in *Ecrits sur la musique*.

20. Crow, "The Oath of the Horatii," p. 460. Crow is speaking of a symbolic shift in representation within the sphere of art itself, usually described as the change from rococo to neoclassicism. I am arguing that this transformation has a wider cultural application, with gender implications.

21. Dowd identifies four factors contributing to the classical revival: court influence exerted through official channels, the philosophy of the Enlightenment, the rise of art criticism, and the international aesthetic and archaeological interest emanating from Rome. In other words, there was an interaction between official and oppositional forces; see David Lloyd Dowd, *Pageant-Master of the Republic: Jacques-Louis David and the French Revolution*. See also Harold T. Parker, *The Cult of Antiquity and the French Revolutionaries*.

22. In addition, the links between bourgeois thought and aristocratic ideas were reinforced by the paradoxes of political opposition under absolutism. Eighteenth-century French liberalism was, to a great degree, the product, expression, residue of the resistance of the parlements—the old regional law courts of Old Regime France—to all government attempts to undercut the privileges of the nobility, especially the gross inequalities in tax obligations. Because of their power to delay the enactment of any law, the parlements could obstruct reforms. The parlements (especially the parlement of Paris) came increasingly to rely on popular support, even to engineer mass public disturbances in the streets of Paris. Ironically, in their confrontations with the crown, the parlements used the vocabulary of liberty to defend their own privileges. They represented their own privilege as a defense of the nation against royal despotism even as the crown in its desperate search for new sources of revenue proposed a more equitable system of taxation and application of the law. Until the late 1780s, the parlementaires succeeded in preempting the field of political dissent. Eighteenth-century liberals had to balance a commitment to universal rights and liberties with a defense of nobility as an insti-

tution; Crow, "The Oath of the Horatii," p. 438. See also Nannerl Keohane, *Philosophy and the State in France: The Renaissance to the Enlightenment*.

23. Crow, "The Oath of the Horatii," p. 442.

24. Ibid.

25. Although Habermas stresses the interaction between the political and literary-cultural public spheres, he does identify some elements of a specifically political public sphere: "We speak of the political public sphere in contrast, for instance, to the literary one, when public discussion deals with objects connected to the activity of the state. Although state authority is so to speak the executor of the political public sphere, it is not a part of it. To be sure, state authority is usually considered 'public' authority, but it derives its task of caring for the well-being of all citizens primarily from this aspect of the public sphere. Only when the exercise of political control is effectively subordinated to the democratic demand that information be accessible to the public, does the political public sphere win an institutionalized influence over the government through the instrument of law-making bodies. The expression 'public opinion' refers to the tasks of criticism and control which a public body of citizens informally — and, in periodic elections, formally as well — practices vis-à-vis the ruling structure organized in the form of a state. Regulations demanding that certain proceedings be public (*Publizitätsvorschriften*), for example those providing for open court hearings, are also related to this function of public opinion. The public as a sphere which mediates between society and state, in which the public organizes itself as the bearer of public opinion, accords with the principle of the public sphere — that principle of public information which once had to be fought for against the arcane policies of monarchies and which since that time has made possible the democratic control of state activities"; Habermas, "The Public Sphere," pp. 49–50.

26. Crow, "The Oath of the Horatii," pp. 443–444.

27. If women are a metonym for the Old Regime, it is also true that men could attack the crown without having to name their object. This was especially useful before the emergence of broad popular support for the republican party, that is, in the days when most reformers looked to a constitutional monarchy as a solution to despotism.

28. Jack Goody, *The Domestication of the Savage Mind*, p. 15. Goody expands on this argument: "Culture, after all, is a series of communicative acts, and differences in the mode of communication are often as important as differences in the mode of produc-

tion, for they involve developments in the storing, analysis, and creation of human knowledge, as well as the relationships between the individuals involved. The specific proposition is that writing, and more especially alphabetic literacy, made it possible to scrutinise discourse in a different kind of way by giving oral communication a semi-permanent form; this scrutiny favoured the increase in the scope of critical activity, and hence of rationality, scepticism, and logic. . . . It increased the potentialities of criticism because writing laid out discourse before one's eyes in a different kind of way; at the same time increased the potentiality for cumulative knowledge, especially knowledge of an abstract kind, because it changed the nature of communication beyond that of face-to-face contact as well as the system for the storage of information; in this way a wider range of 'thought' was made available to the reading public. No longer did the problem of memory storage dominate man's intellectual life; the human mind was freed to study static 'text' (rather than be limited by participation in the dynamic 'utterance'), a process that enabled man to stand back from his creation and examine it in a more abstract, generalised, and 'rational' way. By making it possible to scan the communications of mankind over a much wider time span, literacy encouraged, at the very same time, criticism and commentary on the one hand and the orthodoxy of the book on the other"; *Domestication*, p. 37.

29. English Showalter, Jr., "Authorial Self-Consciousness in the Familiar Letter: The Case of Madame de Graffigny," *Yale French Studies* 71 (1986), p. 125. According to Amelia Gere Mason, Mme de Lambert "wrote much later in life on educational themes, for the benefit of her children and for her own diversion; but she yielded to the prejudices of her age against the woman author, and her works were given to the world only through the medium of friends to whom she had read or lent them"; Mason, *The Women of the French Salons*, p. 136.

30. See Barbara G. Mittman, "Women and the Theatre Arts," pp. 155–169, and associated articles for a fine overview of the period, in *French Women and the Age of Enlightenment*, ed. Samia I. Spencer. On worldliness, see Peter Brooks, *The Novel of Worldliness*.

31. Michael Fried, *Absorption and Theatricality: Painting and Beholder in the Age of Diderot*, p. 168.

32. Elizabeth L. Eisenstein, *The Printing Press as an Agent of Change*, vols. 1 and 2. See also Lucien Febvre and Henri-Jean Martin, *The Coming of the Book: The Impact of Printing, 1450–1800*.

33. See Habermas, *L'espace public*, chaps. 1 and 3. One could speak, as well, of the political implications of the printed word. State record keeping was long associated with an appreciation of the social power of writing. State officials were initially drawn from that restricted sector of the population which had access to advanced education. Writing aided in the administration of tax collection, accounting, census taking, surveillance, and criminal and property law and therefore favored the development of state structure. But, as noted above, writing also fosters critical, nontraditional consciousness. The growth of the bourgeois public sphere as a counterpublic sphere inside absolutism demonstrates that writing and literacy also gave rise to antagonistic forces—that is, the insistence of critical public opinion on publicity, public access, and scrutiny of the secret conduct of the absolutist state was a function of an expanded range of printed materials available to a widening reading public. On state structure, see Jack Goody, "The State, the Bureau and the File," in *The Logic of Writing and the Organization of Society.*

34. Preface to *Press and Politics in Pre-Revolutionary France*, p. xii.

35. William Doyle, *Origins of the French Revolution*, chap. 4. On sexual differences, see Furet and Ozouf, *Reading and Writing*, pp. 32–34. On the general topic of literacy, see Darnton, *The Literary Underground*; Furet and Ozouf, *Reading and Writing*, pp. 32–34; Klaits, *Printed Propraganda*.

36. Daniel Roche observes that "growing literacy, increasing reading, pictures and songs all meant that in Paris the man in the street more or less had to read"; Daniel Roche, "Reading Habits," in *The People of Paris: An Essay in Popular Culture in the 18th Century*, p. 233. Yet class factors were overriding. To be sure, there was a world of difference between utilitarian and practical reading and its more accomplished forms. It is uncontestable, too, that education was a critical factor in the differential reception of printed matter. Walter J. Ong proposes that women writers in the early modern period generally worked from outside the oral tradition because of the simple fact that girls were not commonly subjected to the orally (and Latin) based rhetorical training that boys got in school. He attributes to such nonrhetorical styles the development of the novel as more like a conversation than a platform performance; Walter J. Ong, *Orality and Literacy: The Technologizing of the Word*, pp. 111–112.

37. Georges Duby and Robert Mandrou, *A History of French Civilization*, p. 387. Maité Albistur and Daniel Armogathe, *His-*

*toire du féminisme français*, vol. 1: *Du moyen âge à nos jours*, p. 253. In *Women of the French Revolution*, Winifred Stephens reports that Robespierre, despite his attitude during the Revolution to women's assertion of their rights, defended women's membership in the Academy, thereby winning the future political support of Mme Robert.

38. Doyle, *Origins of the French Revolution*, p. 80.

39. Cited in Eisenstein, *The Printing Press*, p. 132.

40. This observation is made by Dena Goodman in her unpublished study of correspondence as a feature of the eighteenth-century salon, "Salons and Letters: Women and the Project of Enlightenment."

41. Showalter discusses the editorial function in these terms, but he also queries whether there could have been any completely naive or "unself-conscious" letter writing during the eighteenth century. He observes that, due to the literary success of the posthumous publication of Mme de Sévigné's letters, *after* 1725 every literate French man or woman writing a private letter would have been aware of the possiblity of publication, intended or not. But he also concludes that letter writers could have felt conscious of themselves as authors without that awareness visibly affecting their letter writing. Graffigny's correspondence remained unknown until the present day; Showalter, "Authorial Self-Consciousness," pp. 115, 129.

42. I am grateful to Dena Goodman for calling to my attention this last, extremely important distinction. Janet Gurkin Altman also observes: "The history of letter books during and after the eighteenth century is marked by that age's deepened awareness of the relational differences between oral conversation, handwriting, and print as modes of interpersonal communcation, as representations of temporally specific experience, and as conveyors of social values"; Janet Gurkin Altman, "The Letter Book as a Literary Institution 1539–1789: Toward a Cultural History of Published Correspondences in France," *Yale French Studies* 71 (1986), p. 60.

43. Brooks, *The Novel of Worldliness*, p. 6.

44. Only Mme de Châtelet—known best for her liaison with Voltaire—achieved some fame in French intellectual circles and was elected to the Bologna Academy of Sciences. Her one published book on the metaphysics of natural science (the *Institutions de physique*) also appeared in translation. In addition, she coauthored anonymously Voltaire's popularization of Newtonian physics. Nevertheless, her life is a record of the discrimination suffered by an eighteenth-century woman of science. See the fine arti-

cle by Linda Gardiner, "Women in Science," in *French Women and Enlightenment*, ed. S. Spencer.

45. Mason, *Women of the French Salons*, p. 161.

46. Cited in Duby and Mandrou, *A History of French Civilization*, p. 386.

47. Darnton, *The Literary Undergound*, pp. 23-24.

48. One could say that the phallic imagery of the pen had a particularly resonant meaning here. On this issue, see "Toward a Feminist Poetics," in Sandra Gilbert and Susan Gubar, *The Madwoman in the Attic: The Woman Writer and the Nineteenth-Century Literary Imagination*.

49. Cited in Darnton, *The Literary Underground*, p. 35. Darnton speaks of this type of rhetorical posturing as "gutter Rousseauism," a term taken from the appellation first given to Restif de la Bretonne (see Chapter 4), "Rousseau du ruisseau."

50. Nina Rattner Gelbart, *Feminine and Opposition Journalism in Old Regime France: Le journal des dames*, p. 11. Gelbart's study demonstrates a surprisingly high degree of tolerance for frondeur and even radical thought in certain aristocratic circles, indeed among royalty. Like the Fronde, this opposition hoped to unite popular and privileged opposition: "The *Journal des dames*, although many times suspended for its insubordination, circulated with the patronage and protection of certain blue bloods: . . . It was even presented at court to Louis XV in 1765, and although it was silenced and remained in eclipse throughout Chancellor Maupeou's royalist coup, during its last four years its title page boasted that Queen Marie Antoinette herself had accepted its dedication"; ibid., p. 12. Despite its conventional beginnings, the *Journal des dames* soon departed from the conservative format and content of other publications edited by men for a female readership.

51. Nina Rattner Gelbart, "The *Journal des dames* and Its Female Editors: Politics, Censorship, and Feminism in the Old Regime Press," in *Press and Politics in Pre-Revolutionary France*, ed. Censer and Popkin, pp. 25–27.

52. Ibid., pp. 73–74.

53. Ibid., p. 41.

54. Ibid., pp. 71, 59, 72. Gelbart remarks that Mme de Montanclos appealed to Marie Antoinette, after her accession to queen in 1774, to help women to reclaim their dignity: "The paper attacked court frivolity, moral dissipation, and *le luxe* more forcefully than ever. That the new queen was neither virtuous nor maternal did not stop the baronne de Prinzen [Montanclos] from calling on her

to 'reverse the goût de siècle' by making feminine modesty, seriousness, and fidelity fashionable"; ibid., p. 58–59. Other authors also testify to Rousseau's influence among women in these years. Barbara Brookes reports that, in his remarks of 1787 in defense of women's rights, Condorcet seemed painfully aware that he might find little sympathy among his women readers. He even insisted, therefore, that he was speaking of women's equality, and not of their empire — and even acknowledged that some could suspect him of a secret desire to diminish it. Because he recognized women's support for the ideas of Rousseau, Condorcet doubted they would declare in his favor. But he claimed that it is better to speak the truth, even if it exposes one to ridicule; see Barbara Brookes, "The Feminism of Condorcet and Sophie de Grouchy," p. 330.

55. Gelbart, *Feminine and Opposition Journalism*, p. 229.

56. Eisenstein, *The Printing Press*, pp. 133–134.

57. Duby and Mandrou, *A History of French Civilization*, p. 327.

58. See Philippe Ariès's thesis on the discovery of childhood, *Century of Childhood*.

59. See Habermas, *L'espace public*, pp. 54–61; Eagleton, *The Rape of Clarissa: Writing, Sexuality and Class Struggle in Samuel Richardson*.

60. Altman adds: "Publicly recognized epistolarians whose letter books are held up as models for prose style are all members of the same sex, share similar political persuasions and social codes, and are situated in clear positions of subordination to ruling class patrons"; Altman, "The Letter Book," p. 45.

61. Ibid., p. 56.

62. Voltaire and Rousseau, literary legends in their own time, were the objects of letters books — either purloined or wholly fabricated — that purported to document their lives through authentic letters. Altman, like Showalter, speaks of a new functional split occurring between author and editor, and of an incipient professionalization of the work of editorship; Altman, "The Letter Book," pp. 59–60. See also Roland Mortier, *L'originalité. Une nouvelle catégorie esthétique au siècle des lumières* (Geneva: Droz, 1982).

63. Brooks, *The Novel of Worldliness*, p. 148.

64. Jean-Jacques Rousseau, *The Confessions of Jean-Jacques Rousseau*, p. 17; "Les confessions," in *Oeuvres complètes*, vol. 1, ed. Bernard Gagnebin and Marcel Raymond, p. 5.

65. For this argument, see Darnton's very valuable "Readers Respond to Rousseau," in *The Great Cat Massacre and Other Episodes in French Cultural History*.

66. Ibid., p. 231. In his *Confessions*, Rousseau noted with great satisfaction that his novel *La nouvelle Héloïse*, which intentionally rejected le monde, nevertheless had overwhelmed the ladies of society. In the self-congratulatory language of masculine self-restraint, seduction, and conquest, he writes, "opinions differed among men of letters, but in the world [le monde] the verdict was unanimous, and the women especially were wild about the book and its author. Such was their infatuation indeed that there were few of them, even of the highest rank, whose conquest I could not have made if I had attempted it"; Rousseau, *Confessions*, p. 504; *Oeuvres complètes*, vol. 1, p. 545.

67. Darnton, "Readers Respond," p. 251.

## Chapter 3

1. Josette Féral, "The Powers of Difference," in *The Future of Difference*, ed. Hester Eisenstein and Alice Jardine, p. 88.

2. In deriving the nature of a theoretical public, I have benefited from Huet's discussion of Sébastian Mercier's theory of the spectator and Rousseau's political reason; see Huet, *Rehearsing the Revolution*.

3. Joel Schwartz argues forcefully that Rousseau envisions a political role for women in the public sphere, but one that is covert rather than open, secret rather than formal. While I also argue that Rousseau offers women an important place in the new society, I differ with Schwartz on the meaning of women's exclusion from public life. I do not concur with his high estimation for Rousseau's solution to the exigencies of modern existence, nor do I regard covert influence as real power. My own point of departure is women's dismissal from political life. Schwartz has, however, advanced the discussion by situating sexual politics as a central, not a peripheral, element of Rousseau's theory. His analysis is also unusual in giving Rousseau's republicanism pride of place. I regard this as a refreshing alternative to those commentaries that discuss Rousseau almost entirely from the standpoint of liberal theory. But Schwartz fails to provide his readers with an adequate appreciation of the historical context in which Rousseau writes, particularly vis-à-vis the nuanced and influential (not stereotyped) role of women in the absolutist and bourgeois public spheres. Moreover, his extremely comprehensive and subtle interpretation reads as a modern-day defense of Rousseau's central thesis on behalf of a sexual division of labor, and for the interdependence of the sexes pred-

icated on different—and, from a feminist point of view, necessarily unequal—sexual roles. He presents Rousseau as a theorist of equality with difference, a patriarchal opponent of women and a forerunner of feminism. These are complicated claims that cannot be fully addressed here, yet I wonder whether Schwartz's position can be sustained once feminism is treated as itself a complex set of arguments including but not reducible to radical feminism; and I doubt that early modern women were as much victims of their nature or biology as Schwartz would have us believe. See Joel Schwartz, *The Sexual Politics of Jean-Jacques Rousseau*.

4. See Chapters 2, 4, and 6, where I mention Rousseau's enormous impact on pre- and post-revolutionary thought. See also David Williams, "The Fate of French Feminism: Boudier de Villemert's *Ami des femmes*," *Eighteenth-Century Studies* 14:1 (Fall 1980); Jean H. Bloch, "Women and the Reform of the Nation," in *Women and Society in Eighteenth-Century France*, ed. Eva Jacobs et al.; Ruth Graham, "Rousseau's Sexism Revolutionized," in *Woman in the 18th Century and Other Essays*, ed. Paul Fritz and Richard Morton.

5. In other words, I do not think that the central contradiction in Rousseau's theory can be dismissed as mere misogyny (Eva Figes) nor reduced to a functionalist strain in his thinking which runs throughout the Western tradition of political thought (Susan Moller Okin). I also do not share Jean Bethke Elshtain's optimism that feminists may deploy Rousseau's politics without its more disagreeable perspectives on women, for it is precisely that version of politics which is thoroughly inflected with a gender politics. See Eva Figes, *Patriarchal Attitudes*; Okin, *Women in Western Political Thought*; Elshtain, *Public Man, Private Woman*; Schwartz, *The Sexual Politics of Jean-Jacques Rousseau*.

6. On Rousseau's profound influence on the oppositional and revolutionary publics of the late eighteenth century, see James Miller, *Rousseau: Dreamer of Democracy*; Carol Blum, *Rousseau and the Republic of Virtue: The Language of Politics in the French Revolution*.

7. Jean-Jacques Rousseau, *First and Second Discourses*, p. 89; idem, "Discours sur l'origine et les fondemens de l'inégalité parmi les hommes," in *Oeuvres complètes*, vol. 3, p. 119.

8. Rousseau, *Second Discourse*, p. 89, emphasis added; *Oeuvres complètes*, vol. 3, pp. 119–120.

9. Similarly, in *Emile*, Rousseau insists that conduct be shaped through love; Jean-Jacques Rousseau, *Emile; or On Education*, p. 51; idem, "Emile ou de l'éducation," in *Oeuvres complètes*, vol. 4, p. 249.

10. Rousseau, *Emile*, p. 365; *Oeuvres complètes*, vol. 4, pp. 702–703.

11. Rousseau, *Second Discourse*, p. 90; *Oeuvres complètes*, vol. 3, p. 120.

12. Ibid., p. 111; *Oeuvres complètes*, vol. 3, p. 139.

13. Rousseau, *Emile*, p. 474; *Oeuvres complètes*, vol. 4, p. 859.

14. Saint-Preux, too, undertakes journeys prior to his recall to Clarens by Julie in *La nouvelle Héloïse*. And Rousseau begins his own voyage of self-discovery with this (possibly disingenous) note of regret at leaving the life of a respectable Genevan artisan behind him: "I should have been a good Christian, a good citizen, a good father of a family, a good friend, a good workman, a good man in every way. I should have been happy in my condition, and should perhaps have been respected. Then, after a life—simple and obscure, but also mild and uneventful—I should have died peacefully in the bosom of my family. Soon, no doubt, I should have been forgotten, but at least I should have been mourned for as long as I was remembered." *The Confessions of Jean-Jacques Rousseau*, p. 51; idem, "Les confessions," in *Oeuvres complètes*, vol. 1, pp. 43–44.

15. Rousseau, *Emile*, p. 59; *Oeuvres complètes*, vol. 4, p. 277. On Rousseau's contradictory relationship to Geneva, see Miller, *Rousseau: Dreamer of Democracy*. In reality, of course, Rousseau owed much not only to the cities that received him and his works with interest, but also to the patronage of several aristocratic women. He was, moreover, no stranger to salon life, as a reading of his autobiographical accounts reveals.

16. Fried, *Absorption and Theatricality*, p. 167. See also translator's note to *Letter* on the meaning of spectacle; Jean-Jacques Rousseau, *Politics and the Arts: Letter to M. d'Alembert on the Theatre*; idem, "Lettre à d'Alembert sur les spectacles," in *Contrat social, ou Principes du droit politique*.

17. Fried, *Absorption and Theatricality*, p. 168.

18. Rousseau, *Letter*, pp. 82–83; "Lettre," p. 189.

19. These phrases for women and their demands appear throughout Rousseau's writings. For examples, see *Emile*, p. 46; *Oeuvres complètes*, vol. 4, p. 258.

20. Rousseau, *Letter*, p. 64; "Lettre," p, 174.

21. Rousseau, *Emile*, p. 376; *Oeuvres complètes*, vol. 4, p. 718.

22. Rousseau, *Letter*, p. 49; "Lettre," p. 161.

23. Rousseau, *Emile*, p. 387; *Oeuvres complètes*, vol. 4, p. 738.

24. Ibid., p. 388; *Oeuvres complètes*, vol. 4, p. 739. Elsewhere in the book, Rousseau devotes pages to a discussion of contemporary

childrearing practices. He strongly condemns the popular habits of wetnursing and swaddling babies.

25. Ibid., p. 40; *Oeuvres complètes*, vol. 4, p. 250.

26. In the *Second Discourse*, Rousseau observes the evils of civilization: "To be and to seem became two altogether different things; and from this distinction came conspicuous ostentation, deceptive cunning, and all the vices that follow from them. . . . Having formerly been free and independent, behold man due to a multitude of new needs, subjected so to speak to all of nature and especially to his fellowmen, whose slave he becomes in a sense even in becoming their master," pp. 155–156; *Oeuvres complètes*, vol. 3, pp. 174–175.

27. Rousseau, *Letter*, p. 79; "Lettre," p. 186.

28. Ibid., pp. 80–81; "Lettre," p. 187. Rousseau's portrait of the orator necessarily effaces all the rules of rhetorical argument the orator had to obey. In any event, his remarks on oratory are best seen in the context of the contrast between classicism and preciosity I developed in Chapters 1 and 2. Also, much more could be said about the reversal Rousseau observes between the proper roles of actor and spectator, which is consistent with his theme of the deplorable condition of modern man, who lives only in the reputation of others. For a discussion of Rousseau's views on theater, see David Marshall, "Rousseau and the State of Theater," *Representations* 13 (Winter 1986).

29. Rousseau, *Letter*, p. 90; "Lettre," p. 195.

30. Ibid., p. 91; "Lettre," p. 196.

31. Ibid., p. 87; "Lettre," p. 193.

32. Ibid., p. 88, emphasis added; "Lettre," p. 194.

33. Ibid., p. 87; "Lettre," pp. 192–193. See also Jean Starobinski, *Jean-Jacques Rousseau: La transparence et l'obstacle, suivi de sept essais sur Rousseau*.

34. Rousseau, *Letter*, p. 84; "Lettre," p. 190.

35. See Rousseau, *Second Discourse*, p. 134; *Oeuvres complètes*, vol. 3, pp. 157–158.

36. Yet Rousseau also believes that men are subject to diminished and sporadic desire rather than bestial overexcitement. Schwartz points out how complicated in actuality is Rousseau's view of male and female sexuality. He locates two competing versions. In the *Second Discourse*, for example, Rousseau holds to a kind of instinctual, physical mutuality of desire; the natural female is not more modest than the male, and human sexual behavior is not very different from that of the animals. In *Emile* and the *Letter*, however, Schwartz finds Rousseau defending the

natural status of modesty and consequently arguing for the sexual differentiation of males and females. Curiously, however, Rousseau "does not say that sexual acts are successful because men are stronger than women. He says instead that they are successful only *if* men are stronger than women. Men are potentially stronger than women; the problem is to actualize the potential. For woman's desire is permanent, whereas man's desire is temporary. Successful sexual acts require the arousal of the male, which is to say that unsuccessful sexual acts result from his failure to be aroused." In other words, "the guarantee of sexual success (that is, the sexual act's attainment of its natural end) is, then, male arousal. The sexual act is a social relationship, requiring the cooperation of two individuals. Of the two individuals, the female's performance is guaranteed, but not the male's. . . . Paradoxically, the weakness of male desire gives the male priority in the relationship; because he is weak, the female must please him." The male is physically stronger, but weaker in his desires. "He desires to be desired more than he truly desires." And, "because his desire is weaker, the male must seem to be the stronger. Female modesty, the resistance to male sexual advances which is then overcome, gives the male the desired appearance of strength"; Schwartz, *The Sexual Politics of Jean-Jacques Rousseau*, pp. 34–35. Given all this, however, I am arguing that Rousseau walks a thin line: to inflame male desire is to run the risk of overexcitement, of pain and conflict, not pleasure and delight, and indeed of pure hedonism rather than family life (with its reproductive requirements). It is for this reason that Rousseau can worry simultaneously about excessive sexuality and diminished desire. He also attempts to overcome the possibility of women's sexual rule over men (due to their advantage in the field of desire) and proposes a consensual model of mutual sexual relations. He presents the sexual relationship as a political relationship in which men and women alternate in ruling and being ruled. But in his speculations on love he never truly retreats from the masculine standpoint. Given the impasse posited for male desire and Rousseau's belief that men will always require a measure of resistance in order to procreate (properly), I am arguing that for Rousseau violence and sexual domination must necessarily accompany civilized love, and that the implications are far from equal (as he would want us to believe).

37. Author's note, *Letter*, p. 85; "Lettre," p. 191.

38. Rousseau, *Emile*, p. 359; *Oeuvres complètes*, vol. 4, p. 695.

39. Fried, *Absorption and Theatricality*, pp. 168–169.

40. Rousseau, *Emile*, p. 358; *Oeuvres complètes*, vol. 4, pp. 693–694.

41. Ibid., p. 359; *Oeuvres complètes*, vol. 4, p. 695.

42. Ibid., p. 360; *Oeuvres complètes*, vol. 4, p. 695 .

43. Ibid., p. 404; *Oeuvres complètes*, vol. 4, p. 761.

44. Ibid., pp. 404–405; *Oeuvres complètes*, vol. 4, p. 762.

45. Ibid., p. 405; *Oeuvres complètes*, vol. 4, pp. 762–763.

46. Ibid., p. 370; *Oeuvres complètes*, vol. 4, p. 710.

47. Rousseau, *Confessions*, p. 48; *Oeuvres complètes*, vol. 1, p. 41.

48. Ibid.

49. Rousseau, *Emile*, p. 401; emphasis added; *Oeuvres complètes*, vol. 4, p. 757. He goes on to say that "birth, wealth, rank, and opinion will in no ways enter in our decision," emphasizing that character, compatibility, and suitability are the most decisive factors.

50. Ibid., pp. 413–414; *Oeuvres complètes*, vol. 4, p. 775. On the guest, see Tony Tanner, *Adultery in the Novel: Contract and Transgression*, pp. 24–52.

51. Rousseau, *Emile*, p. 415; *Oeuvres complètes*, vol. 4, p. 777.

52. Ibid., p. 416; *Oeuvres complètes*, vol. 4, p. 778.

53. Ibid; *Oeuvres complètes*, vol. 4, p. 777.

54. Fried, *Absorption and Theatricality*, pp. 168.

55. Catherine Bodard Silver, "Salon, Foyer, Bureau: Women and the Professions in France," *American Journal of Sociology* 78:4 (1972–73), p. 844.

56. Things work out relatively well for Sophie, who is never really forced to confront seriously her own resistance to her assigned position in the patriarchal structure. Julie, Rousseau's other heroine, does not fare so well. In the end, submission to the father's word costs Julie her life, thus, according to Tony Tanner, revealing that the secret of marriage is its adulterous, chaotic core. What Rousseau offers Julie is a hand in structuring her own fate — that is, she learns to will her own domination and to abandon freedom; domestic harmony is her reward. For a provocative discussion of *La nouvelle Héloïse*, see Tanner, *Adultery in the Novel*. See also Susan Moller Okin's fine account of the fate of Rousseau's romantic heroines, and of the unpublished sequel to Emile, *Les solitaires*, wherein "Paris, the cesspit of civilization, proves their [Sophie and Emile's] downfall"; *Women in Western Political Thought*, p. 170, pp. 167–193.

57. See Chapter 1, note 37.

58. Rousseau, *Letter*, pp. 87–88; "Lettre," pp. 193–194.

59. Rousseau, *Emile*, p. 46; *Oeuvres complètes*, vol. 4, p. 258.

60. Ibid., p. 48; *Oeuvres complètes*, vol. 4, p. 261.

61. Rousseau, *Letter*, p. 85. Elsewhere, Rousseau defends himself against the charge that the family is merely an invention of the social laws, a ruse to protect (male) property and the institution of patriarchy; ibid., p. 83; "Lettre," pp. 189, 191.

62. See Rousseau, *Emile*, p. 361; *Oeuvres complètes*, vol. 4, pp. 697–698.

63. Rousseau, *Letter*, p. 93; "Lettre," p. 198. See also Fried, *Absorption and Theatricality*.

64. Rousseau, *Letter*, p. 99; "Lettre," p. 203.

65. Ibid., p. 63; "Lettre," p. 173.

66. Rousseau, *Emile*, pp. 367, 403; *Oeuvres complètes*, vol. 4, pp. 706, 758.

67. Rousseau, *Letter*, pp. 100–101; "Lettre," p. 204.

68. Ibid., pp. 101–102; "Lettre," p. 205.

69. Ibid., p. 105; "Lettre," p. 208.

70. Author's note, *Letter*, p. 103; "Lettre," p. 206.

71. Ibid., p. 109; "Lettre," p. 211.

72. Ibid., pp. 104–105; emphasis added; "Lettre," p. 207. Rousseau makes good use of the opposition between classicism and preciosity.

73. Ibid., p. 106; "Lettre," p. 209.


*Chapter 4*

1. At least not in its pristine, absolutist form. The restored monarchy of the nineteenth century was a constitutional monarchy.

2. As an institution, the salon outlasted the Revolution, but it never again achieved the cultural prominence it enjoyed during the Old Regime.

3. The long-standing controversy over whether the French Revolution deserves to be called a "bourgeois" revolution has focused on the question of the Revolution's social origins. The revisionist charge that the revolutionaries were not uniformly bourgeois in origin has been widely accepted. On the other hand, Marxists, neo-Marxists, and non-Marxist scholars continue to agree on the bourgeois outcomes of the Revolution. I follow the latter line of argumentation, especially since my concern is with the political and cultural consequences of the Revolution, and less so with its economic origins. Also, when cultural questions are highlighted, there do not seem to be such strong oppositions between, say, Marx's interpretation of the Revolution and that of Furet, who is usually

taken to be an antagonist of the reigning Marxist formulations of the Revolution. Furet even returns to the writings of the young Marx to buttress his rejection of the Marxist orthodoxies; see Furet, *Interpreting the Revolution*. For a survey of the debate, see Doyle, *Origins of the French Revolution*.

4. See Hunt, *Politics, Culture, and Class*.

5. Ibid., p. 32.

6. Jules Michelet, *History of the French Revolution*, ed. Gordon Wright, p. 201; idem, *Histoire de la Révolution française*, vol. 1, p. 233. Along with society women, market women, and prostitutes, the neighborhoods and sites of the Palais Royal and the Temple were frequented by or even became the domiciles of certain women journalists during the eighteenth century; see Nina Rattner Gelbart, "The *Journal des dames*," pp. 24–75.

7. Cahiers de doléances were an old institution which otherwise would not have been authorized by the monarchy. Yet in contrast to past cahiers, authorship was undoubtedly broadened by eighteenth-century changes associated with the development of the bourgeois public sphere. The bourgeoisie were simply more numerous than the medieval burghers, who had represented a town as a feudal lord would represent the interests of an estate.

8. See Furet, *Interpreting the Revolution*, pp. 40–43; Michel Vovelle, *The Fall of the French Monarchy, 1787–1792*, pp. 93–96.

9. According to Winifred Stephens, ever since the institution of the Estates General by Philippe le Bel, in 1302, certain women possessed the right of representation based on a property qualification and had from time to time made use of it. The royal decree which summoned the States General, after a lapse of one hundred and seventy-five years, contained a clause that called upon all women, lay or religious who held seignorial fiefs, to appoint proxies, chosen from the nobility in the case of lay-women, from the clergy in the case of nuns, to represent them in the electoral colleges. Consequently, certain members of the National Assembly owed their election partly to women's votes; Winifred Stephens (Whale), *Women of the French Revolution*, pp. 238–239.

10. Petitions, usually humble petitions, are requests and thus suggest a relationship of deference. Cahiers, in contrast, suggest a common participation, part of a process of forming something like a general will. Insofar as women's petitions are called cahiers (as they were during the Revolution), this may suggest a never-realized potential for women to have been included in the "official" political process.

11. On the shift from a moral economy to a political economy,

and women's shifting position, see E. P. Thompson, "The Moral Economy of the English Crowd in the Eighteenth Century," *Past and Present* 50 (1971); Louise A. Tilly, "The Food Riot as a Form of Political Conflict in France," *Journal of Interdisciplinary History* 2 (1971); Charles Tilly, "Food Supply and Public Order in Modern Europe," in *The Formation of National States in Western Europe,* ed. Charles Tilly; Olwen Hufton, *The Poor of Eighteenth Century France, 1750–1789;* idem, "Women and the Family Economy in Eighteenth Century France," *French Historical Studies* 9 (Spring 1975); George Rudé, *The Crowd in the French Revolution.*

12. "The Specific Grievances of the Merchant Flower Sellers of the City and Faubourgs of Paris," "Petition of Women of the Third Estate to the King," and "The Fishwives of Paris Pay Homage to the Third Estate," in *Women in Revolutionary Paris, 1789–1795, Selected Documents,* trans. and ed. Darline Gay Levy, Harriet Branson Applewhite, and Mary Durham Johnson, pp. 22–26, 18–21, 27–28. For a wider selection, see: *Les femmes dans la Révolution française* (Paris: EDHIS, 1982); and Paule-Marie Duhet, ed., *Cahiers de doléances des femmes en 1789 et autres textes* (Paris: des femmes, 1981), which contains "Petition des femmes du Tiers-Etat au Roi" and "Cahier de doléances des Bouquetières" discussed here, pp. 25–29, 31–37.

13. Levy, Applewhite, and Johnson, eds., *Women in Revolutionary Paris,* pp. 19–20.

14. Ibid., p. 34. See also Rudé, *The Crowd in the French Revolution,* p. 67.

15. Harriet B. Applewhite and Darline Gay Levy, "Reponses to the Political Activism of Women of the People in Revolutionary Paris, 1789–1793," in *Women and the Structure of Society: Selected Research from the Fifth Berkshire Conference on the History of Women,* ed. Barbara J. Harris and JoAnn K. McNamara, p. 220.

16. Siméon-Prosper Hardy, from "Mes loisirs," cited in Levy, Applewhite, and Johnson, eds., *Women in Revolutionary Paris,* p. 35.

17. The implication of their rhetoric seems to be that the king, like a common baker, must be subject to popular surveillance without which he might be capable of a conspiracy against the people.

18. See Jules Michelet, *The Women of the French Revolution,* p. 42.

19. Galina Osipovna Sokolnikova (Serebriakova), *Nine Women Drawn from the Epoch of the French Revolution,* p. 20. Méricourt had already participated in the taking of the Bastille on July 14,

1789, and would later receive a heroine's welcome in Paris at the Jacobin Club after her arrest and release by the Austrians. She was a strong advocate of women's equality who tried unsuccessfully to found a women's society. She belonged to the Société fraternelle and the Amis de la loi and was close to the Girondin politician Brissot.

20. Applewhite and Levy, "Responses to Political Activism," p. 223.

21. Jean-Joseph Mounier, from *Exposé de la conduite de M. Mounier dans l'Assemblée nationale, et des motifs de son retour en Dauphiné*, cited in Applewhite and Levy, "Responses to Political Activisim," p. 221.

22. From *Révolutions de Versailles, dédiées aux dames françoises*, no. 1, cited in Darline Gay Levy and Harrriet Branson Applewhite, "Women of the Popular Classes in Revolutionary Paris, 1789–1795," in *Women, War and Revolution*, ed. Carol R. Berkin and Clara M. Lovett, p. 15.

23. Applewhite and Levy, "Responses to Political Activism," pp. 222–223.

24. Charge given to the Comité des recherches of the Paris municipality, in *Procédure-criminelle, instruite au Châtelet de Paris, sur la dénonciation des faits arriveés à Versailles dans la journée du 6 octobre 1789*, cited in Applewhite and Levy, "Responses to Political Activism," p. 222. The charge of masquerade is especially common in the historiography of the Revolution. The feminist historian Natalie Zemon Davis, for example, explains the Châtelet investigators' charge by way of a long tradition of female dress and titles in riots according to which, merely as a woman acting in a disorderly way, a female persona authorized resistance. Males drew on the sexual power and energy of unruly women and their license to promote fertility, to defend the community's interests and standards, and to tell the truth about unjust rule; Davis, *Society and Culture*, pp. 147–150.

25. Michelet, *Women of the French Revolution*, p. 72.

26. Edmund Burke, *Reflections on the Revolution in France*, in *Reflections on the Revolution in France, Edmund Burke; and The Rights of Man, Thomas Paine*, p. 85. In the following paragraphs, I draw from Ronald Paulson's excellent discussion of the gender implications of Burke's and Wollstonecraft's portrayals of the October Days: *Representations of Revolution, 1789–1820*.

27. Mary Wollstonecraft, *A Vindication of the Rights of Men (1790)*, pp. 67–68.

28. Brookes speculates that the lycée and the Condorcet salon

were important in offering an opportunity for serious study to women who were deprived of such a challenging education; see "The Feminism of Condorcet and Sophie de Grouchy," p. 325. I have chosen to discuss Condorcet's essay of 1790. However, Brookes gives an excellent account of Condorcet's several writings on the woman question within the context of his personal, literary, and political affiliations. She demonstrates that Condorcet's increasingly radical view of liberal democracy was accompanied by the extension of his ideas about the political role of women"; ibid., p. 327.

29. Marie Jean Antoine Nicolas de Caritat, Marquis de Condorcet, "Sur l'admission des femmes au droit de cité" (3 July 1790), *Oeuvres*, vol. 10, pp. 119–130; "On the Admission of Women to the Rights of Citizenship (1790)," in Condorcet, *Selected Writings*, ed. Keith Michael Baker, pp. 97–104.

30. The Society of 1789 was founded early in 1790 by a group of moderates closely associated with Lafayette in attempt to counterbalance the more radical influences developing within the Jacobin Club. Its goal was the restoration of order and the achievement of peaceful constitutional change in accordance with the principles of 1789. As the society lost influence, its more liberal members (including those who, like Condorcet, also belonged to the Cercle Social) drifted away from the remaining more conservative members.

31. See Condorcet, Second Letter, in "Lettres d'un bourgeois de New-haven à un citoyen de Virginie" (1787), *Oeuvres*, vol. 9, pp. 10–56. See note 9 above.

32. Condorcet, "Admission of Women," p. 100; *Oeuvres*, vol. 10, p. 126.

33. Ibid., p. 98; *Oeuvres*, vol. 10, p. 122.

34. According to Levy, Applewhite, and Johnson, France before the Revolution had no national legal system, so that the legal status of women differed from province to province. In general, forms of legal equality originating in the Middle Ages had been abolished or were no longer applied in the eighteenth century. For example, noblewomen had lost seigneurial rights to plead cases or adjudicate disputes within their territories, and Parisian working women had lost most of their exclusively female guilds that protected their economic rights; *Women in Revolutionary Paris*, p. 6.

35. Condorcet, "Admission of Women," p. 103; *Oeuvres*, vol. 10, p. 130.

36. Mary Wollstonecraft, too, ridicules the exclusion of women from political representation. She allows "that women ought to

have representatives, instead of being arbitrarily governed without having any direct share allowed them in the deliberations of government," and she satirizes women's misfortunes: "But, as the whole system of representation is now, in this country, only a convenient handle for despotism, they need not complain, for they are as well represented as a numerous class of hard working mechanics, who pay for the support of royalty when they can scarcely stop their children's mouths with bread"; Mary Wollstonecraft, *A Vindication of the Rights of Woman: An Authoritative Text, Backgrounds, Criticisms,* ed. Carol H. Poston, p. 147.

37. Condorcet, "Admission of Women," p. 101; *Oeuvres,* vol. 10, p. 128.

38. Condorcet's views on the important subject of property were in transition. Initially a defender of property requirements, he moved toward a more democratic position, opposing these provisions in the Constitution of 1791. Nevertheless, it has proven difficult to date the point at which he abandoned the idea of propertied suffrage. See the fine discussion of this topic in Brookes, "The Feminism of Condorcet and Sophie de Grouchy," p. 333.

39. Condorcet, "Admission of Women," pp. 99–100; *Oeuvres,* vol. 10, p. 125.

40. Ibid., p. 100; *Oeuvres,* vol. 10, p. 125.

41. Ibid.; *Oeuvres,* vol. 10, p. 126.

42. Ibid., p. 101; *Oeuvres,* vol. 10, p. 127.

43. Ibid., p. 102; *Oeuvres,* vol. 10, pp. 128–129.

44. In Paris since 1774, Palm was connected with the circle of Mme de Condorcet and appeared as an orator on behalf of women's causes in revolutionary club circles in 1790. In 1791 she made a direct appeal to the revolutionary legislators on behalf of women's rights. Those arrested also included the wife of a butcher who was active in section politics, the wife of a wine merchant, and the owner of Hébert's print works. A cook arrested for insulting a national guardsman who had participated in the events at the Champ de Mars described herself as one of the *bons patriotes.* She had frequented the Palais Royal and the Tuileries and attended the Cordeliers Club, although she was not a member; see Levy and Applewhite, "Women of the Popular Classes," pp. 17–18; idem, "A Cook Testifies on Her Participation at the Champ de Mars," in *Women in Revolutionary Paris,* pp. 81–82.

45. See Evelyne Sullerot, *Histoire de la presse féminine, des origines à 1848.*

46. In the following account, I draw on Gary Kates' excellent overview of the Cercle Social. Its origins were as a small, secret

society of Parisian politicians advocating representative democracy during the Paris municipal revolution of 1789–90. The Confédération des amis de la vérité, founded in 1790, became one of the largest clubs of the Revolution (3,000–6,000 members) and was famous for its radical views on land reform, religion, women's rights, and democracy; the Confédération was suppressed after the massacre at the Champs de Mar. Finally, between the summer of 1791 and the summer of 1793, the publishing company Imprimerie du Cercle Social was created. Kates notes that "the *Cercle Social* became the Girondins' most enduring attempt to develop a discourse that claimed to speak for the nation"; Gary Kates, *The Cercle Social, the Girondins, and the French Revolution*, p. 10. For a discussion of feminism, see ibid., pp. 117–127.

47. Gita May, *Madame Roland and the Age of Revolution*, pp. 231, 251. Mme Roland is especially intriguing as a figure who straddles the tensions between liberal rights and republican notions of womanhood, and between standards of femininity in the absolutist and bourgeois pubic spheres. She fashioned a republican salon where, as Gita May recounts, she "did not dare to display the social graces and amenities so highly prized under the Old Régime .... Manon's was a decidedly political salon with a spartan flavor. She officiated with tact and, what was even more appreciated, in silence. Unlike Mme de Staël, she did not crave to be the center of attraction at all times. A woman's place, she continued to hold, was definitely in the background. In her *Memoirs* she tells us she never allowed herself to utter a word until the meetings were over. Deliberately seating herself outside the circle of men, she quietly did needlework or wrote letters while the debates went on.... It goes without saying, however, that such an attempt at self-effacement did not prevent her from exercising a certain influence on the men who regularly met in her salon"; ibid., pp. 184–185.

48. From Etta Palm d'Aelders, *Appel aux françoises sur la régénération des moeurs et la nécessité de l'influence des femmes dans un gouvernement libre*, cited and discussed by Kates, *The Cercle Social*, p. 123.

49. Discussed by Kates, *The Cercle Social*, p. 124. See also Etta Palm d'Aelders, *Prospectus pour le Cercle patriotique des amies de la vérité*.

50. Levy, Applewhite, and Johnson, eds., "Etta Palm d'Aelders Proposes a Network of Women's Clubs to Administer Welfare Programs in Paris and Throughout France," in *Women in Revolutionary Paris*, pp. 68–69.

51. Ibid., p. 69.

52. Ibid., pp. 70–71.

53. Ibid., "A Call for an End to Sexual Discrimination," p. 76; Palm, *Appel*, pp. 37–40.

54. Cited in Albert Soboul, *The French Revolution, 1787–1799: From the Storming of the Bastille to Napoleon*, p. 183.

55. Jane Abray, "Feminism in the French Revolution," *American Historical Review* 80:1 (February 1975), p. 54.

56. See James F. Traer, *Marriage and the Family in Eighteenth-Century France.*

57. For an excellent study of this important topic, which regrettably does not address the topic of gender, see Blum, *Rousseau and the Republic of Virtue.*

58. Olympe de Gouges, "The Declaration of the Rights of Woman," in *Women in Revolutionary Paris*, p. 96; idem, *Déclaration des droits de la femme à la reine*, pp. 20–22.

59. See Stephens, *Women of the French Revolution*, p. 247. Stephens mentions that Gouges had suffered the refusal of her plays by the Comédie Française and other Paris theaters, and also in London where she brought one of her productions, *L'esclavage des nègres*. Further, Gelbart reports that Mme de Montanclos came to know Olympe de Gouges, who was suffering indignities at the hands of the comédiens and even the comédiennes. But, while Gouges berated the female actors who she felt should demonstrate solidarity with female playwrights, Mme de Montanclos attacked the men in power for their illegal procedures. The two women shared another important connection, the friendship of Louis-Sébastian Mercier. Mercier helped Gouges with her numerous political pamphlets, and especially with her plays, one of which was called *Les comédiens démasqués*. He sympathized with female playwrights and journalists and he wrote with great sensitivity about the threats posed to men by women with literary or political ambitions. Gelbart, *Feminine and Opposition Journalism*, pp. 204, 213, and see chap. 6.

60. This gesture did not precipitate her arrest, although she was charged at her trial with being a royalist and harboring federalist sympathies; see "The Trial of a Feminist Revolutionary," in *Women in Revolutionary Paris*, pp. 254–259.

61. Gouges, "Declaration," pp. 87–88, 89; *Déclaration*, pp. 1–4, 6–7.

62. Wollstonecraft, *A Vindication*, p. 53.

63. Gouges, "Declaration," p. 91; *Déclaration*, p. 9.

64. Ibid., p. 96; *Déclaration*, pp. 21–22.

65. Wollstonecraft, *A Vindication*, p. 5. Wollstonecraft's work

appeared in London in 1792. It was so provocative and popular that a second edition appeared in the same year, and Paris, Dublin, and American editions quickly followed. Thus her work was known in France, where she resided between December 1792 and 1795.

66. Ibid., p. 5.

67. Theodor Gottlieb von Hippel, *On Improving the Status of Women*, pp. 120, 121. On controversies regarding oath taking, see Abray, "Feminism in the French Revolution," p. 55.

68. Hippel, *Improving*, p. 122. Wollstonecraft despairs of there being only menial occupations open to women, and of the poor treatment educated women receive when forced to take employment as governesses; *A Vindication*, p. 148.

69. Hippel, *Improving*, p. 132.

70. Ibid. Musing on the question of woman's inclusion in the political community as well as her maternal responsibilities, Hippel also proposed the reform of childrearing, so that men might share this responsibility and so that women would not be precluded from playing a larger social role. He asked: "And is the mother to deny herself the privilege of becoming acquainted with . . . [larger societal] circles? Is she to raise her children for society without ever learning herself what society is?" ibid., p. 172.

71. Wollstonecraft, *A Vindication*, p. 4.

72. Ibid., pp. 7, 5–6.

73. Ibid., p. 6.

74. Ibid., pp. 4, 8.

75. Ibid., p. 137.

76. Ibid., pp. 24, 17.

77. Ibid., p. 4.

78. Ibid., p. 29.

79. Ibid., p. 68.

80. Ibid., p. 61.

81. Ibid., pp. 21, 45.

82. Mary Poovey, *The Proper Lady and the Woman Writer: Ideology as Style in the Works of Mary Wollstonecraft, Mary Shelley, and Jane Austen*, p. 79.

83. Wollstonecraft, *A Vindication*, p. 26.

84. Ibid., p. 141.

85. Ibid., p. 62; see also Poovey, *The Proper Lady*, p. 27.

86. On some occasions Wollstonecraft speaks self-consciously as a woman on behalf of her sex, but more often she adopts a neutral voice, an implicit asexual ideal, as in the opening dedication: "I call with the firm tone of humanity; for my arguments, Sir, are dictated by a disinterested spirit—I plead for my sex—not for my

self." Wollstonecraft praises Catherine Macaulay not merely for her intellectual achievements but for her (neutral) strong and clear style of writing, where "no sex appears." Wollstonecraft, *A Vindication*, p. 3, p. 105.

87. Poovey, *The Proper Lady*, p. 80.

88. Cora Kaplan, "Wild Nights: Pleasure/Sexuality/Feminism," in *Formations of Pleasure*.

89. Wollstonecraft, *A Vindication*, p. 10.

90. She endorses Talleyrand's scheme for free public education, insisting that education be mixed and open to all classes. All should dress alike and be submitted to the same discipline, until the age (after nine years) when girls and boys intended for domestic employments or mechanical trades are to be removed for such instruction in the afternoon sessions; see Wollstonecraft, *A Vindication*, p. 168.

91. Ibid., pp. 168–169.

92. This despite her personal experiences of opening a girls' school, caring for a sister and a female friend, and serving as a governess. On Wollstonecraft's life, see Claire Tomalin, *The Life and Death of Mary Wollstonecraft*; and Margaret George, *One Woman's "Situation": A Study of Mary Wollstonecraft*.

93. Wollstonecraft, *A Vindication*, pp. 127, 164.

94. Hippel, *Improving*, pp. 129, 139.

95. Wollstonecraft, *A Vindication*, p. 167.

96. Ibid., p. 142.

97. See Tanner, *Adultery in the Novel*.

98. Wollstonecraft, *A Vindication*, pp. 194, 186.

99. In Chapter 6, I discuss Auguste Comte's version of the denial of political freedom to women. Comte, however, was not concerned with political representation in the same way as nineteenth-century liberals who argued that women could be represented adequately through a household suffrage. This latter method entailed that the (propertied) male take account of the interests of other family members and then cast a ballot on behalf of marital rather than (his) individual will.

100. Mary Durham Johnson, "Old Wine in New Bottles: The Institutional Changes for Women of the People during the French Revolution," in *Women, War and Revolution*, ed. Carol R. Berkin and Clara M. Lovett, pp. 121–122; Corrado, "Revolution and Retreat, " in ibid., p. 218.

101. The Constitution of 1793, which also incorporated many of the demands of the popular movement, was submitted for popular ratification and approved by an overwhelming margin. How-

ever, its implementation was first postponed until peace had been restored and then suspended entirely during the period of the Jacobin dictatorship. Its guarantee of private property was criticized at the time by the enragés, but this radical document became the symbol of political democracy throughout the first half of the nineteenth century, as during the Revolution itself.

102. Soboul, *The French Revolution*, pp. 315–317.

103. Those few national workshops, for example, that did employ working women paid a lower wage than those employing males for comparable work. And, when education was wrested from exclusive church control, there were too few qualified laywomen to staff the public schools. See Johnson, "Old Wine in New Bottles," in *Women, War and Revolution*, ed. Berkin and Lovett; idem, "Patriotism and Antipatriotism in the Classroom: The Case of Citoyenne Raubour," in *Women in Revolutionary Paris*, ed. Levy, Applewhite, and Johnson.

104. On women soldiers, see Abray, "Feminism in the French Revolution," p. 49; on modernization of the army and elimination of female camp followers, see Johnson, "Old Wine in New Bottles," in *Women, War and Revolution*, ed. Berkin and Lovett, p. 123; on early modern military institutions, see Barton C. Hacker, "Women and Military Institutions in Early Modern Europe: A Reconnaissance," *Signs* 6:4 (1981).

105. Margaret George, "The 'World Historical Defeat' of the *Républicaines-Révolutionnaires*," *Science and Society* 40:4 (Winter 1976–1977), p. 411.

106. The process whereby crowds seized goods and sold them at what they deemed to be the just price. See documents in sect. III of Levy, Applewhite, and Johnson, eds., *Women in Revolutionary Paris*.

107. The Society, closely allied with the enragés or most radical elements among the sans-culottes, is discussed by Scott H. Lyttle, "The Second Sex (September 1793)," *Journal of Modern History* 26 (1955); Olwen Hufton, "Women in Revolution," *Past and Present* 53 (November 1971); R. B. Rose, *The Enragés: Socialists of the French Revolution?*; George, "*Républicaines-Révolutionnaires*"; Abray, "Feminism in the French Revolution"; Levy, Applewhite, and Johnson, eds., *Women in Revolutionary Paris*; Levy and Applewhite, "Women of the Popular Classes."

108. "The Regulations of the Society of Revolutionary Republican Women," in *Women in Revolutionary Paris*, p. 161.

109. Reported in Lyttle, "The Second Sex," p. 21.

110. Cited in Rose, *Enragés*, p. 60. Chabot doubtlessly was

referring to women's participation and leading role in the sugar riots of 1792, and to other instances of *taxation populaire* during subsistence crises.

111. Cited in Abray, "Feminism in the French Revolution," p. 58.

112. Levy and Applewhite, "Women of the Popular Classes," p. 23. See also M. George, *"Républicaines-Révolutionnaires,"* pp. 431–432. Lacombe appeared before the Committee of General Security and was released when a search of her papers found no incriminating evidence.

113. See selections on the cockade law and the disturbances over the cockade and the red bonnet in Levy, Applewhite, and Johnson, eds., *Women in Revolutionary Paris*, pp. 197–212.

114. One member of the Convention hesitated, calling out: "I don't see on what principle we can lean to retire women from peaceful assembly. Unless you are going to deny that women are part of humanity, can you refuse them this right common to all thinking beings? . . . When one Society is found wanting . . . it can be handled by the police." The doubter was brushed aside by Bazire, who said, "Of course we can do this, we are the revolutionary government, we do as we please"; George, *"Républicaines-Révolutionnaires,"* p. 435.

115. Reported in Abray, "Feminism in the French Revolution," p. 58.

116. "The National Convention Outlaws Clubs and Popular Societies of Women," in Levy, Applewhite, and Johnson, eds., *Women in Revolutionary Paris*, pp. 215–216.

117. Ibid., pp. 216–217.

118. Levy and Applewhite, "Women of the Popular Classes in Revolutionary Paris," p. 25.

119. Levy, Applewhite, and Johnson, eds., *Women in Revolutionary Paris*, p. 223.

120. From *Les révolutions de Paris*, cited in George, *"Républicaines-Révolutionnaires,"* p. 436.

121. From *Moniteur*, cited in Abray, "Feminism in the French Revolution," p. 53. See also Levy, Applewhite, and Johnson, eds., *Women in Revolutionary Paris*, p. 272.

122. For a thorough discussion of changes in family law, see James F. Traer, *Marriage and the Family*.

123. Applewhite and Levy, "Responses to Political Activism," p. 220.

124. For an invaluable analysis of the way the political discourse of the 1790s was structured by notions of transparency, publicity, vigilance, and terror, see Hunt, *Politics, Culture, and Class*.

125. Mary Wollstonecraft, *An Historical and Moral View of the Origin and Progress of the French Revolution and the Effect It Has Produced on Europe*, pp. 430, 426.
126. Ibid., pp. 437, 450.
127. Ibid., pp. 457–458.
128. Ibid., pp. 453–454.
129. Ibid., pp. 452–453.


*Chapter 5*

1. The painting was first exhibited in Rome, where it aroused enormous interest and admiration. It has been claimed since by republicans and Marxists as a revolutionary work, and, David — soon to be a Convention member and supporter of Robespierre — has been celebrated as a consistently revolutionary artist. Latter-day critics (especially Brookner, Rosenblum), however, have disputed David's republicanism in the years before 1789. The debate turns on whether oath taking had republican or merely patriotic overtones, and whether the painting's subject matter speaks to public or private notions of nobility, which in turn either affirm or subvert the monarchical and aristocratic structures of Old Regime France. Thomas Crow has argued rather convincingly for the older "political" position, but on wholly different grounds. While sharing his view of David as a painter of the non-courtly, oppositional public sphere, I also see the painting as a powerful representation (and forecast) of woman's place in the new order created by the Revolution. In this respect, the artist's classicizing orientation (whether deemed republican or monarchist) must be understood as having especially consequential implications for women; see Crow, "The Oath of the Horatii"; idem, *Painters and Public Life*; Anita Brookner, *Jacques-Louis David*; Robert Rosenblum, *Transformations in Late Eighteenth Century Art*; Hugh Honour, *Neoclassicism*.
2. Jean Starobinski, *1789: The Emblems of Reason*, p. 102. Starobinski also remarks: "Through an intervention from on high, in the name of a transcendent God, the coronation ceremony invested the monarch with the supernatural insignia of his power. The revolutionary oath created sovereignty, whereas the monarch received it from Heaven"; ibid., p. 101.
3. On the painting's sexual polarity, see Rosenblum, *Transformations*, pp. 70–71; Crow, "The Oath of the Horatii," p. 457; Brookner, *David*, p. 83; Paulson, *Representations of Revolution*,

pp. 29–30; Norman Bryson, *Tradition and Desire: From David to Delacroix.*

4. Crow, "The Oath of the Horatii," pp. 461, 460.

5. Bryson, *Tradition and Desire*, pp. 73–74.

6. For a provocative statement of the relationship between political revolution and male hysteria, see Neil Hertz, "Medusa's Head: Male Hysteria under Political Pressure," *Representations* 4 (Fall 1983).

7. Paulson, *Representations of Revolution*, p. 16. See also James A. Leith, *The Idea of Art as Propaganda in France.*

8. Maurice Agulhon, *Marianne into Battle: Republican Imagery and Symbolism in France, 1789–1880*, pp. 18, 15. Agulhon points to a double allegory: Liberty represents an eternal value, but also the newly constituted regime of the French Republic. He suggests further that Liberty draws on civic imagery of the ancient Republic—thus being a product of elite culture—but also on a set of popular images, part of a repertory of live allegory on which the Revolution also draws; ibid., p. 14. Agulhon traces the different postures Liberty takes, reflecting the active stage of revolt and the more passive stage of reconstructing law within the revolution itself. Finally, he refers to the tension between Liberty—especially, as a tranquil, aloof, and statuesque visage—and Hercules, a more masculine image of the people united with strength. On the latter, see Hunt, *Politics, Culture, and Class*, chap. 3; Eric Hobsbawm, "Man and Woman in Socialist Iconography," *History Workshop* 6 (Autumn 1978); and Maurice Agulhon, "On Political Allegory: A reply to Eric Hobsbawm," *History Workshop* 8 (Autumn 1979).

9. Marina Warner, *Monuments and Maidens: The Allegory of the Female Form*, pp. xix–xx.

10. I have benefited from Nancy Fitch's insights into this feature of the Revolution. The use of theatrical metaphors is especially prominent in the article by Margaret George, "*Républicaines-Révolutionnaires.*"

11. "Citoyenne Lacombe's Report to the Society of Revolutionary Republican Women Concerning What Took Place September 16 at the Jacobin Society," in Levy, Applewhite, and Johnson, eds., *Women in Revolutionary Paris.*

12. "Claire Lacombe's Associates in the *Société des Citoyennes Républicaines Révolutionnaires* Testify against Her," in ibid., p. 181.

13. Hunt, *Politics, Culture, and Class*, pp. 31, 62.

14. Jules Michelet, *Women of the French Revolution*, p. 76. Michelet's formulation is not unlike the romantic, positivist ver-

sion of republicanism associated best with Auguste Comte, to be discussed in Chapter 6.

15. Ibid., p. 80

16. Ibid., p. 82. It is of some consequence that Michelet's remorse here is occasioned by a description of the festivals of 1790, the first to be submitted to a process of regularization, discipline, and systematization. It is significant that men in uniform (soldiers, national guard, and officials) were at the heart of these ceremonies, which occurred simultaneously all over France; Hunt, *Politics, Culture, and Class*, p. 60. See also Ozouf, *La fête révolutionnaire*.

17. Agulhon, *Marianne into Battle*, p. 22.

18. R. B. Rose proposes that Claire Lacombe, the beautiful actress and former leader of the Society of Revolutionary Republican Women, played Liberty at the great festival of November 10, 1793, at Notre Dame, organized by Hébert, Chaumette, and the radical Paris city government just weeks after the banning of the Society by the Convention; Rose, *Enragés*, p. 69 — Rose's source is Baron M. De Villiers, *Histoire des clubs de femmes et des légions d'amazones* (Paris, 1910), pp. 269–270. Other historical accounts fail to confirm Rose's statement, although we do know that after the demise of the Society and the cessation of radical women's activities, Lacombe resumed her former career of acting in Paris and Nantes. The historiographic topics raised here are interesting: How are popular traditions represented within political discourses of one or another persuasion? What is the relationship between real women and the allegory of liberty. Maurice Agulhon comments that there is a well-established tradition of the denigration of popular revolutionary movements, one in which the role of the goddess of Liberty can only be played by a woman of "easy virtue"; Agulhon, "On Political Allegory," p. 169. One wants to question further, then, the implications of Lacombe's alleged performance as Liberty.

19. Hunt, *Politics, Culture, and Class*, p. 64. As Hunt points out, the contradictions of this situation were manifest. The official view discouraged all carnival masks and disguises, regarding them as synonymous with moral and political evil of all kinds. But it was difficult to suppress the popular connection between revolutionary festival and carnival. It is not surprising, then, that Liberty was chosen much like a carnival queen, the most beautiful woman of the village or the neighborhood. "The people had made her their own queen for a day. In this way, the radical didactic impulse to repress all idols was appropriated and inverted by pop-

ular rituals of festivity." On the other hand, Hunt observes the discipline that accompanied the adoption of the new revolutionary symbolism. She explores the contradiction between didacticism and transparency in wholly political terms as an instance of the alienation of political authority from its source in the people; ibid., pp. 67, 65, 59–60. See also Ozouf, *La fête révolutionnaire*.

20. Méricourt, a Girondist supporter, was whipped and seriously injured in the National Assembly by Revolutionary Republican Women. She was committed to a hospital, and she died there years later, it is claimed, of her wounds. Others speculate that she may have been a victim of syphilis.

21. Johnson, "Old Wine in New Bottles," in *Women, War and Revolution*, ed. Berkin and Lovett, p. 111.

22. Hunt, *Politics, Culture, and Class*, pp. 116, 96–97.

23. Ibid., p. 104.

24. Jennifer Harris reports that the bonnet rouge, possibly the most potent symbol of freedom from tyranny to appear in the years 1789–94, was the spontaneous identifying dress of the sans-culottes. It was, however, rarely worn by the revolutionary bourgeoisie, and its adoption as compulsory wear for Jacobins was quite definitely rejected by Robespierre himself, due doubtlessly to its close identification with the most radical sections of the popular movement. The women's insistence on this militant costume should therefore be seen within a highly politicized context. Harris also distinguishes various uniforms: that of patriotic republican girls worn at almost all national festivals after the Fête de la Fédération of July 14, 1790—white dress decorated by the tricolor; the militant woman's uniform (as worn by Théroigne de Méricourt)—blue gown and jacket with military details and a short cap trimmed with tricolor feathers, a *cocarde* similar to those worn by deputies of the Convention, a pistol and sabre; and the dress of the militant sans-culotte favored by the Society of Revolutionary Republican Women. Finally, Harris notes that one item of women's dress of working-class origin did come to be adopted by the revolutionaries—a type of bonnet composed of a cotton headsquare wound once or twice around the head to form a single point on the crown. This latter bonnet is worn by Mme Roland in a terracotta plaque of 1793 by J. Chinard and in oil portraits of her from this period, and female spectators are depicted in this headdress in other images from the period; Jennifer Harris, "The Red Cap of Liberty: A Study of Dress Worn by French Revolutionary Partisans 1789-94," *Eighteenth-Century Studies* 14:3 (Spring 1981).

25. Johnson, "Old Wine in New Bottles," in *Women, War and Revolution*, ed. Berkin and Lovett, p. 121.

26. Hunt, *Politics, Culture, and Class*, p. 113.

27. Huet, *Rehearsing the Revolution*, p. 35, and passim.

28. Ibid., p. 41.

29. *Archives nationales*. F7.4774.9.d. I am grateful to Nancy Fitch for this reference.

*Chapter 6*

1. Claire Goldberg Moses, *French Feminism in the Nineteenth Century*, pp. 14–15.

2. Ibid., p. 18 and passim, for an excellent overview of the provisions of the Civil Code and its impact on women and family life. See also Susan Groag Bell and Karen M. Offen, eds., *Women, the Family, and Freedom: The Debate in Documents*, vol. 1: *1750–1880*, pp. 39–40.

3. Moses, *French Feminism*, p. 6. The wide embrace of codes of domesticity has been discussed by Margaret H. Darrow, "French Noblewomen and the New Domesticity, 1750-1850," *Feminist Studies* 5:1 (Spring, 1979); and Elizabeth Fox-Genovese and Eugene Genovese, *Fruits of Merchant Capital: Slavery and Bourgeois Property in the Rise and Expansion of Capitalism*.

4. See the fine essay on republicanism by Siân Reynolds, "Marianne's Citizens? Women, the Republic and Universal Suffrage in France," in *Women, State and Revolution: Essays on Power and Gender in Europe since 1789*, ed. Siân Reynolds, p. 113.

5. K. Steven Vincent, *Pierre-Joseph Proudhon and the Rise of French Republican Socialism*, pp. 6-7. On French republicanism, see Claude Nicolet, *L'idée républicaine en France: Essai d'histoire critique*; Roger Henry Soltau, *French Political Thought in the 19th Century*.

6. The insightful term "anticipatory conservative" belongs to Gertrud Lenzer; see the introduction to Lenzer, ed., *Auguste Comte and Positivism: The Essential Writings*, p. xxxiii. Lenzer's volume is an annotated compilation of various nineteenth-century English translations of Comte's writings, including the Bridges edition of the Second System (see note 8 below).

7. For two excellent accounts, see Moses, *French Feminism*; and Albistur and Armogathe, *Histoire du féminisme français*, vol. 2.

8. "Influence féminine du positivisme," in Auguste Comte, "Système de politique positive ou traité de sociologie," in *Oeuvres d'Auguste Comte*, vol 7, pp. 204-273. The nineteenth-century (and, to date, only available) English edition translated by Bridges et al.

renders this title "The Influence of Positivism upon Women," thereby altering Comte's emphasis; see Comte, *System of Positive Polity*, vol. 1.

9. Comte, *System of Positive Polity*, p. 55; *Oeuvres*, vol. 7, pp. 68, 70.

10. Albistur and Armogathe, *Histoire du féminisme français*, p. 453. In Paris alone, 171 new newspapers and some 200 to 450 political clubs came into existence between March and mid-June; Moses, *French Feminism*, p. 128. See also Peter H. Amann, *Revolution and Mass Democracy: The Paris Club Movement in 1848*.

11. See Comte, *System of Positive Polity*, pp. 208–219, 257–321; *Oeuvres*, vol. 7, pp. 258–273, 321–399.

12. This story has only begun to be uncovered. For some indications of positivist influence on the international women's movement of the nineteenth century, see Bell and Offen, eds., *Women, the Family, and Freedom*, vol. 1; William Leach, *True Love and Perfect Union: The Feminist Reform of Sex and Society*, offers a suggestive account of the extent to which positivist ideas penetrated the American feminist movement. For Mill's critical appraisal of Comte, see John Stuart Mill, *Auguste Comte and Positivism*. For one nineteenth-century woman's reply to Comte, see Jenny P. d'Hericourt, *A Woman's Philosophy of Woman; or, Woman Affranchised. An Answer to Michelet, Proudhon, Girardin, Legouvé, Comte, and Other Modern Innovators*.

13. Comte, *System of Positive Polity*, pp. 56, 87; *Oeuvres*, vol. 7, pp. 71, 111.

14. Comte qualifies this last remark by noting that women will be part of his coalition only once the work of regeneration is first explained to them; ibid., pp. 164–165; *Oeuvres*, vol. 7, pp. 204–205.

15. Ibid., p. 169; *Oeuvres*, vol. 7, p. 210.

16. Ibid., p. 198; *Oeuvres*, vol. 7, p. 247.

17. This, it should be said, is the province of material force, numbers, and wealth. Thus to capital is reserved the administration of power; ibid., p. 171; *Oeuvres*, vol. 7, pp. 212–213.

18. Leszek Kolakowski discusses the role assigned womanhood in the new faith in *The Alienation of Reason: A History of Positivist Thought*, pp. 62–63.

19. Comte, *System of Positive Polity*, p. 189; *Oeuvres*, vol. 7, p. 236.

20. Ibid., p. 170; *Oeuvres*, vol. 7, p. 211.

21. Ibid., pp. 198–199; *Oeuvres*, vol. 7, p. 247.

22. Ibid., p. 169, emphasis added; *Oeuvres*, vol. 7, p. 210.

23. Ibid., pp. 289–290; *Oeuvres*, vol. 7, p. 361.

24. Ibid. p. 169; *Oeuvres*, vol. 7, p. 210. Even though he rejects Condorcet's liberalism, his parliamentarianism, and, above all, his feminism, Comte refers often to Condorcet as a predecessor, honoring his efforts to arrive at a systematic science of society. For Comte's view of the slogans of liberty, equality, and fraternity, see ibid., "Conclusion: The Religion of Humanity," pp. 257–321; "Conclusion générale du discours préliminaire: Religion de l'humanité," *Oeuvres*, vol. 7, pp. 321–399.

25. In his 1847 break with Comte, John Stuart Mill charged the positivist with being an opponent of liberty. He objected to the despotism of society and its Religion of Humanity over the individual; see Mill, *Auguste Comte*. These charges have been repeated endlessly in the literature. For example, Leszek Kolakowski assays Comte's philosophy in a similar manner when he writes: "Comte's philosophy does away with human subjectivity entirely. Personality in the subjective sense is a speculative fiction from the point of view of the criteria of positive science; it is also a fiction from a sociological view, and can be treated as such in projects for social reconstruction . . . . Positivist criteria, in characterizing the human individual exclusively by his objectively ascertainable place in inter-individual communication, have invalidated, so to speak, subjective individuality as a possible object of study"; Kolakowski, *The Alienation of Reason*, p. 69.

26. Comte, *System of Positive Polity*, p. 199; *Oeuvres*, vol. 7, p. 248.

27. Ibid., p. 259; *Oeuvres*, vol. 7, p. 324.

28. From *System of Positive Polity*, quoted by Lenzer, ed., *Auguste Comte and Positivism*, p. xxxiii.

29. See *The Positive Philosophy of Auguste Comte*, vol. 1, 2d ed., chaps. 1–2; *Oeuvres*, vol. 1, chaps. 1–2. On Comte's method, see Jürgen Habermas, *Knowledge and Human Interests*; Ronald Fletcher, "Introduction," in *The Crisis of Industrial Civilization: The Early Essays of Auguste Comte*; Brian Fay, *Social Theory and Political Practice*.

30. *The Positive Philosophy of Auguste Comte*, p. 12; *Oeuvres*, vol. 1, p. 40.

31. Comte, *System of Positive Polity*, p. 167; *Oeuvres*, vol. 7, p. 208.

32. Ibid., p. 186; *Oeuvres*, vol. 7, pp. 231–232.

33. Ibid., p. 187; *Oeuvres*, vol. 7, p. 232.

34. Ibid., p. 188; *Oeuvres*, vol. 7, p. 234.

35. Ibid., pp. 193, 196; *Oeuvres*, vol. 7, pp. 241, 244.

36. Ibid., p. xix; *Oeuvres*, vol. 7, p. 13.

37. "Is There a Woman in This Text?" *New Literary History* (1982), p. 118.

38. Ibid., pp. 139, 119.

39. Flora Tristan, *The London Journal of Flora Tristan, 1842; or, The Aristocracy and the Working Class of England;* idem, *Promenades dans Londres ou L'aristocracie et les prolétaires anglais,* ed. François Bédaria; idem, *The Workers' Union;* idem, *Union ouvrière: Suivie de lettres de Flora Tristan,* ed., Daniel Armogathe and Jacques Grandjonc. Tristan's journal of her tour of France has recently been published; see idem, *La tour de France,* 2 vols., ed. Jules-L. Peuch. For biographical remarks on Tristan's life, I have drawn from the excellent introductions by Jean Hawkes and Beverly Livingston to the English translations of her major works, cited here, as well as from Moses, *French Feminism,* pp. 107–116; and Dominique Desanti, *A Woman in Revolt: A Biography of Flora Tristan.*

40. Tristan's first major publication was a two-volume work entitled *Les pérégrinations d'une paria* (1838), which stemmed from her unsuccessful journey to Peru to claim her paternal inheritance.

41. Tristan, *The London Journal,* p. 5; *Promenades,* p. 55. Tristan's commitment to the radical transformation of society was emboldened after her visit to London. There she observed the stunning contrasts of human misery and great wealth. Her widely read journalistic account is a direct precursor of Friedrich Engels' *The Condition of the Working Class in England* (1845).

42. Tristan, *The Workers' Union,* p. 57; *Union ouvrière,* pp. 165–166.

43. Ibid., p. 88; *Union ouvrière,* p. 212.

44. Ibid., p. 42; *Union ouvrière,* p. 147.

45. Ibid., p. 47; *Union ouvrière,* p. 150.

46. S. Joan Moon, "Feminism and Socialism: The Utopian Synthesis of Flora Tristan," in *Socialist Women: European Socialist Feminism in the Nineteenth and Early Twentieth Centuries,* ed. Marilyn J. Boxer and Jean H. Quataert, pp. 40–41. Beverley Livingston, Tristan's translator, also observes, "Since the fundamental familial structure went unchallenged in her analysis, the traditional division of labor remained virtually intact"; introduction to *The Workers' Union,* pp. xxiii–xxiv.

47. Tristan, *The Workers' Union,* p. 80; *Union ouvrière,* pp. 194–195.

48. Ibid. p. 83; *Union ouvrière,* pp. 204–205.

49. Ibid, p. 87; *Union ouvrière,* p. 210.

50. From *The Workers' Union*, cited in Moon, "Feminism and Socialism," p. 37.

51. Tristan, *The London Journal*, pp. 256–257; *Promenades*, p. 276.

52. Cited by Jean Hawkes, Translator's Introduction to *The London Journal*, p. xxix. In her appeal to the bourgeoisie in *The Workers' Union*, Tristan denies that she is "a revolutionary or an anarchist or a bloodthirsty person" even if her demeanor and activities might so appear. Tristan presents herself as one of the "sighted" ones among this class, those who are capable of seeing the need for aiding the working class; "To the Bourgeois," pp. 133–134; *Union ouvrière*, pp. 261–264.

53. See Moon, "Feminism and Socialism," p. 41.

54. Cited in Beverley Livingston, Introduction to *The Workers' Union*, pp. xv–xvi; Tristan, *Le tour*, pp. 102, 139.

## Conclusion

1. I am thinking here of the theses of such French writers as Luce Irigaray, Helene Cixous, Julia Kristeva, the psyche-et-pol group, and their English interpreters, especially Juliet Mitchell and Jacqueline Rose. Similarly, American writers such as Michelle Zimbalist Rosaldo and Sherri Ortner have spoken of a universal public–domestic split corresponding to male–female relations. And the anthropologist Edwin Ardener has postulated the universal male control of symbolic production.

2. Norman O. Brown, *Love's Body*; Sigmund Freud, *Civilization and its Discontents*; idem, *Totem and Taboo*; Juliet Mitchell and Jacqueline Rose, eds., *Feminine Sexuality: Jacques Lacan and the école freudienne*.

3. Hanna Fenichel Pitkin, *The Concept of Representation*, pp. 8–9.

4. Jürgen Habermas, "Hegel's Critique of the French Revolution," in *Theory and Practice*, p. 141.

5. Jürgen Habermas, "Natural Law and Revolution," in *Theory and Practice*, p. 120.

# Bibliography

Abensour, Léon, *La femme et le féminisme avant le révolution*. Paris: Editions Ernest Leroux, 1923.

Abray, Jane. "Feminism in the French Revolution." *American Historical Review* 80:1 (February 1975), 43–62.

d'Aelders, Etta Palm. *Appel aux françoises sur la régénération des moeurs et la nécessité de l'influence des femmes dans un gouvernement libre*. Paris: ICS, 1791.

_____. *Prospectus pour le Cercle patriotique des amies de la vérité*. Paris: ICS, 1791.

Agulhon, Maurice. *Marianne into Battle: Republican Imagery and Symbolism in France, 1789–1880*. Trans. Janet Lloyd. Cambridge: Cambridge University Press; Paris: Editions de la Maison des Sciences de l'Homme, 1981.

_____. "On Political Allegory: A reply to Eric Hobsbawm." *History Workshop* 8 (Autumn 1979), 167–173.

Albistur, Maité, and Daniel Armogathe. *Histoire du féminisme français*, 2 vols. Paris: Des femmes, 1977.

Altman, Janet Gurkin. "The Letter Book as a Literary Institution, 1539–1789: Toward a Cultural History of Published Correspondences in France." *Yale French Studies* 71 (1986), 17–62.

Amann, Peter H. *Revolution and Mass Democracy: The Paris Club Movement in 1848*. Princeton, N.J.: Princeton University Press, 1975.

Anderson, Perry. *Lineages of the Absolutist State*. London: NLB, 1974.

Apostolidès, Jean-Marie. *Le roi-machine: Spectacle et politique au temps de Louis XIV*. Paris: Minuit, 1981.

Applewhite, Harriet B., and Darline Gay Levy. "Responses to the

253

Political Activism of Women of the People in Revolutionary Paris, 1789–1793." In *Women and the Structure of Society: Selected Research from the Fifth Berkshire Conference on the History of Women.* Ed. Barbara J. Harris and JoAnn K. McNamara, pp. 215–231. Durham, N. C.: Duke University Press, 1984.

Arendt, Hannah. *The Human Condition.* Chicago: University of Chicago Press, 1958.

——. *On Revolution.* New York: Viking, 1963.

——. *Rahel Varnhagen: The Life of a Jewish Woman.* New York: Harcourt Brace Jovanovich, 1974.

Ariès, Philippe. *Centuries of Childhood: A Social History of Family Life.* Trans. Robert Baldick. New York: Vintage, 1962.

Backer, Anne Liot. *Precious Women: A Feminist Phenomenon in the Age of Louis XIV.* New York: Basic Books, 1974.

Baker, Keith Michael. *Condorcet: From Natural Philosophy to Social Mathematics.* Chicago: University of Chicago Press, 1975.

——. "On the Problem of the Ideological Origins of the French Revolution." In *Modern European Intellectual History: Reappraisals and New Perspectives.* Ed. Dominic LaCapra and Steven L. Kaplan, pp. 197–219. Ithaca, N.Y.: Cornell University Press, 1982.

——. "Politics and Public Opinion under the Old Regime: Some Reflections." In *Press and Politics in Pre-Revolutionary France.* Ed. Jack R. Censer and Jeremy D. Popkin, pp. 204–246. Berkeley: University of California Press, 1987.

Barber, Elinor. *The Bourgeoisie in Eighteenth Century France.* Princeton, N.J.: Princeton University Press, 1955.

Bataille, Georges. *Erotism: Death and Sensuality.* Trans. Mary Dalwood. San Francisco: City Lights Books, 1986.

Bell, Susan Groag, and Karen M. Offen, eds. *Women, the Family, and Freedom: The Debate in Documents,* vol. 1: 1750–1880. Stanford, Calif.: Stanford University Press, 1983.

Benjamin, Walter. "Paris, Capital of the Nineteenth Century." In *Reflections: Essays, Aphorisms, Autobiographical Writings.* Trans. Edmund Jephcott. Ed. Peter Demetz. New York: Harcourt Brace Jovanovich, 1978 (orig. 1955).

Bidelman, Patrick Kay. *Pariahs Stand Up! The Founding of the Liberal Feminist Movement in France, 1858–1889.* Westport, Conn.: Greenwood, 1982.

Bloch, Jean H. "Women and the Reform of the Nation." In *Women and Society in Eighteenth-Century France.* Ed. Eva Jacobs et al., pp. 3–18. London: Athlone Press, 1979.

Bloch, Marc. *The Royal Touch: Sacred Monarchy and Scrofula in England and France.* Trans. J. E. Anderson. London: Routledge and Kegan Paul; Montreal: McGill-Queens University Press, 1973 (orig. 1924).

Bloch, Maurice, and Jean H. Bloch. "Women and the Dialectics of Nature in Eighteenth-Century French Thought." In *Nature, Culture and Gender.* Ed. Carole P. MacCormack and Marilyn Strathern, pp. 25–41. Cambridge: Cambridge University Press, 1980.

Blum, Carol. *Rousseau and the Republic of Virtue: The Language of Politics in the French Revolution.* Ithaca, N.Y.: Cornell University Press, 1986.

Bodek, Evelyn Gordon. "Salonnières and Bluestockings: Educated Obsolescence and Germinating Feminism." *Feminist Studies* 3:3/4 (Spring–Summer 1976), 185–199.

Bouloiseau, Marc. *The Jacobin Republic, 1792–1794.* Trans. Jonathan Mandelbaum. Cambridge: Cambridge University Press, 1983 (orig. Paris: Editions de la Maison des Sciences de l'Homme, 1973).

Bouten, Jacob. *Mary Wollstonecraft and the Beginnings of Female Emancipation in France and England.* Amsterdam: H. J. Paris v/h Firma A. H. Kruyt, 1922.

Bridenthal, Renate, and Claudia Koonz, eds. *Becoming Visible: Women in European History.* Boston: Houghton Mifflin, 1977.

Brookes, Barbara. "The Feminism of Condorcet and Sophie de Grouchy," *Studies on Voltaire and the Eighteenth Century* 189 (1980), 297–362. Oxford: The Voltaire Foundation at the Taylor Institution.

Brookner, Anita. *Jacques-Louis David.* New York: Harper and Row, 1980.

Brooks, Peter. *The Novel of Worldliness.* Princeton, N.J.: Princeton University Press, 1969.

Brown, Norman O. *Love's Body.* New York: Vintage Books, 1966.

Bryson, Norman. *Tradition and Desire: From David to Delacroix.* Cambridge: Camridge University Press, 1984.

———. *Word and Image: French Painting of the Ancien Régime.* Cambridge: Cambridge University Press, 1981.

Burke, Edmund. *Reflections on the Revolution in France.* In *Reflections on the Revolution in France, Edmund Burke; and The Rights of Man, Thomas Paine.* Garden City, N.Y.: Doubleday, 1961 (orig. 1790).

Cassirer, Ernst. *The Philosophy of the Englightenment.* Trans. Fritz C. A. Koelln and James P. Pettegrove. Princeton, N.J.: Princeton University Press, 1951 (orig. 1951).

Censer, Jack R., and Jeremy D. Popkin, eds. *Press and Politics in Pre-Revolutionary France.* Berkeley: University of California Press, 1987.

Cerati, Marie. *Le club des citoyennes républicaines révolutionnaires.* Paris: Editions Sociales, 1966.

Clark, Alice. *The Working Life of Women in the Seventeenth Century.* London: Routledge, 1919.

Clark, Lorenne M. G., and Lynda Lange, eds. *The Sexism of Social and Political Theory: Women and Reproduction from Plato to Nietzsche.* Toronto: University of Toronto Press, 1979.

Clawson, Mary Ann. "Early Modern Fraternalism and the Patriarchal Family." *Feminist Studies* 6:2 (Summer 1980), 368–391.

Clinton, Katherine B. *"Femme et philosophe:* Enlightenment Origins of Feminism." *Eighteenth-Century Studies* 8:3 (Spring 1975), 283–299.

Comte, Auguste. *Oeuvres d'Auguste Comte,* vols. 1, 7, 8. Paris: Anthropos Paris, 1969–1970.

———. *The Positive Philosophy of Auguste Comte,* 2 vols., 2d ed. Trans. and ed. Harriet Martineau. London: Trübner, 1875 (orig. 1830–1842).

———. *System of Positive Polity,* 4 vols. Trans. John Henry Bridges. London: Longmans, Green, 1875 (orig. 1851).

Condorcet, Marie Jean Antoine Nicolas de Caritat, Marquis de. "On the Admission of Women to the Rights of Citizenship." In Condorcet, *Selected Writings.* Ed. Keith Michael Baker, pp. 97–104. Indiannapolis, Ind.: Bobbs-Merrill, 1976 (orig. 1790).

———. "Sur l'admission des femmes au droit de cité" (3 July 1790), pp. 119–130 in *Oeuvres,* vol. 10, facsimile of Paris edition 1847–1849. Stuttgart-Bad Cannstatt: Friedrich Frommann Verlag (Günther Holzboog), 1968.

Corrado, Barbara Pope. "Revolution and Retreat: Upper-Class French Women after 1789." In *Women, War and Revolution.* Ed. Carol R. Berkin and Clara M. Lovett, pp. 215–236. New York and London: Holmes and Meier, 1980.

Crow, Thomas. "The Oath of the Horatii in 1785: Painting and Pre-Revolutionary Radicalism in France." *Art History* 1:4 (December 1978), 424–471.

———.*Painters and Public Life in Eighteenth-Century Paris.* New Haven, Conn.: Yale University Press, 1985.

Darnton, Robert. *The Literary Underground of the Old Regime.* Cambridge, Mass.: Harvard University Press, 1982.

———. "Policing Writers in Paris circa 1750." *Representations* 5 (Winter 1984), 1–32.

_____. "Readers Respond to Rousseau: The Fabrication of Romantic Sensitivity." In *The Great Cat Massacre and Other Episodes in French Cultural History.* New York: Vintage, 1984.

Darrow, Margaret H. "French Noblewomen and the New Domesticity, 1750–1850." *Feminist Studies* 5:1 (Spring 1979), 41–65.

Davis, Natalie Zemon. *Society and Culture in Early Modern France.* Stanford, Calif.: Stanford University Press, 1975.

_____. "Women's History in Transition: The European Case." *Feminist Studies* 3:4 (Summer 1976), 83–103.

_____. "Women in the Crafts in Sixteenth-Century Lyon." *Feminist Studies* 8:1 (Spring 1982), 47–80.

Desanti, Dominique. *A Woman in Revolt: A Biography of Flora Tristan.* Trans. Elizabeth Zelvin. New York: Crown, 1976.

Dewey, John. *The Public and Its Problems.* Chicago: Swallow Press, 1954.

Diderot, Denis. *Oeuvres complètes,* vol. 10. Introd. Roger Lewinter. Société encyclopédique française and le Club français du livre, 1971.

_____. "On Women," in *Dialogues.* Trans. Francis Birrell. London: George Routledge, 1927 (orig. 1772).

Dowd, David Lloyd. *Pageant-Master of the Republic: Jacques-Louis David and the French Revolution.* Lincoln: University of Nebraska Press, 1948.

Doyle, William. *Origins of the French Revolution.* Oxford: Oxford University Press, 1980.

Duby, Georges, and Robert Mandrou. *A History of French Civilization.* Trans. James Blakely Atkinson. New York: Random House, 1964 (orig. 1958).

Duhet, Paule-Marie, ed. *Cahiers de doléances des femmes en 1789 et autres textes.* Paris: Des femmes, 1981.

Duncan, Carol. "Fallen Fathers: Images of Authority in Pre-Revolutionary French Art." *Art History* 4:2 (June 1981), 186–202.

Eagleton, Terry. *The Function of Criticism: From "The Spectator" to Post-Structuralism.* London: Verso/NLB, 1984.

_____. *The Rape of Clarissa: Writing, Sexuality and Class Struggle in Samuel Richardson.* Minneapolis: University of Minnesota Press, 1982.

Eisenstein, Elizabeth L. *The Printing Press as an Agent of Change: Communications and Cultural Transformations in Early Modern Europe,* 2 vols. Cambridge: Cambridge University Press, 1979.

_____. *The Printing Revolution in Early Modern Europe.* Cambridge: Cambridge University Press, 1983.

Eisenstein, Zillah. *The Radical Future of Liberal Feminism.* New York and London: Longman, 1981.

Elias, Norbert. *The Civilizing Process,* 2 vols. Trans. Edmund Jephcott. New York: Pantheon, 1978, 1982 (orig. 1939).

———. *The Court Society.* Trans. Edmund Jephcott. New York: Pantheon, 1983 (orig. 1969).

Elshtain, Jean Bethke, ed. *The Family in Political Thought.* Amherst: University of Massachusetts Press, 1982.

———. *Public Man, Private Woman: Women in Social and Political Thought.* Princeton, N.J.: Princeton University Press, 1981.

Evans, Richard. *The Feminists.* New York: Barnes and Noble; London: Croom Helm, 1977.

Fay, Brian. *Social Theory and Political Practice.* London: George Allen and Unwin, 1975.

Febvre, Lucien, and Henri-Jean Martin. *The Coming of the Book: The Impact of Printing, 1450–1800.* Trans. David Gerard. Ed. Geoffrey Nowell-Smith and David Woolton. London: Verso, 1976 (orig. 1958).

*Les femmes dans la Révolution française.* Paris: EDHIS, 1982.

Féral, Josette. "The Powers of Difference." In *The Future of Difference.* Ed. Hester Eisenstein and Alice Jardine, pp. 88–94. Boston: G. K. Hall, 1980.

Figes, Eva. *Patriarchal Attitudes.* Greenwich, Conn.: Fawcett, 1970.

Fletcher, Ronald. "Introduction," in *The Crisis of Industrial Civilization: The Early Essays of Auguste Comte.* Trans. Henry Dix Dutton. London: Heinemann Educational Books, 1977.

Foucault, Michel. *The Birth of the Clinic: An Archaeology of Medical Perception.* Trans. A. M. Sheridan Smith. New York: Vintage, 1973 (orig. 1963).

———. *Discipline and Punish: The Birth of the Prison.* Trans. Alan Sheridan. New York: Vintage, 1977 (orig. 1975).

———. *The Order of Things: An Archaeology of the Human Sciences.* New York: Vintage, 1970.

Fox-Genovese, Elizabeth. "Property and Patriarchy in Classical Bourgeois Political Theory." *Radical History Review* 4 (1977), 36–59.

Fox-Genovese, Elizabeth, and Eugene D. Genovese. *Fruits of Merchant Capital: Slavery and Bourgeois Property in the Rise and Expansion of Capitalism.* Oxford: Oxford University Press, 1983.

Freud, Sigmund. *Civilization and Its Discontents.* Trans. James Strachey. New York: Norton, 1961 (orig. 1930).

_____. *Dora: An Analysis of a Case of Hysteria.* Ed. Philip Rief. New York: Collier, 1963 (orig. 1905).

_____. *Totem and Taboo.* Trans. James Strachey. New York: Norton, 1950 (orig. 1912).

Fried, Michael. *Absorption and Theatricality: Painting and Beholder in the Age of Diderot.* Berkeley: University of California Press, 1980.

Furet, François. *Interpreting the French Revolution.* Trans. Elborg Forster. Cambridge: Cambridge University Press, 1981 (orig. Paris: Editions de la Maison des Sciences de l'Homme, 1978).

Furet, François, and Jacques Ozouf. *Reading and Writing: Literacy in France from Calvin to Jules Ferry.* Cambridge: Cambridge University Press, 1982 (orig. Paris: Editions de la Maison des Sciences de l'Homme, 1977).

Furet, François, and Denis Richet. *French Revolution.* Trans. Stephen Hardman. New York: Macmillan, 1970.

Gardiner, Linda. "Women in Science." In *French Women and Enlightenment.* Ed. Samia I. Spencer, pp. 181–193. Bloomington: Indiana University Press, 1984.

Gelbart, Nina Rattner. *Feminine and Opposition Journalism in Old Regime France: Le journal des dames.* Berkeley: University of California Press, 1987.

_____. "The *Journal des dames* and Its Female Editors: Politics, Censorship, and Feminism in the Old Regime Press." In *Press and Politics in Pre-Revolutionary France.* Ed. Jack R. Censer and Jeremy D. Popkin, pp. 24–74. Berkeley: University of California Press, 1987.

George, Margaret. *One Woman's "Situation": A Study of Mary Wollstonecraft.* Urbana: University of Illinois Press, 1970.

_____. "The 'World Historical Defeat' of the Républicaines-Révolutionnaires." *Science and Society* 40:4 (Winter 1976–1977), 410–437.

Gilbert, Sandra, and Susan Gubar. *The Madwoman in the Attic: The Woman Writer and the Nineteenth-Century Literary Imagination.* New Haven, Conn.: Yale University Press, 1979.

Goncourt, Edmond de, and Jules de Goncourt. *La femme au dix-huitième siècle.* Paris: Flammarion, 1982 (orig. 1862).

_____. *The Woman of the Eighteenth Century: Her Life, from Birth to Death, Her Love and Her Philosophy in the Worlds of Salon, Shop and Street.* Trans. Jacques Le Clercq and Ralph Roeder. New York: Minton, Balch, 1927 (orig. 1862).

Goodman, Dena. "Salons and Letters: Women and the Project of Enlightenment." Unpublished ms.

Goody, Jack. *The Domestication of the Savage Mind.* Cambridge: Cambridge University Press, 1977.

———. *The Logic of Writing and the Organization of Society.* Cambridge: Cambridge University Press, 1986.

Goubert, Pierre. *The Ancien Régime: French Society 1600–1750.* Trans. Steve Cox. New York: Harper and Row, 1973 (orig. 1969).

Gouges, Olympe de. *Déclaration des droits de la femme à la reine.* Bibliothèque Nationale Lb39 9989 (orig. 1791).

———. "The Declaration of the Rights of Woman," in *Women in Revolutionary Paris, 1789–1795, Selected Documents.* Ed. and trans. Darline Gay Levy, Harriet Branson Applewhite, and Mary Durham Johnson. Urbana: University of Illinois Press, 1979.

Graham, Ruth. "Rousseau's Sexism Revolutionized." In *Woman in the 18th Century and Other Essays.* Ed. Paul Fritz and Richard Morton, pp. 127–139. Toronto: Hakkert, 1976.

Greenblatt, Stephen. *Renaissance Self-Fashioning: From More to Shakespeare.* Chicago: University of Chicago Press, 1980.

Habermas, Jürgen. *L'espace public: Archéologie de la publicité comme dimension constitutive de la société bourgeoise.* Trans. Marc B. de Launay. Paris: Payot, 1978 (orig. *Strukturwandel der Öffentlichkeit: Untersuchungen zu einer Kategorie der bürgerlichen Gesellschaft.* Neuwied and Berlin: Hermann Luchterhand, 1962).

———. "Hannah Arendt's Communications Concept of Power." *Social Research* 44 (Spring 1977), 3–24.

———. *Knowledge and Human Interests.* Trans. Jeremy J. Shapiro. Boston: Beacon, 1971 (orig. 1968).

———. "The Public Sphere: An Encyclopedia Article (1964)." Trans. Peter Hohendahl. *New German Critique* 3 (Fall 974), 45–55.

———. *Theory and Practice.* Trans. John Viertel. Boston: Beacon, 1973 (orig. 1971).

———. *The Theory of Communicative Action,* vol. 1: *Reason and the Rationalization of Society.* Trans. Thomas McCarthy. Boston: Beacon Press, 1984 (orig. 1981).

Hacker, Barton C. "Women and Military Institutions in Early Modern Europe: A Reconnaissance." *Signs* 6:4 (1981), 643–671.

Hamilton, Roberta. *The Liberation of Women: A Study of Patriarchy and Capitalism.* London: George Allen and Unwin, 1978.

Harris, Jennifer. "The Red Cap of Liberty: A Study of Dress Worn by French Revolutionary Partisans, 1789–94." *Eighteenth-Century Studies* 14:3 (Spring 1981), 283–312.

Harth, Erica. *Ideology and Culture in Seventeenth-Century France.* Ithaca, N.Y.: Cornell University Press, 1983.

Hartsock, Nancy C. M. "Prologue to a Feminist Critique of War and Politics." In *Women's View of the Political World of Men.* Ed. Judith Hicks Stiehm, pp. 121–150. Dobbs Ferry, N.Y.: Transnational, 1984.

Hause, Steven C., and Anne R. Kenney. *Women's Suffrage and Social Politics in the French Third Republic.* Princeton, N.J.: Princeton University Press, 1984.

Herbert, Robert L. David. *Voltaire, Brutus and the French Revolution.* New York: Viking Press, 1973.

d'Hericourt, Madame Jenny. *A Woman's Philosophy of Woman; or, Woman Affranchised: An Answer to Michelet, Proudhon, Girardin, Legouvé, Comte, and Other Modern Innovators.* Reprint of last Paris edition (1864). Westport, Conn.: Hyperion Press, 1981.

Hertz, Deborah. *Jewish High Society in Old Regime Berlin.* New Haven, Conn.: Yale University Press, 1988.

———. "Salonières and Literary Women in Late Eighteenth Century Berlin." *New German Critique* 14 (Spring 1978), 97–108.

Hertz, Neil. "Medusa's Head: Male Hysteria under Political Pressure." *Representations* 4 (Fall 1983), 27–54.

Hippel, Theodor Gottlieb von. *On Improving the Status of Women.* Trans. Timothy F. Sellner. Detroit, Mich.: Wayne State University, 1979 (orig. 1792).

Hobsbawm, Eric. "Man and Woman in Socialist Iconography." *History Workshop* 6 (Autumn 1978), 121–138.

Hohendahl, Peter Uwe. *The Institution of Criticism.* Ithaca, N.Y.: Cornell University Press, 1982.

Homans, Margaret. *Women Writers and Poetic Identity: Dorothy Wordsworth, Emily Brontë, and Emily Dickinson.* Princeton, N.J.: Princeton University Press, 1980.

Honour, Hugh. *Neo-classicism.* Harmondsworth: Penguin Books, 1968.

Horkheimer, Max, and Theodor W. Adorno, *Dialectic of Enlightenment.* Trans. John Cumming. New York: Seabury Press, 1972 (orig. 1944).

Huet, Marie-Hélène. *Rehearsing the Revolution: The Staging of Marat's Death, 1793–1797.* Trans. Robert Hurley. Berkeley: University of California Press, 1982.

Hufton, Olwen. *The Poor of Eighteenth-Century France, 1750–1789.* Oxford: Clarendon Press, 1974.

———. "Women and the Family Economy in Eighteenth-Century France." *French Historical Studies* 9 (Spring 1975), 1–22.

———. "Women in Revolution." *Past and Present* 53 (1971), 90–108.

Hunt, H. J. *Le socialisme et le romantisme en France: Etude de la presse socialiste de 1830 à 1848.* Oxford: Clarendon Press, 1935.

Hunt, Lynn. "Engraving the Republic: Prints and Propaganda in the French Revolution." *History Today* 30 (October 1980), 11–17.

———. "Hercules and the Radical Image in the French Revolution." *Representations* 1:2 (Spring 1983), 95–117.

———. *Politics, Culture, and Class in the French Revolution.* Berkeley: University of California Press, 1984.

———. "Review Essay of *Penser la Révolution française.*" *History and Theory* 20 (1981), 313–323.

———. "The Rhetoric of Revolution in France." *History Workshop Journal* 15 (1983), 78–94.

Hunt, Margaret, Margaret Jacob, Phyllis Jack, and Ruth Perry. *Women and the Enlightenment.* New York: The Institute for Research in History; Haworth, 1984.

Jackson, Catherine Charlotte, Lady. *The Old Regime: Courts, Salons, and Theatres.* New York: Henry Holt, 1882.

Jacobus, Mary. "Is There a Woman in This Text?" *New Literary History* 14:1 (Autumn 1982), 117–142.

———, ed. *Women Writing and Writing about Women.* London: Croom Helm; New York: Barnes and Noble, 1979.

Johnson, Mary Durham. "Old Wine in New Bottles; The Institutional Changes for Women of the People during the French Revolution." In *Women, War and Revolution.* Ed. Carol R. Berkin and Clara M. Lovett, pp. 107–144. New York and London: Holmes and Meier, 1980.

Kantorowicz, Ernst H. *The King's Two Bodies: A Study in Medieval Political Theology.* Princeton, N.J.: Princeton University Press, 1957.

Kaplan, Cora. "Language and Gender." In *Papers on Patriarchy: Conference London 1976.* London: Women's Publishing Collective, 1976.

———. "Wild Nights: Pleasure/Sexuality/Feminism." In *Formations of Pleasure*, pp. 15–35. London: Routledge and Kegan Paul, 1983.

Kates, Gary. *The Cercle Social, the Girondins, and the French Revolution.* Princeton, N.J.: Princeton University Press, 1985.

Kelly(-Gadol), Joan. "Did Women Have a Renaissance?" In *Becoming Visible: Women in European History.* Ed. Renate Bridenthal and Claudia Koonz, pp. 137–164. Boston: Houghton Mifflin, 1977.

———. "Early Feminist Theory and the Querelle des Femmes, 1400–1789." *Signs* 8:1 (Autumn 1982), 4–28.

Keohane, Nannerl. *Philosophy and the State in France: The*

*Renaissance to the Enlightenment.* Princeton, N.J.: Princeton University Press, 1980.

Keuls, Eva C. *The Reign of the Phallus: Sexual Politics in Ancient Athens.* New York: Harper and Row, 1985.

Klaits, Joseph. *Printed Propaganda under Louis XIV: Absolute Monarchy and Public Opinion.* Princeton, N.J.: Princeton University Press, 1976.

Knödler-Bunte, Eberhard. "The Proletarian Public Sphere and Political Organization: An Analysis of Oskar Negt and Alexander Kluge's *The Public Sphere and Experience.*" *New German Critique* 4 (Winter 1975), 52–75.

Kofman, Sarah. *Aberrations: Le devenir-femme d'Auguste Comte.* Paris: Flammarion, 1978.

Kolakowski, Leszek. *The Alienation of Reason: A History of Positivist Thought.* Trans. Norbert Guterman. Garden City, N.Y.: Doubleday, 1968 (orig. 1966).

Lacan, Jacques. *Ecrits: A Selection.* Trans. Alan Sheridan. New York: Norton, 1977 (orig. 1966).

Ladurie, Emmanuel Le Roy. "Versailles Observed: The Court of Louis XIV in 1709." In *Mind and Method of the Historian.* Trans. Siân Reynolds and Ben Reynolds, pp. 149–174. Chicago: University of Chicago Press, 1981 (orig. 1978).

Landes, Joan B. "Feminism and the Internationals." *Telos* 49 (Fall 1981), 117–126.

———. "Women and the Public Sphere: A Modern Perspective." *Social Analysis: Journal of Cultural and Social Practice* 15 (August 1984), 20–31.

Leach, William. *True Love and Perfect Union: The Feminist Reform of Sex and Society.* New York: Basic Books, 1980.

Leavis, Q. D. *Fiction and the Reading Public.* London: Chatto and Windus, 1932.

Lefebvre, Georges. *The French Revolution,* vol. 1: *From Its Origins to 1793.* Trans. Elizabeth Moss Evanson. London: Routledge and Kegan Paul; New York: Columbia University Press, 1962 (orig. 1951).

———. *The French Revolution,* vol. 2: *From 1793 to 1799.* Trans. John Hall Stewart and James Friguglietti. London: Routledge and Kegan Paul; New York: Columbia University Press, 1964 (orig. 1951).

Leith, James A. *The Idea of Art as Propaganda in France.* Toronto: University of Toronto Press, 1965.

Lenzer, Gertrud, ed. *Auguste Comte and Positivism: The Essential Writings.* New York: Harper and Row, 1975.

Levy, Darline Gay, and Harriet Branson Applewhite. "Women of the Popular Classes in Revolutionary Paris, 1789-1795." In *Women, War and Revolution.* Ed. Carol R. Berkin and Clara M. Lovett, pp. 9-36. New York and London: Holmes and Meier, 1980.

Levy, Darline Gay, Harriet Branson Applewhite, and Mary Durham Johnson, eds. and trans. *Women in Revolutionary Paris, 1789-1795, Selected Documents.* Urbana: University of Illinois Press, 1979.

Lougee, Carolyn C. *Le paradis des femmes: Women, Salons, and Social Stratification in Seventeenth-Century France.* Princeton, N.J.: Princeton University Press, 1976.

Lyttle, Scott H. "The Second Sex (September 1793)." *Journal of Modern History* 26 (1955), 14-26.

McCarthy, Thomas. *The Critical Theory of Jürgen Habermas.* Cambridge, Mass.: M.I.T. Press, 1978.

Maclean, Ian. *Woman Triumphant: Feminism in French Literature, 1610-1652.* Oxford: Clarendon Press, 1977.

Macpherson, C. B. *The Theory of Possessive Individualism.* Oxford: Clarendon Press, 1962.

Maland, David. *Culture and Society in Seventeenth-Century France.* New York: Charles Scribner's Sons, 1970.

Marin, Louis. "The Inscription of the King's Memory: On the Metallic History of Louix XIV." *Yale French Studies* 59 (1980), 17-36.

———. *Le portrait du roi.* Paris: Minuit, 1981.

Marshall, David. "Rousseau and the State of Theater." *Representations* 13 (Winter 1986), 84-114.

Marx, Karl. *The Eighteenth Brumaire of Louis Bonaparte.* New York: International Publishers, 1963 (orig. 1852).

Mason, Amelia Gere. *The Women of the French Salons.* New York: Century, 1891.

May, Gita. *Madame Roland and the Age of Revolution.* New York: Columbia University Press, 1970.

Michelet, Jules, *La femme.* Introduction by Thérèse Moreau. Paris: Flammarion, 1981.

———. *Histoire de la Révolution française,* rev. ed. 9 vols. Paris: Librairie Abel Pilon, A. Le Vasseur, Successeur, Editeur, n.d.

———. *History of the French Revolution.* Ed. Gordon Wright. Translated by Charles Cocks. Chicago: University of Chicago Press, 1967 (orig. 1847-1853).

———. *The Women of the French Revolution.* Trans. Meta Roberts Penington. Philadelphia: Henry Carey Baird, 1855.

Mill, John Stuart. *Auguste Comte and Positivism.* Ann Arbor: University of Michigan Press, 1961 (orig. 1865).

Miller, James. *Rousseau: Dreamer of Democracy.* New Haven, Conn.: Yale University Press, 1984.

Mills, C. Wright. *The Power Elite.* New York: Oxford University Press, 1956.

Mitchell, Juliet, and Jacqueline Rose, eds. *Feminine Sexuality: Jacques Lacan and the école freudienne.* Trans. Jacqueline Rose. New York: Norton; Pantheon, 1982.

Mittman, Barbara G. "Women and the Theatre Arts." In *French Women and the Age of Enlightenment.* Ed. Samia I. Spencer, pp. 155–169. Bloomington: Indiana University Press, 1984.

Monter, William. "Women in Calvinist Geneva (1550–1800)." *Signs* 6:2 (1980), 189–209.

Montesquieu, Charles-Louis de Secondat, Baron de. *Oeuvres complètes,* 2 vols. Ed. Roger Caillois. Paris: Gallimard, 1949–1951.

———. *Persian Letters.* Trans. C. J. Betts. Harmondsworth: Penguin, 1973 (orig. 1721).

———. *The Spirit of Laws: A Compendium of the First English Edition.* Ed. David Wallace Carrithers. Berkeley: University of California Press, 1977 (orig. 1748).

Montrose, Louis Adrian. "'Shaping Fantasies': Figurations of Gender and Power in Elizabethan Culture." *Representations* 1:2 (Spring 1983), 61–94.

Moon, S. Joan. "Feminism and Socialism: The Utopian Synthesis of Flora Tristan." In *Socialist Women: European Socialist Feminism in the Nineteenth and Early Twentieth Centuries.* Ed. Marilyn J. Boxer and Jean H. Quataert, pp. 19–50. New York: Elsevier, 1978.

Moses, Claire Goldberg. *French Feminism in the Nineteenth Century.* Albany: State University of New York Press, 1984.

———. "Saint-Simonian Men/Saint-Simonian Women: The Transformation of Feminist Thought in 1830s' France." *Journal of Modern History* 54:2 (June 1982), 240–267.

Mukerji, Chandra. *From Graven Images: Patterns of Modern Materialism.* New York: Columbia University Press, 1983.

Myktyka, Larysa. "Lacan, Literature and the Look: Women in the Eye of Psychoanalysis." *Sub-Stance* 39 (1983), 49–57.

Nicolet, Claude. *L'idée républicaine en France; Essai d'histoire critique.* Paris: Gallimard, 1982.

Norton, Theodore Mills. "The Public Sphere: A Workshop." *New Political Science* 11 (Spring 1983), 75–84.

Okin, Susan Moller. *Women in Western Political Thought.* Princeton, N.J. Princeton University Press, 1979.

Ong, Walter J. *Orality and Literacy: The Technologizing of the Word.* London and New York: Methuen, 1981.

Ortner, Sherry. "The Virgin and the State." *Feminist Studies* 4:3 (October 1978), 19–36.

Ozouf, Mona. *La fête révolutionnaire, 1789–1799.* Paris: Gallimard, 1976.

Parker, Harold T. *The Cult of Antiquity and the French Revolutionaries.* Chicago: University of Chicago Press, 1937.

Pateman, Carole. "The Disorder of Women: Women, Love, and the Sense of Justice." *Ethics* 91 (October 1980), 20–34.

Paulson, Ronald. *Representations of Revolution (1789–1820).* New Haven, Conn: Yale University Press, 1983.

Pinchbeck, Ivy. *Women Workers and the Industrial Revolution, 1750–1850.* New York: Augustus M. Kelley, 1969.

Pitkin, Hanna Fenichel. *The Concept of Representation.* Berkeley: University of California Press, 1972.

———. *Fortune Is a Woman: Gender and Politics in the Thought of Niccolò Machiavelli.* Berkeley: University of California Press, 1984.

Pocock, J. G. A. *The Machiavellian Moment: Florentine Political Thought and the Atlantic Republican Tradition.* Princeton, N.J.: Princeton University Press, 1975.

———. *Virtue, Commerce, and History: Essays on Political Thought and History, Chiefly in the Eighteenth Century.* Cambridge: Cambridge University Press, 1985.

Poovey, Mary. *The Proper Lady and the Woman Writer: Ideology as Style in the Works of Mary Wollstonecraft, Mary Shelley, and Jane Austen.* Chicago: University of Chicago Press, 1984.

Reynolds, Siân. "Marianne's Citizens? Women, the Republic and Universal Suffrage in France." In *Women, State and Revolution: Essays on Power and Gender in Europe since 1789.* Ed. Siân Reynolds, pp. 101–122. Amherst: University of Massachusetts Press, 1987.

Roche, Daniel. *The People of Paris: An Essay in Popular Culture in the 18th Century.* Trans. Marie Evans in association with Gwynne Lewis. Berkeley: University of California Press, 1987 (orig. 1981).

Rose, R. B. *The Enragés: Socialists of the French Revolution?* Melbourne: Melbourne University Press, 1965.

Rosenblum, Robert. *Transformations in Late Eighteenth Century Art.* Princeton, N.J.: Princeton University Press, 1967.

Rousseau, Jean-Jacques. *Oeuvres complètes,* 4 vols. Ed. Bernard Gagnebin and Marcel Raymond. Paris: Gallimard, 1959–1969.

———. *The Confessions of Jean-Jacques Rousseau.* Trans. J. M. Cohen. Harmondsworth: Penguin, 1953 (orig. 1770).

____. *Contrat social ou principes du droit politique*. Paris: Garnier Frères, 1931.

____. *Emile; or, On Education*. Ed. and trans. Alan Bloom. New York: Basic, 1979 (orig. 1762).

____. "Essai sur l'origine des langues." In Jean-Jacques Rousseau, *Ecrits sur la musique*. Paris: Stock/Musique, 1983.

____. "Essay on the Origin of Languages," in *On The Origin of Language*. Trans. John H. Moran and Alexander Gode. New York: Frederick Ungar, 1966 (orig. 1817?).

____. *The First and Second Discourses*. Ed. Roger D. Masters. Trans. Roger D. Masters and Judith R. Masters. New York: St. Martin's, 1964 (orig. 1750, 1754).

____. *La nouvelle Héloïse: Julie, or the New Eloise. Letters of Two Lovers, Inhabitants of a Small Town at the Foot of the Alps*. Trans. and abr. Judith H. McDowell. University Park: Pennsylvania State University Press, 1964 (orig. 1761).

____. *On the Social Contract; with Geneva Manuscript and Political Economy*. Ed. Roger D. Masters. Trans. Judith R. Masters. New York: St. Martin's Press, 1978 (orig. 1762, 1756).

____. *Politics and the Arts: Letter to M. d'Alembert on the Theatre*. Trans. Allan Bloom. Ithaca, N.Y.: Cornell University Press, 1960 (orig. 1758).

Rudé, George. *The Crowd in the French Revolution*. Oxford and New York: Oxford University Press, 1959.

Sahlins, Marshall. *Historical Metaphors and Mythical Realities*. Ann Arbor: University of Michigan Press, 1981.

____. *Islands of History*. Chicago: University of Chicago Press, 1985.

Saisselin, R. G. "Neo-classicism: Images of Public Virtue and Realities of Private Luxury." *Art History* 4:1 (March 1981), 14–36.

Schwartz, Joel. *The Sexual Politics of Jean-Jacques Rousseau*. Chicago: University of Chicago Press, 1984.

Sennett, Richard. *The Fall of Public Man: On the Social Psychology of Capitalism*. New York: Vintage, 1976.

Shanley, Mary L., and Peter G. Stillman. "Political and Marital Despotism: Montesquieu's *Persian Letters*." In *The Family in Political Thought*. Ed. Jean Bethke Elshtain, pp. 30–95. Amherst: University of Massachusetts Press, 1982.

Shklar, Judith. *Men and Citizens*. Cambridge: Cambridge University Press, 1969.

Showalter, English, Jr. "Authorial Self-Consciousness in the Familiar Letter: The Case of Madame de Graffigny." *Yale French Studies* 71 (1986), 113–130.

Silver, Catherine Bodard. "Salon, Foyer, Bureau: Women and the Professions in France." *American Journal of Sociology* 78:4 (1972–73), 836–851.

Smith, Bonnie. *Ladies of the Leisure Class: The Bourgeoises of Northern France in the Nineteenth-Century.* Princeton, N.J.: Princeton University Press, 1981.

Soboul, Albert. *The French Revolution, 1787–1799: From the Storming of the Bastille to Napoleon.* Trans. Alan Forrest and Colin Jones. New York: Vintage, 1975 (orig. 1962).

_____. *The Sans-Culottes: The Popular Movement and Revolutionary Government, 1793–1794.* Trans. Remy Inglis Hall. Garden City, N.Y.: Doubleday, 1972 (orig. 1968).

Sokolnikova (Serebriakova), Galina Osipovna. *Nine Women Drawn from the Epoch of the French Revolution.* Trans. H. C. Stevens. Freeport, N.Y.: Books for Libraries Press, 1932; reprint, 1969.

Soltau, Roger Henry. *French Political Thought in the 19th Century.* New York: Russell and Russell, n.d.

Sowerwine, Charles. *Sisters or Citizens? Women and Socialism in France since 1876.* Cambridge: Cambridge University Press, 1982.

Spencer, Samia I., ed. *French Women and the Age of Enlightenment.* Bloomington: Indiana University Press, 1984.

Stanton, Domna. *The Aristocrat as Art: A Study of the Honnête Homme and the Dandy in Seventeenth- and Nineteenth-Century French Literature.* New York: Columbia University Press, 1980.

_____. "The Fiction of Préciosité and the Fear of Women." *Yale French Studies* 62 (1981), 107–134.

Starobinski, Jean. *Jean-Jacques Rousseau: La transparence et l'obstacle, suivi de sept essais sur Rousseau.* Paris: Gallimard, 1971.

_____. *1789: The Emblems of Reason.* Trans. Barbara Bray. Charlottesville: University of Virginia Press, 1982 (orig. 1973).

Stephens (Whale), Winifred. *Women of the French Revolution.* London: Chapman and Hall, 1922.

Stiehm, Judith Hicks, ed. *Women's Views of the Political World of Men.* Dobbs Ferry, N.Y.: Transnational, 1984.

Strumingher, Laura S. *Women and the Making of the Working Class: Lyon 1830–1870.* St. Alban's, Vt., and Montreal: Eden, 1979.

Sullerot, Evelyne. *Histoire de la presse féminine en France, des origines à 1848.* Paris: Armand Colin, 1966.

Tanner, Tony. *Adultery in the Novel: Contract and Transgression.* Baltimore, Md.: Johns Hopkins University Press, 1979.

Terdiman, Richard. *Discourse/Counter-Discourse: The Theory and Practice of Symbolic Resistance in Nineteenth-Century France.* Ithaca, N.Y.: Cornell University Press, 1985.

Thompson, E. P. "The Moral Economy of the English Crowd in the Eighteenth Century." *Past and Present* 50 (1971), 76–136.

Tilly, Charles. "Food Supply and Public Order in Modern Europe." In *The Formation of National States in Western Europe.* Ed. Charles Tilly, pp. 380–455. Princeton, N.J.: Princeton University Press, 1975.

Tilly, Louise A. "The Food Riot as a Form of Political Conflict in France." *Journal of Interdisciplinary History* 2 (1971):23–57.

Tilly, Louise A., and Joan W. Scott. *Women, Work, and Family.* New York: Holt, Rinehart and Winston, 1978.

Todd, Janet M., ed. *A Wollstonecraft Anthology.* Bloomington: Indiana University Press, 1977.

Tomalin, Claire. *The Life and Death of Mary Wollstonecraft.* New York: Harcourt Brace Jovanovich, 1974.

Traer, James F. *Marriage and the Family in Eighteenth-Century France.* Ithaca, N.Y.: Cornell University Press, 1980.

Tristan, Flora. *The London Journal of Flora Tristan, 1842; or, The Aristocracy and the Working Class of England. A Translation of Promenades dans Londres.* Trans. Jean Hawkes. London: Virago, 1982.

——. *Promenades dans Londres; ou, L'aristocracie et les prolétaires anglais.* Ed. François Bédaria. Paris: La Découvérte/ Maspero, 1983.

——. *La tour de France,* 2 vols. Ed. Jules-L. Peuch. Paris: François Maspero, 1980.

——. *Union ouvrière: Suivie de lettres de Flora Tristan.* Ed. Daniel Armogathe and Jacques Grandjonc. Paris: des femmes, 1986 (orig. 1843).

——. *The Workers' Union.* Trans. Beverley Livingston. Urbana: University of Illinois Press, 1983.

Vincent, K. Steven. *Pierre-Joseph Proudhon and the Rise of French Republican Socialism.* New York and Oxford: Oxford University Press, 1984.

Vovelle, Michel. *The Fall of the French Monarchy, 1787–1792.* Trans. Susan Burke. Cambridge: Cambridge University Press, 1984 (orig. Paris: Editions de la Maison des Sciences de l'Homme, 1972).

Warner, Marina. *Monuments and Maidens: The Allegory of the Female Form.* New York: Atheneum, 1985.

Watt, Ian. *The Rise of the Novel: Studies in Defoe, Richardson and Fielding.* Berkeley: University of California Press, 1957.

Weber, Max. "Politics as a Vocation." In *From Max Weber: Essays in Sociology.* Trans. and ed. H. H. Gerth and C. Wright Mills, pp. 77–128. New York: Oxford University Press, 1946.

Williams, David. "The Fate of French Feminism: Boudier de Ville-mert's *Ami des femmes." Eighteenth-Century Studies* 14:1 (Fall 1980), 37–55.

_____. "The Politics of Feminism in the French Enlightenment." In *The Varied Pattern: Studies in the Eighteenth Century.* Ed. Peter Hughes and David Williams, pp. 333–351. Toronto: Hakkert, 1971.

Wollstonecraft, Mary. *An Historical and Moral View of the Origin and Progress of the French Revolution and the Effect It Has Produced in Europe.* New York: Scholars' Facsimiles and Reprints, 1975 (orig. 1794).

_____. *Letters: Written during a Short Residence in Sweden, Norway, and Denmark.* Ed. Carol H. Poston. London: University of Nebraska Press, 1976 (orig. 1796).

_____. *A Vindication of the Rights of Men (1790).* Gainesville, Fla.: Scholars' Facsimiles and Reprints, 1960.

_____. *A Vindication of the Rights of Woman: An Authoritative Text, Backgrounds, Criticisms.* Ed. Carol H. Poston. New York: Norton, 1975 (orig. 1792).

Woronoff, Denis. *The Thermidorean Regime and the Directory, 1794–1799.* Trans. Julian Jackson. Paris: Editions de la Maison des Sciences de l'Homme; Cambridge: Cambridge University Press, 1984.

Yeatman, Anna. "Despotism and Civil Society: The Limits of Patriarchal Citizenship." In *Women's Views of the Political World of Men.* Ed. Judith Hicks Stiehm, pp. 151–176. Dobbs Ferry, N.Y.: Transnational, 1984.

_____. "Gender and the Differentiation of Social Life into Public and Domestic Domains." *Social Analysis: Journal of Cultural and Social Practice* 15 (August 1984), 32–49.

# Index

271

**Library of Congress Cataloging-in-Publication Data**

Landes, Joan B., 1946–
    Women and the public sphere in the age of the French Revolution.

    Bibliography: p.
    Includes index.
    1. Women in public life — France — History — 18th century. 2. France — History —
Revolution, 1789–1799 — Women. 3. Women — France — History — 18th century.
4. Women's rights — France — History — 18th century. I. Title.
HQ1391.F7L36   1988        305.4′0944        88-3723
ISBN 0-8014-2141-1   (alk. paper)
ISBN 0-8014-9481-8   (pbk. : alk. paper)

276